ISAIAH'S VISION AND THE FAMILY OF GOD

KATHERYN PFISTERER DARR

•

WESTMINSTER JOHN KNOX PRESS
Louisville, Kentucky

Isaiah's Vision and the Family of God

© 1994 Katheryn Pfisterer Darr

First edition

Published by Westminster John Knox Press,
Louisville, Kentucky

This book is printed on acid-free paper that meets the American National Standards Institute Z39.48 standard. ∞

PRINTED IN THE UNITED STATES OF AMERICA
2 4 6 8 9 7 5 3 1

Library of Congress Cataloging-in-Publication Data

Darr, Katheryn Pfisterer, 1952-
  Isaiah's Vision and the Family of God / Katheryn Pfisterer Darr. — 1st ed.
      p.   cm. — (Literary currents in biblical interpretation)
  Includes bibliographical references (pp. 258-270) and indexes.
  ISBN 0-664-25537-X (pbk. : alk. paper)

  1. Bible. O.T. Isaiah—Criticism, interpretation, etc. I. Title.
BS1515.2.D37 1994
224'.106—dc20   94-15669

For my husband, John A. Darr,
and our son, Joshua Pfisterer Darr,
my family and my joy.

CONTENTS

SERIES
PREFACE

New currents in biblical interpretation are emerging. Questions about origins—authors, intentions, settings—and stages of composition are giving way to questions about the literary qualities of the Bible, the play of its language, the coherence of its final form, and the relations between text and readers.

Such literary criticism is rapidly acquiring sophistication as it learns from major developments in secular critical theory, especially in understanding the instability of language and the key role of readers in the production of meaning. Biblical critics are being called to recognize that a plurality of readings is an inevitable and legitimate consequence of the interpretive process. By the same token, interpreters are being challenged to take responsibility for the theological, social, and ethical implications of their readings.

Biblical interpretation is changing on the practical as well as the theoretical level. More readers, both inside and outside the academic guild, are discovering that the Bible in literary perspective can powerfully engage people's lives. Communities of faith where the Bible is foundational may find that literary criticism can make the Scripture accessible in a way that historical criticism seems unable to do.

Within these changes lie exciting opportunities for all who seek contemporary meaning in the ancient texts. The goal of the series is to encourage such change and such search, to breach the confines of traditional biblical criticism, and to open channels for new currents of interpretation.

—THE EDITORS

PREFACE

n *The Writing Life,* Annie Dillard describes the joy and freedom
attending the creation of a book:

> Putting a book together is interesting and exhilarating. It is
> sufficiently difficult and complex that it engages all your
> intelligence. It is life at its most free. Your freedom as a writer
> is not freedom of expression in the sense of wild blurting; you
> may not let rip. It is life at its most free, if you are fortunate
> enough to be able to try it, because you select your materials,
> invent your task, and pace yourself. (1989:11)

Dillard's own writings are not the stuff of the guild. In writing
this book (which is), however, I have experienced large measures of the exhilaration she describes, and also some of the
frustration that, in this particular quote, she does not acknowledge.

Throughout the task, I have received the invaluable assistance of my husband, John A. Darr, Associate Professor of New
Testament at Boston College. His influence as a scholar is
apparent on virtually every page, for I adopt, with little adaptation, the reader-oriented method he developed in his 1987
dissertation, and further refined in a 1992 monograph. Though
our paths are on different sides of the line separating the
Testaments, we are familiar enough with each other's terrain to
understand and appreciate our respective journeys. Both of us
know that some days, writing a paragraph is a victory. Our son,
Joshua, also abetted the writing of this book with hugs and
encouraging words.

In 1989, I received a Research Grant from the American
Academy of Religion. During the 1990-91 academic year,
Boston University awarded me both a sabbatical, and a
year-long appointment as Junior Fellow in the Society of Fel-
lows, the Humanities Foundation. Both the funds, and the
break from teaching responsibilities, helped launch me on this

project. My colleague, Dr. Simon B. Parker, read through the manuscript with his usual, considerable care. My scholarship is always the better for his efforts. Dr. David Gunn, my editor, provided invaluable assistance, encouragement, and suggestions along the way. The Reverend Steve Bishop, a Master's degree student at Boston University School of Theology, proved an able proofreader. Special words of appreciation go to C. Bob Darrell, Professor of English at Kentucky Wesleyan College, who meticulously edited a large portion of the manuscript and, as always, strengthened my writing.

Finally, I express my ongoing gratitude to all those who, by their teaching, writing, and encouragement, have equipped me for the great joy of studying Isaiah—in many ways ancient Israel's crowning literary achievement—and for sharing my understanding of Isaiah's vision.

—KATHERYN PFISTERER DARR

INTRODUCTION

This book has grown from two convictions. The first affirms that sequential readers of Isaiah discover unfolding themes, motifs, etc., that are likely overlooked in the course of purely pericopal readings. The second insists that figurative language is *strategic* language, that is, that metaphors and related tropes invite readers to particular perceptions of reality. Combined, these two convictions have resulted in a reader-oriented construal of Isaiah that focuses especially upon its recurring female and child tropes and the themes to which they are integral.

During the past two decades, increasing numbers of specialists have begun asking fresh questions about the formation and unity of Isaiah. Some scholars seek to recover those historical processes by which Isaian oracles were shaped and supplemented until the scroll attained its final form. Others focus upon recurring words, themes, and motifs that bridge the book's "parts" and contribute to its intelligibility when read as a single literary work. Against this background, Chapter 1 undertakes two tasks: first, it describes a reader-oriented approach that takes seriously both the roles of reader, text, and extratext in construing meaning, and the sequential and cumulative nature of the reading process; second, it presents our understandings of how metaphor and related tropes function.

In Chapter 2, we turn to Isaian references to children. Examining the relevant texts reveals some of ancient Israel's stereotypical associations with children, and also how those associations function within their respective literary contexts. Recurring metaphorical depictions of Israel as God's rebellious children are a key element in a larger theme, Isaiah's "rhetoric of rebellion," which we trace in the second half of the Chapter.

Chapter 3 examines Isaiah's figurative references to women. Like Chapter 2, it identifies stereotypical associations with females and explains how such ideas contribute to the meaning and function of specific texts. Here, we discover Isaian authors exploiting common, long-lived associations with women toward strategic ends.

Chapters 4 and 5 trace the "ladies' lots," that is, the fates of Zion and her rival cities. Focusing upon Isaiah's female city imagery brings into relief issues crucial to Isaiah as a whole: Zion's relationship to her God, and her ultimate position among the nations. Personified Jerusalem's story does not reach its conclusion until Isaiah 66. In Chapter 5, however, we stop short of that climactic text, for its full import cannot be grasped until we have first examined a proverb uttered by King Hezekiah at a crucial juncture in Jerusalem's history. That task, the focus of Chapter 6, leads us to both biblical and extrabiblical texts that illumine the meaning and function of the King's enigmatic proverb, "Babes are positioned for birth, but there is no strength to deliver" (37:3b). That proverb also has implications for the much-debated question of how Hezekiah is presented, and judged by sequential readers, in Isaiah 1—39.

Finally, at the conclusion of Chapter 6, we examine two other Isaian texts that echo in striking ways the imagery of Hezekiah's metaphorical proverb. Together, these three texts constitute yet another recurring theme, the "(in)ability-to-bring-to-birth," that contributes to Isaiah's intelligibility when read as a complex literary unity.

The book of Isaiah has been read and interpreted from a host of perspectives over thousands of years. Though we make no claim to identify *the* meaning of Isaiah, our selected tropes and themes prove crucial to what is certainly one of Isaiah's central affirmations, that is, that those in Zion who repent of Israel's history of rebellion and live in obedience to God's teaching can, with confidence and joy, await the fulfillment of Yahweh's plan. Those who persist in rebelling against God, by contrast, will endure the punishment pronounced already in Isaiah 1. Readers of Isaiah's astonishingly rich and complex "vision" must decide which course to choose.

1

READING
ISAIAN
METAPHORS

More than a century of Isaiah scholarship supports the claim that in biblical studies, no less than in other fields, our presuppositions and methods shape the questions we ask;[1] and the questions we ask inevitably influence the answers we discern in the text. Early historical critics of Israel's prophetic literature, for example, set as their primary goal recovering the prophets' authentic words against their original historical settings.[2] They sought to chip away later supplements from "genuine" utterances in order that the prophets' own religious beliefs, personalities, and historical circumstances might be revealed. To borrow from a description of sculpting attributed to the great Italian artist, Michelangelo, these scholars carved into the textual block until they reached a particular prophet's "skin" and then stopped. When their work was completed, the statue before them looked precisely like their images of Amos, or Ezekiel, or "Deutero-Isaiah." But littered around its base lay chunks and shards of discarded text.

Some contemporary biblical scholars, frustrated by the atomistic and speculative tendencies of historical-critical methods, have abandoned them for a variety of literary-critical ones. Certainly alternative approaches can yield fresh and significant insights into the biblical books. But historical criticism and literary criticism are not *inevitably* antithetical (as proponents of each sometimes suggest). Some literary-critical approaches, including our own, rely upon historical-critical discoveries.[3] In this study I set aside certain traditional agendas, such as distinguishing between "authentic" and "inauthentic" materials, seeking to associate each pericope with a particular historical setting, and tracing Isaiah's history of composition. But I do not, on that account, devalue the vast contributions of historical criticism to biblical scholarship. To the contrary, reconstructing *historical* knowledge of ancient Israel's literary conventions, including its stereotypical associations with entities occurring in figurative uses of language, will prove essential to our task.

DISASSEMBLING AND RECONSTRUCTING ISAIAH

Already in the eighteenth century, critics advanced theories of dual Isaian authorship (Döderlein 1789; Eichhorn 1780-83), arguing that chapters 40–66 reflected an exilic rather than a pre-exilic setting, and identifying striking differences between these and preceding chapters. Traditional scholars responded by pointing to Isaiah's explicit claims (1:1; 2:1; 13:1) to be the vision of a single eighth-century prophet—an assertion ostensibly supported by both New Testament and rabbinical writings. Similarities in language and concepts confirmed Isaian authorship, they insisted, whereas the admittedly real differences between chapters 1–39 on the one hand and 40–66 on the other could be explained as shifts in subject matter and authorial intent (Childs 1979:316-17). As multiple author theories gained ground in Isaiah studies, however, these traditional arguments were forced to retreat.

Like their eighteenth-century counterparts, contemporary scholars frequently point to similarities in imagery, motifs, themes, and concepts spanning major sections of the scroll. Their studies (and my own), however, presuppose not single but multiple authorship: Isaian unity does not require sole authorship by the prophet Isaiah. Rather, unity and coherence are sought "in the 'reciprocal relationships' between the literary blocks of First (1–39), Second (40–55), and Third (56–66) Isaiah" (Seitz 1988:17).

The Unity of Isaiah:
Diachronic and Synchronic Approaches

"The common starting point among scholars interested in the formation of the Book of Isaiah," R. Rendtorff writes, "is the conviction, or at least the assumption, that the present shape of the book is not the result of more or less accidental or arbitrary developments but rather . . . of deliberate and intentional literary and theological work" (1991b:9).[4] Following Rendtorff, I distinguish between two approaches current in contemporary Isaiah studies.[5] The difference between these approaches becomes clear when we express each as a question. On the one hand, diachronic approaches ask, "In what stages did the text reach its final form?" On the other hand, synchronic approaches ask, "What does the text (in all its complexity) mean in its given final shape?" (1991b:22).[6]

An imposing group of scholars has addressed Rendtorff's first question.[7] Because our study focuses upon Isaiah as a literary whole, however, I shall not detail the results of their primarily diachronic investigations.[8] Diachronic and synchronic interests can converge, of course, since focusing upon one provokes questions and sparks insights regarding the other.[9] Nevertheless, our approach owes more to the work of critics pursuing Rendtorff's second, synchronic question. B. Anderson (1988:17) points to the promise of such an approach:

> The established practice of separating [Isaiah] into several discrete parts, each of which is viewed in isolation from the whole, is giving way to exploratory efforts to understand the overall unity and the theological dynamic of the Isaiah tradition. Indeed, it is an illuminating experience to lay aside most of the commentaries of the past and read through in one sitting the Book of Isaiah with a kind of "second naiveté."

Diachronic Approaches and Redaction Criticism

Most contemporary specialists are less likely than their predecessors simply to dismiss textual elements that, in their judgment, reflect the efforts of later disciples (collectors) or redactors. M. Sweeney (1988:2) notes scholarship's shifting attitude:

> Past scholarship viewed redactors in opposition to authors. Their basic task was not creative, like that of authors, but mechanical. . . . They were viewed as technicians, "scissors and paste men" who may add irrelevant and dull comments to their material, frequently distorting its message, but who had very little of theological worth to say. . . . [But] later scholars have recognized redactors as creative theologians who give a "new interpretation" to the older materials which they transmit.

Hence, while some critics continue giving pride of place to what they regard as a prophet's *ipsissima verba*, many others have moved beyond that task to reconstructing how earlier materials subsequently were reinterpreted, shaped, and supplemented in light of changing times and religio-social perspectives. Redaction criticism provides invaluable clues to those ongoing processes—historical, literary, hermeneutical—that turned earlier prophetic utterances into fresh words with inexhaustible meanings (see Knierim 1985:150-58).

In his *Introduction to the Old Testament as Scripture* (1979), B. Childs considered the implications of reshaping the Isaiah traditions. He did not doubt the original independence of three, or at least two, of the scroll's major sections. To the contrary, he confidently speculated that the Deutero-Isaian corpus once contained specific information about its historical context, but that this information was subsequently all but expunged, causing chapters 40–55 to lose their "original historical particularity" (1979:325-26). With that secondary juxtaposition, however, the message of Deutero-Isaiah assumed "a new role within the canon" (325); and proper construal *required* its being read and interpreted in the literary context of the entire work, since it now functioned as "a prophetic word of promise offered to Israel by the eighth-century prophet, Isaiah of Jerusalem" (325):

> A message which originally functioned in a specific exilic context in the middle of the sixth century has been detached from this historical situation to become fully eschatological. In its new context its message no longer can be understood as a specific commentary on the needs of exiled Israel, but its message relates to the redemptive plan of God for all of Israel. . . . [T]he loss of an original historical context has given the material an almost purely theological shape. (1979:326)

The so-called "Proto-Isaian" corpus remained, in Childs' view, malleable enough to be influenced by Deutero- and perhaps Trito-Isaiah as well. Many other scholars have concluded that Isaiah demonstrates "far greater redactional purpose and inner-exegetical significance" than was recognized previously (Seitz 1990:239), so that readers must keep firmly in mind its thematic and other intertextual linkages. P. Ackroyd argued that Isaiah 1–12 were consciously shaped with the entire corpus in view (1978:47). R. Clements discerns evidence of a Babylonian redaction of the Proto-Isaian corpus (1985:101), but also insists that certain "prominent and fundamental themes" in Deutero-Isaiah are conscious, redactional allusions back to the scroll's first major section. The motif of Israel's blindness and deafness, to cite but a single example, had its Isaian origin in the eighth-century prophet's commissioning (Isa 6:9-10). It continues as an important concern in Deutero-Isaiah's oracles (Isa 42:18-19; 43:8; cf. 44:18; and see also Isa 35:5 and 29:18).

Redaction-critical analysis of Isaiah's compositional history carries important implications for understanding the growth of the scroll's recurring features. Nevertheless, scholars looking askance at other historical-critical methods can also be wary of redaction criticism, since it often leads to intricate, conflicting reconstructions of the stages by which a highly complex literary entity like Isaiah attained its final form. This is by no means surprising, of course; any biblical scholar seeking to recover a book's precanonical history should acknowledge the hypothetical nature of his or her conclusions. More often than not, either we lack adequate data to confirm our theories "beyond a reasonable doubt," or the available data can reasonably be construed in more than one way. Moreover, as B. Childs has noted, biblical redactors apparently labored to *conceal*, rather than to highlight, their efforts (1979:59).

In *Reading Isaiah*, E. Conrad argues that redaction criticism merely shifts the critic's attention from authors to redactors:

> the aim is to recover the intentions of the redactors in the development of the book and the historical background of the redactional process, rather than the intentions of the prophet Isaiah and the prophet's historical background. . . . The book is now understood to be a unified whole, not an anthology or collection. . . . The demotion of the original intentions of Isaiah as embedded in his "authentic" words is clearly evident in Clements's opinion [1985:100] that "the later, redactional stages in the formation of the book have contributed more to an understanding of what it means than can usefully be gleaned by modern attempts to reconstruct the story of the 'life and times' of Isaiah of Jerusalem in the eighth century B.C." (1991:17-18)

Clements drew this conclusion, Conrad contends, because "when redactors are allowed to rewrite creatively the prophet's words and subsequent editions of the book, the search for the prophet in the book is frustrated" (1991:18): "Fohrer associated revelation with prophetic experience," he writes. "Clements associates it with a redactional Heilsgeschichte" (18).

For Conrad, continued reliance upon historical-critical methodologies, including redaction criticism, further widens existing gaps between "communities of interpretation outside the theological community" and the academic guild. To help close such gaps he proposes adopting an "objective" theory from contemporary, secular literary analysis[10]—one based on the presupposition that "the text is an object to be studied in its own right without reference to external factors such as author intention and historical background" (1991:27).

Synchronic Approaches

In "The Book of Isaiah: A Complex Unity" (1991b), R. Rend-torff both summarizes the results and defends the legitimacy of recent, synchronic readings of Isaiah:

> [A] changing view on the Book of Isaiah should allow, and even require, studies on topics, themes, expressions, and even ideas characteristic for the book as a whole or significant parts of it, without at the same time discussing the questions of redaction or composition. A synchronic reading, if carried out with the necessary sophistication, should have its own right. (1991b:20; see also 1984; 1991a)

B. G. Webb's synchronic approach, for example, traces Zion's transformation in Isaiah:

> Taken together, the title in 1.1 and its echo in 2.1 indicate that while the vision concerns Judah and Jerusalem in particular and takes its rise during the reigns of certain kings in the eighth century BCE, it includes within its scope all nations and reaches to the very eschaton itself. Temporally, the vision moves between the twin poles of 'the days of Uzziah . . .' (1.1) and 'the latter days' (2.1). Nationally, it is centred on 'Judah and Jerusalem'. . . . The eschaton towards which the book as a whole moves is a new cosmos centred on a new Jerusalem/Zion (cf. 2.1-4). (1990:68-69)

Zion's centrality within Isaiah is also indicated by R. J. Clifford's synchronic analysis. He argues that three Deutero-Isian themes which, at first flush, seem alien to the received Isaiah tradition—that is, the exodus-conquest, creation, and Cyrus as

Yahweh's king (1993:2)—actually derive from that tradition and develop some aspect of Zion in "its manifold meanings of temple, temple city, or people" (3).

Like both Webb and Clifford, I shall argue that Jerusalem's fate is a dominant concern throughout Isaiah. Indeed, I would affirm with C. Seitz that in Isaiah, "the second major character alongside God is Zion" (1988:122). I trace Lady Zion's fate, however, not only within its primary locus, the Yahweh-Israel-Zion triad, but also as it relates to what I term the "ladies' lots," i.e., the fates of *other* cities in Israel's ancient Near Eastern world (Chapters 4 and 5). Their futures, like Zion's, are part of Yahweh's plan for Israel and the nations. Contextualizing the Zion traditions among other Isaian city oracles, we discover significant, but hitherto overlooked, patterns emerging that inform our understanding of the entire work.[11]

In his monograph, E. Conrad has produced an essentially synchronic reading of Isaiah 1–66 (1991); and his efforts disclose both important insights into the book's overall structure, and intriguing connections among its parts. Conrad's method entails gathering texts from throughout portions of Isaiah according to certain rubrics: he analyzes the significance of the scroll's royal narratives for its overall organization (while noting especially the pivotal role of the Hezekiah narrative in Isaiah 36–39); he traces the intermittent motif of Yahweh's world-wide military strategy; he explores the significance of first person pronouns (especially in the book's initial and concluding chapters), arguing that their presence provides an important clue to the book's orality and structure; and he insists that the prophet's "vision" is part of, but not coextensive with, Isaiah's sixty-six chapters (it is confined, rather, to chapters 6–39 and set in the past). When the vision is read (in response to the command in 40:6), the implied audience brings that vision into its own, present context.

Though frequently insightful, Conrad's views do not uniformly persuade. In particular, his assertion that the implied audience understands Isaiah's vision to begin only with 6:1 (despite the assertions of Isa 1:1 and 2:1) and to conclude at 39:8 is not so compelling as he suggests. Since both the superscription in 1:1 and the *historical narratives* within chapters 1–39 (e.g., chapters 6–8, 20, and 36–39) locate the prophet

Isaiah's *activity* from the death of King Uzziah (6:1) to his announcement of events lying beyond Hezekiah's not-too-distant death (Isa 39:5-7), we should *not* be surprised that subsequent chapters contain no historical narratives in which the prophet himself plays a role. Isaiah's *vision*, however, "concerning Judah and Jerusalem," which he saw "in the days of Uzziah, Jotham, Ahaz, and Hezekiah, Kings of Judah" (1:1), is *not* restricted to that same time span. To the contrary, it already transcends the perimeters of the prophet's own lifetime in Isaiah 13–14, with the announcement that Babylon will ultimately be destroyed by the Medes (13:17).

Disputes concerning the extent of Isaiah's unfolding vision notwithstanding, it suffices at this point simply to concur with Conrad, Rendtorff, and others that a synchronic reading can proceed without necessarily exploring the redactors' contributions to Isaiah's composition. No less than Conrad, I pursue a text's "aesthetic momentum, not its historical development" (1992:29). But while Conrad describes his method as comprising "primarily objective theories of interpretation in combination with pragmatic [i.e., reader-oriented] ones" (28-29), I try always to remember that readers are required to actualize that potential aesthetic momentum. With W. Iser, I agree that "the text is not a solid object whose meaning is self-evidencing. Rather, it has gaps, indeterminacies, portions which are not written but only implied. In order to produce the literary *work* . . ., the reader must go through the temporal, sequential process of filling these gaps left in the text." (Iser 1972:279; in J. A. Darr 1992:29).

Finally, P. Miscall's synchronic readings of Isaiah explore certain recurring metaphors (e.g., light, darkness, fire, water) and their associated commonplaces (positive and negative). In "Isaiah: The Labyrinth of Images" (1991), he adopts a labyrinth metaphor to describe an approach that moves indiscriminately across Isaiah's surface and explores its poetic imagery without regard to sequence, since readers can enter and exit the text at any number of different points:

> I start with the image of light from Isa 2:5 and, using selected examples, trace it back-and-forth through the book. But, like a journey through the Labyrinth, the tracing doesn't lead to a center or to a definite entrance or exit; rather, it constructs a Labyrinth which also serves as an image for the reading of

Isaiah. This tracing, this reading, crosses the limits of "light" for it quickly expands to an increasing number of images, e.g., darkness, fire, dryness and water, to a variety of themes, e.g., rescue and destruction, and to wordplay on the terms used for the images and the themes. (1991:103)

The labyrinth offers an especially apt allegory for reading, Miscall claims, because the latter is not a "specifically directed procedure," but a "reader-directed process" in which one "decides which textual threads to pick up and follow, how far to follow each one and whether to tie them all together at some end or center or just leave them lying on the page" (107). To the extent that Miscall's approach focuses upon poetic imagery and is "reader-directed," it resembles my own. But *caveat emptor!* Adopting a labyrinth metaphor permits the text no directive power. Moreover, the labyrinth's intricate, interconnecting passages are a perfect place to become lost, and perhaps to be eaten by the Minotaur lurking within. Our reader seeks consistency, coherence, closure. He wishes to "get through" the text, just as the labyrinth's potential victims seek to survive the maze.

In a 1993 essay, "Isaiah: New Heavens, New Earth, New Book," Miscall reflects upon relations between texts when the author of one has "borrowed" from another (1993:44). Sometimes texts are intentionally constructed to displace earlier ones: "to recognize that a text is related to another text is both to affirm and to deny the earlier text. It is affirmed as a type of model and source, while it is denied by being made secondary to the later text, precisely by being regarded as a model and a source that has been superseded" (44).

Hence, biblical authors sometimes "trope on tropes," seeking to trump an earlier text's authority (45):

instead of a stream of tradition that flows on and into the text, we have texts that displace and decenter one another—we do not have to follow historical priority here—by dispersing and disseminating each other's parts or elements: letters, words, sentences, themes, images, characters and plot.

Isaiah, for example, seeks to displace the Genesis creation account: "the letters, words and themes of Genesis 1 are dispersed throughout Isaiah; this is a new creation, a new book, and not just a translation of Genesis 1" (1993:48). The process begins already in Isa 1:2 with its references to the heavens and earth and continues with recurring images of darkness, light, water, etc. Of course, both Genesis 1 and Isaiah "trope" other ancient Near Eastern creation texts as well. Nevertheless, the relationship of Isaiah to Genesis (and other texts) is, Miscall claims, aggressively self-assertive: "This is a new book and a new vision of the heavens and the new earth which the Lord is creating; the things of the past, whether acts, words or books, are to be forgotten. Read Isaiah and not these other books!" (1991:55).

Miscall concedes, of course, that the biblical authors could evoke thoughts of earlier texts toward other ends, for example, to underscore and supplement shared ideas, images, themes, motifs, and interpretations. Along the way, I, too, attend to relationships pertaining between Isaian and other biblical and extra-biblical texts sharing our selected metaphors and themes.

READING ISAIAH

As noted, most biblical scholars no longer limit their interests to the retrieval of a prophet's original words, disencumbered of later accretions. To the contrary, recent Isaian scholarship displays abundant interest in redactors as gifted literary artists and theologians in their own right. Although not disparaging the results of diachronic, redaction-critical analyses, I choose to focus upon the reader who construes the text in its final form. That reader may, to a significant degree, be influenced by the redactors' decisions, their strategic invitations to interpret texts and position themselves *vis à vis* those texts in certain ways rather than in others. But because readers themselves play a role in actualizing texts (see below), we must leave open the possibility that they discern relationships between texts not, consciously or unconsciously, in the redactors' thoughts. In other words, redaction criticism cannot, in and of itself, exhaust a discussion of Isaian unity, since sequential readers can interrelate texts in ways that redactors never envisioned.

My method permits us to attend to such linkages, largely irrespective of attempts to read redactors' minds. Consider, for example, Isa 2:5-22 with its threat that Yahweh "has a day" against "all that is proud and lofty" (vs. 12). These various symbols of grandiosity—cedars of Lebanon, high mountains, lofty towers—include the "ships of Tarshish," vessels proverbial for their size, beauty, and richly-laden holds. Whether redactors intended a connection between 2:16 and a sequentially much later text is, of course, impossible to prove. For the reader recalling this early threat, however, Yahweh's "day" comes with the opening words of Isaiah 23: "Wail, O ships of Tarshish, for your fortress is destroyed" (vs. 1a, repeated in vs. 14). By Isa 60:9, those same ships, now in Yahweh's service, bring home Israel's most precious possessions—its children, gold and silver.

In what follows, we shall consider the special challenges of a reader-oriented approach seeking to describe how sequential readers actualized a text like Isaiah. With that task come important questions. We must determine, for example, how, and to what extent, the reader-oriented approach here adopted must be adapted for our task. J. A. Darr's literary method, set out both in his dissertation (1987) and in a recent monograph (1992), was designed with the Lukan narratives in mind. Can it profitably be applied to Isaiah, a lengthy and complex text shaped over hundreds of years and more poetry than prose?

A READER-ORIENTED METHOD

J. A. Darr's reader-oriented method approaches biblical books (in his case, Luke-Acts; in mine, Isaiah) as potentially coherent literary works,[12] rather than simply as quarries for historical data (1987:11). Acknowledging the legion of literary methods available to would-be critics, Darr stresses the importance of constructing a "text-specific" approach, i.e., one well-suited to a given piece of literature. All too often, he observes, contemporary biblical scholars opt for literary methods developed with modern works and worlds in mind. Students of biblical metaphor, for example, sometimes interpret tropes on the basis of contemporary, rather than ancient Near Eastern, ideas and associations. Yet such anachronistic approaches inevitably prove inadequate. To paraphrase Darr, the complexities of interpreting an ancient religious text like Isaiah cannot be overlooked in our search for viable literary-critical methods (1987:12-13). Rather, we must construct an eclectic approach, whose features we chose in light of specific postulates and the particular text to hand.

Three Critical Premises

Three critical premises ground Darr's method. *First,* he affirms that "literature functions rhetorically," that is, "it achieves certain effects—esthetic, emotional, moral, ideological—in an audience by means of rhetorical strategies" (1987:15).[13] Logologist K. Burke stressed the persuasive nature of language: "Since, in Burke's view, language itself is action, every one of its particular and local manifestations is to be understood as purposive, in all the motivational and 'creative' complexity of that term" (Crocker 1977:340). Such assertions are (at least) as true for poetry as for prose; and they are crucial to my analysis of Isaiah generally and Isaian tropes particularly.

Of course, all communication draws addresser and addressee closer together: the former issues a kind of invitation; the latter expends effort to accept that invitation; and their transaction constitutes the acknowledgement of a community (Cohen 1979:6). As we shall see, however, communication involving figurative uses of language proffers a unique relationship, for metaphors and related tropes invite communication *of a special sort* (6-7). Such invitations are issued, consciously or unconsciously, for specific purposes—to entitle, to persuade, to disguise, to conceal. But beware! Accepting a trope's "special" invitation sometimes proves dangerous (9-10). Like Ehud, who ostensibly approached Eglon to share a secret, but instead planted a sword in his bowels (Judg 3:15-22), so-called "weapon" metaphors (Booth 1979:50-51) invite intimacy in order to deal a deadly thrust.

Second, Darr asserts that meaning results from the "dynamic interaction of both the rhetorical strategies of the text and the interpretive structures (a repertoire of conventions and expectations) of its reader" (1987:16). In other words, *meaning depends not just upon what the text brings to the reader, but also upon what the reader brings to the text.* This second premise presupposes, of course, that critics can gain access to both the text, and (at least aspects of) the reader's extratextual repertoire, including, "(1) language; (2) social norms and cultural scripts; (3) classical or canonical literature; (4) literary conventions (e.g., genres, type scenes, standard plots, stock characters) and reading rules (e.g., how to categorize, rank, and process various textual data); and (5) commonly-known historical and geographical facts" (1992:22). Our knowledge of this repertoire remains partial, of course; like our counterparts engaged in fully historical-critical pursuits, we can never free ourselves of uncertainty, or of the necessity to conjecture. Nonetheless, Darr insists in his *third* premise that a host of *text-specific* factors— historical, social, linguistic, literary—remain relevant for *contemporary* interpretations of ancient texts. True, certain of those factors function transculturally, and so are easily grasped. But it behooves critics also to reconstruct, as best they can, culture-specific factors (including reading conventions) pertaining when a completed Isaiah could be actualized as a coherent literary work.

With these three critical premises in place, Darr locates his literary method, drawing—like Conrad—upon M. H. Abrams' categories in *The Mirror and the Lamp* (Darr 1987:18):

> Abrams' analytic scheme consists of four elements: the work itself, the artist or author, the universe or nature, and the audience. While most critics blend all four of these elements in their interpretive endeavors, each "tends to derive from one of these terms his principle categories for defining, classifying and analyzing a work of art, as well as the major criteria by which he judges its value" [1953:6]. All literary theories, by definition, pay some heed to the text; however, some approaches concentrate on it in isolation (objective theories), whereas others explain the work by relating it to something or someone else—the author (expressive theories), the audience (pragmatic theories), or aspects of the universe (mimetic theories).

Darr's premises place his method along the "pragmatic" axis of Abrams' framework. Pragmatic approaches are scarcely new. They predominated from the time of Horace through the eighteenth century. But they were supplanted in the following two centuries first by expressionism (Romanticism), and then by objectivism (Formalism and the New Criticism), largely as a reflex against Romanticism's tendencies toward "psychologistic and biographical criticism" (1987:23).

Objective theories, by contrast, posit the text's self-sufficiency as an object "solid and material as an urn or icon" (Eagleton 1983:47). The benefits of the New Criticism have been manifold. Critics read, reread, and reify the text as a complete mental "object" whose textual features, including plot, theme, motif, character, point of view, juxtaposition, ambiguity, etc., can be analyzed and described. For example, they may interpret Isa 27:10-11 (women feeding their fires with desiccated branches from the desolate streets of once-fortified cities) in light of a sequentially much later text, Isa 44:9-22 (a craftsman gathering wood to make an idol, but also to fuel his cooking-fire; note the common assertion that these people lack understanding [27:11; 44:18-19]). But our first-time, sequential reader engages Isa 27:10-11 without benefit of the "big-picture." Only in retrospect can he or she reconsider the significance of an earlier text in light of later ones.

With Darr, then, I stand alongside critics such as Iser and W. Booth (1961) who focus upon "the dynamic interaction between text and reader in the temporal, conventional process of reading" (1987:38). True, Iser's system bears a certain, inevitable indeterminacy: "by bringing in the reader as co-creator of the work's meaning, Iser has left himself open to . . . charges of indeterminacy and relativism. . . . Will not each individual reading of a text be different? Are some readings better than others? If so, what criteria are used to make these sorts of judgments?" (1987:30). Though daunting, such questions are better faced head-on than ignored (as if readers played no role in construing a text's meaning). Darr concludes (1987:38–39), "responsibility for maintaining a delicate balance between text and reader in the dialectical production of literary meaning lies with the critic; at this point artistry enters the interpretive enterprise":

> We envision a dialectic in which the text guides, prefigures, and attempts to persuade a reader to choose a particular path or adopt a certain world-view. At the same time, the reader is only using these textual promptings as starting points for filling in the gaps left by the text, forming opinions about characters and events, and anticipating what is to come as the reading progresses. Texts have a certain determinateness, but the meanings derived from these texts are qualified by the receptivity and creativity of the individual reader in an interpretive community.

Focusing upon text, reader, and reading does not, of course, rule out appeals to other elements in the interpretive process. Recall that Darr's eclectic method admits those social, historical, and literary contexts pertaining at the times when biblical books were completed and first read. It remains essentially pragmatic, nonetheless, by virtue of the ways in which these "extrinsic" elements are perceived and utilized: "in essence, author and historical context are brought into the process of interpretation through the portals of text and reader, respectively" (19).

"Optical Lenses" and the Critic's Task

While critics select, order, and balance elements shaping interpretation, their choices are not—protestations notwithstanding—utterly disinterested. To the contrary, "what the critic writes is no less rhetorical than the text itself," since critics actively advance one reading over others (Darr 1987:55):

> the critic is a creative re-reader whose selections specify and limit what is to be perceived and how "best" it is to be understood by others. . . . by reconstructing a particular social-historical setting, identifying specific literary influences, and accentuating select textual phenomena (and ignoring others), the critic attempts to persuade others to accept his or her interpretation. (56-57)

One need look no further than C. Seitz's recent book, *Zion's Final Destiny*, to see that competent critics construe texts in widely-divergent ways. Seitz suggests that the servant described in Isa 52:13–53:12 is none other than Jerusalem herself. Gender is no obstacle to equating the male servant and the female city, Seitz asserts, since "Zion can be depicted as 'son of her womb' . . . in 49:15, without causing undue strain on the other images of wife and mother" (1991:203-4). But in Isaiah, Zion is always female, never male. She is not depicted as "son of her womb" in 49:15; rather, verse 15 foregrounds the bond between mother and infant, only to claim that Yahweh's devotion to and care for Zion exceed even that paradigmatic human tie. Arguments seeking to equate Zion and the servant must treat carefully how tropes function within each literary context.

Darr adopts W. Booth's "optical lens" imagery to describe how critics negotiate a variety of interpretive options. "Our choices of a given inquiry work like our choices of optical instruments," he avers, "each camera or microscope or telescope uncovering what other instruments conceal and obscuring what other instruments bring into focus" (Booth 1983:405). Darr's own "optical instrument" requires the manipulation of four lenses: wide-angle; editorial; objective; and reading (57). The wide-angle lens is located in the eye of the critic. Its field of vision is broadest of the four since it includes all of the information (historical, cultural, social, literary, etc.) that critics bring to a text. The editorial lens, Darr's second optical instrument, probes a smaller field, but at greater depth. It focuses upon the text to hand, yet through it modern critics can discern information unavailable to ancient readers. For Darr's purposes, this lens permits the critic to discern specific, preexisting literary sources employed by the author of Luke-Acts. In our case, the lens sharpens signs of multiple authors and levels of redaction in Isaiah. (Use of the editorial lens may be most evident in our appropriation of phrases like "Proto-," "Deutero-," and "Trito-Isaiah"). In either case, however, evidence observed through this second lens becomes imperceptible through the following two lenses, for, "such knowledge is the prerogative of the critic (and the critic's readers)" (1987:60).

The objective lens enables critics to bring an entire work into focus within the same field (1987:60). Unlike first-time readers (see below), critics read and reread a literary work until it appears a "complete mental object" whose recurring features take their places within the larger overall design. "Through this lens," Darr writes, the critic "scans the entire work (in any sequence—end to beginning, beginning to end, or randomly) in an effort to compare the part to the whole" (60).[14]

Finally, critics shape and position the reading lens, a lens most crucial to our present task. Although not always recognized as such, "the reader" is an interpretive construct:

> the reader is not a given (e.g., an innate property of the text), but rather, is implicitly or explicitly construed by the critic. Such a construal is inevitably based, at least in part, on the critic's own reading experience. Every audience-oriented approach is founded upon preconceived notions of (1) the nature of the reading process (in general, and with regard to the specific work in question), and (2) the identity (competence, learning, knowledge of literary and cultural codes) of the reader. (J. Darr 1987:61)

Of course, critics inevitably create readers (to at least some degree) in their own image. Nevertheless, critic and reader are not simply the same:

if our treatment . . . is to be truly *text-specific*, then the audience to which we refer should fit the cultural profile of the readers for whom the account was written. That is, we must reconstruct—to the fullest extent possible—the extratextual repertoire, literary skills and basic orientation of the original audience. In doing so, our ultimate purpose is hermeneutical, not historical: we are less concerned with discovering the identities of intended addressees than with ascertaining the type and degree of "cultural literacy" the author seems to have assumed for his audience. In other words, the question is not "Who is the reader *per se*?" but rather, "What did a reader have to bring to a text in order to actualize it competently?" (J. Darr 1992:25-26)

First-time readers engaging a text sequentially in a dialogical process must contend with a limited field of vision. They cannot compare parts to whole because, immersed though they be in the text, they are able to actualize it only to the point read *thus far*. But this fourth lens also has implications for modern biblical critics, since peering through it limits their own fields of vision as well.

Identifying the Reader and the Reading Process

Having identified the four lenses in his "optical instrument," Darr both *turns* to a more precise description of the reader, and *returns* to the reading process itself.

The Reader

Our first task is to reconstruct a "text-specific" reader who possesses the extratext (cultural and literary knowledge) required to construe Isaiah satisfactorily. Recall that the question is not "who is the reader *per se*," but rather "what did a reader have to bring to a text in order to actualize it competently" (J. Darr 1992:26). I would add that *redactors* responsible for bringing Isaiah to its final form, as well as those *scribes* and *other specialists* committed to its preservation and promulgation, likely believed their *own* levels of competence to exceed those of non-specialist contemporaries lacking the training, time, and access necessary to read and interpret texts with a similar degree of sophistication. These members of ancient Israel's learned class may well have presumed at least two levels of competency—one possessed by a readership whose general knowledge permitted only a "layperson's" level of understanding, and the other possessed by those whose literary, cultural, and historical competencies enabled more complex and literate readings.

Who is "our reader" of Isaiah's vision? He belongs to post-exilic Israel's cognoscenti, a scribe or religious leader and educator enjoying such legal rights and social standing as were possible at the beginning of the fourth-century BCE,[15] and under Persian rule.[16] Culturally-literate and fully at home within his society, he knows—or at least thinks he knows—basic facts (historical, political, geographical, religious, ethnic) and conventions (social, cultural, literary, etc.) related to Israel and its world. Though this is his first reading of Isaiah, he is familiar with other of Israel's existing religious texts, including the Torah of Moses, certain prophetic collections, psalms, and so on. He also knows the literary "classics" of his larger culture. For the vast majority of his contemporaries, of course, access to Isaiah consists only of listening to brief excerpts in contexts of worship; such a scenario appears in Luke 4:16-20:

> When [Jesus] came to Nazareth, where he had been brought up, he went to the synagogue on the sabbath day, as was his custom. He stood up to read, and the scroll of the prophet Isaiah was given to him. He unrolled the scroll and found the place where it was written:
> "The Spirit of the Lord is upon me,
>> because he has anointed me to bring good news
>>> to the poor.
> He has sent me to proclaim release to the captives
>> and recovering of sight to the blind,
>> to let the oppressed go free,
>> to proclaim the year of the Lord's favor."
> And he rolled up the scroll, gave it back to the attendant, and sat down. The eyes of all in the synagogue were fixed on him.

But our reader, a minority in his society, enjoys the opportunity, access, expertise, and time to read and interpret the unfolding Isaiah scroll on other than just a pericope by pericope basis.[17]

Aspects of the Reading Process

W. Iser describes the dynamic process of reading as follows: "We look forward, we look back, we decide, we change our decisions, we form expectations, we are shocked by their non-fulfillment, we question, we muse, we accept, we reject." (1972:293). From this quotation (and a similar one by S. Fish [1972:126-27]), Darr identifies four complementary and ongoing aspects of reading: anticipation and retrospection; consistency building (gestaltic activity); investment and identification; and defamiliarization (1992:29). I shall briefly discuss each in turn.

Readers moving through a text continually reassess earlier expectations and judgments, forming fresh ones as new insights and data emerge: "In the dialectic of reading," Darr declares, "each word, sentence, or other textual unit both illuminates and is illumined by what precedes it." And the further one reads, the more complex anticipation and retrospection become (1987:64). This is particularly true when one seeks to construe so long and complex a text as Isaiah.[18]

Related to this first aspect is the reader's proclivity toward consistency building: "By correlating discrete elements of the text. . ., and adding extratextual information when necessary, the audience is able to image patterns (what Iser calls *Gestalten*) which cover textual gaps, help to resolve tensions, and clarify ambiguities." (1987:65). Again, consistency building is a more complex process when an extensive and eclectic piece of prophetic literature is at issue, rather than a narrative like Luke-Acts (which tells a continuous story, the life and death of Jesus, and the "history" of the early church). Nevertheless, certain textual features—the initial identification of the scroll's contents as Isaiah's vision (1:1; 2:1; 13:1), the presence of myriad linking words (e.g., *yaqûm*, "they stand up/rise up," at the end of an oracle in Isa 32:8; *qomenah*, "rise up," at the beginning of the next oracle in 32:9), propelling phrases like "on that day" that encourage and facilitate the reader's tendency to move ahead, correlating texts and filling gaps, the chronological arrangement of narratives in which the prophet plays a role (chapters 6, 7, 20, and 36–39), and transitional passages like Isaiah 34–35 and 36–39, encourage readers to construe texts on the basis of preceding chapters and verses.[19]

A third aspect, "investment and identification," refers to the variability of "distance" between the reader and what he is reading. "Consciously or unconsciously," Darr observes, "the reader oscillates between a full-scale involvement in the [world of the text] and a more detached observation of it" (1987:65).

How are readers of Isaiah encouraged to identify with those in their historically-rebellious community who have repented of its obdurate past, live in obedience to Yahweh's Torah, and await a glorious future secure within redeemed Jerusalem, while concomitantly distancing themselves from those whose rebelliousness perdures? Here our focus shifts from the reader to the text: "the *text* provides a series of stimuli which elicit and guide audience responses. In other words, it is a rhetorical framework, designed strategically to foster a sequence of mental images and cognitive acts by the reader. The text also controls point of view, a vital element in the shaping of values" (Darr 1992:32). But text and reader also share an extratext, i.e., common ground that facilitates communication from the outset: "The first-time reader must bring to a text a set of expectations which provide a context for processing it. Such a meeting point between reader and text is provided by the extra-text, the repertoire of shared conventions and canonical works that exists in any literate society" (1987:67). Biblical and extra-biblical literature from Israel's ancient Near Eastern world suggests that audiences prized established literary conventions, e.g., stock story lines and poetic refrains. Yet innovation had its place as well. Indeed, what Iser calls "defamiliarization" (1978:69)—setting the well-known in unfamiliar terrain—could force readers to perceive established elements in new ways. In Isa 42:14, for example, the stereotypical simile "like a travailing woman" functions in an unconventional way. Instead of illumining physiological and psychological reactions to incapacitating fear in the face of impending death (its normal usage), this simile serves as a powerful prelude to Yahweh's awesome and redeeming acts.

Construing Contiguous
Lines of Poetic Texts

Throughout his methodological discussion, Darr describes reading as a complex activity requiring interactions between reader, text, and extratext. Many, if not most, aspects of his method apply to our reading of Isaiah as well, though the latter is mostly poetry with occasional narrative, rather than prose narrative with the occasional piece of poetry.

In *The Dynamics of Biblical Parallelism*, A. Berlin observes how readers seek to construe meaning in the contiguous lines of Hebrew poetry (1985:6). Early on, she quotes W. Empson's comments (1947:24–25) regarding translation of Chinese verse:

> Lacking rhyme, metre, and any overt device such as comparison, these lines are what we should normally call poetry only by virtue of their compactness; two statements are made as if they are connected, and the reader is forced to consider their relations for himself. The reason why these facts should have been selected for a poem is left for him to invent; he will invent a variety of reasons and order them in his own mind. This, I think, is the essential fact about the poetical use of language.

Empson's "compactness" and sense of "connectedness" correspond, Berlin claims, to the "terseness" and "parallelism" that characterize biblical poetry's "paratactic style." She writes: "The lines, by virtue of their contiguity, are perceived as connected, while the exact relationship between them is left unspecified . . . such contiguity creates the impression of connectedness and forces the reader to 'consider their relations for himself' and to 'invent a variety of reasons to explain the relationship'" (1985:6).

Form criticism has done much to distinguish between poetic genres developed and/or employed by Israel's prophets. Moreover, form critics have identified characteristic constituent components of those genres, thereby assisting our efforts to discern where a given oracle, or portion of an oracle, begins and ends. The presence in Isaiah of a wide variety of oracle types, one following immediately upon the other, might seem to mitigate against a sequential construal of its contents. Certainly, it has suggested to many critics that prophetic books consist largely of once-discrete oracles whose juxtapositions occurred only steps removed from their proclamation. As P. Hanson has demonstrated, however, the exilic and post-exilic periods witnessed the combining of originally discrete genres within the confines of a single, extended oracle:

> the structure of literary genres is as subject to transformation over the centuries as is the structure of prosodic units. This does not mean that a priori every complex unit from the sixth century must be regarded as original; . . . It does mean, however, that great risks are involved in the attempt to estab-

lish the limits of post-exilic prophetic units on the basis of pre-exilic models. Those limits legitimately can be determined only on the basis of internal evidence and comparison with other oracles from the same period. (1975:119)

Hence, a sudden shift in genre cannot be interpreted simply as evidence that one oracle has ended or a new oracle begun.[20] To the contrary, the increasing length and complexity of prophetic oracles, coupled with those other textual features referred to, encourage readers to interpret the lines before them in light of sequentially prior ones and irrespective of genre boundaries.[21] Of course, "unifying" Isaiah is not the same as construing a relatively straightforward narrative composed within a brief time span by one author. We should not expect all its parts to fit together *precisely*. Nevertheless, readers who approach Isaiah's vision attempting "to fit everything together in a consistent pattern" (Iser 1972:288; 1978:118-29), and consciously or unconsciously filling textual gaps (assisted by both text and extratext), will discover ample bases for construing it as a coherent literary work, less congruous elements notwithstanding. Recurring female and child tropes are but two features assisting readers in this task.

ISAIAH'S UNFOLDING VISION

Because not every scholar interested in Isian unity views the prophet's vision as contiguous with the sixty-six chapter work, we pause briefly here to describe how our reader understands Isaiah's unfolding vision and his place within it. He knows that Isaiah saw this vision "concerning Judah and Jerusalem" in the days of four Judean kings, but also that it extended far beyond their reigns. He knows that some of the prophet's predictions came to pass already during Isaiah's lifetime (e.g., the humbling of Assyria's arrogant king and destruction of his army [Isaiah 36–37]). Other predictions have been fulfilled during the centuries from Isaiah's death to the reader's own day (e.g., Babylon's overthrow by Cyrus and the exiles' return to Judah). Still others have yet to be fulfilled (e.g., the ultimate glorification of Zion before the nations). Of course, our reader construes all aspects of Isaiah's vision with an eye to their contemporary and future significance. God's word never runs out of relevance. Nevertheless, the sure knowledge that many of Isaiah's prophecies already have been fulfilled functions both to buttress the prophet's authority, and to embolden the reader's belief that the as-yet-unfulfilled aspects of God's plan for Israel and the nations also shall be accomplished. Until that day, our reader lives within Isaiah's unfolding vision and in expectation of its ultimate realization.

PROPHECY AND METAPHOR: FEMALE AND CHILD IMAGERY IN ISAIAH

Central among the vast array of issues addressed in Isaiah are the nature and status of ongoing relationships among Yahweh, Israel (both narrowly and broadly defined), and Judah's capital city, Jerusalem. Isaiah's authors did not, of course, analyze these relationships—which transcended the human realm and were by their nature mysterious—systematically. Rather, they frequently employed tropes derived from everyday familial roles (husband/wife, parent/child) and experiences (e.g., marriage, labor and delivery, disciplining recalcitrant children) to shed light on the powerful bonds they believed existed between Israel and its God. Such relationships and experiences might not themselves be devoid of mystery (e.g., childbirth), but they were better known, or at least more commonly experienced, than the ties they sought to disclose.

Immediately, a number of questions come to mind. Why do certain Isaian texts repeatedly evoke attributes and experiences of children and/or women to describe attributes and experiences of other entities, be they adult males, land, cities, nations, or deities? What culturally-defined, stereotypical associations with these two groups do literal and figurative references evoke? Do *familial* images of children and women within specific Isaian contexts exploit well-established associations with these two groups, highlight previously-suppressed commonplaces (thereby breathing new life into clichés), or create novel insights into past, present, or anticipated phenomena? And if figurative language is strategic speech that invites readers to particular perceptions of reality, then what ends were served best by these particular tropes? Finally, what do certain recurring familial metaphors and models contribute to the reader's construal of

Isaiah as a unified literary composition?[22] Such questions shape our analyses of pertinent Isaian texts.

Figurative Language and Contemporary Theory

Before turning to Isaiah, I pause to describe my theoretical understanding of how readers, ancient and modern, construe figurative uses of language—metaphor, but also simile, synecdoche and metonymy, catachresis, and neologism. Theories of metaphor are properly of interest to many fields of inquiry, including literary criticism, philosophy, mathematics, science, and social and cultural anthropology. The remainder of this chapter addresses three of the many tasks and topics in metaphor studies of special importance for *literary* analysis of Isaiah's child and female tropes: (1) identifying a theory of metaphor that will, with some adaptation, ground our interpretations; (2) describing ways by which we can recover, to the degree possible, our reader's relevant extratextual repertoire—including those associated commonplaces surrounding terms in particular figurative utterances, and vital to its competent construal; and (3) highlighting the significance of figurative language as *strategic speech*, i.e., language inviting readers to different perceptions of reality.

Historically, figurative language has not been the focus of ongoing study and debate within Old Testament studies.[23] In "Meter, Parallelism, and Tropes," P. J. Miller (1983:103–105) called for greater attention to tropes in biblical poetry:

> Our contemporary focus on formal characteristics, figures of speech more than figures of thought, and parallelism has served to obscure the role of figures in biblical poetry. . . . Considerable work has been done in the analysis and categorization of metaphors in general that is capable of being applied to the metaphors of biblical poetry. . . . the figurative language of biblical poetry should be—and of course is—able to tell us much about Israel's experience and how they assimilated and understood it.

In the decade since Miller's article appeared, several scholars have begun focusing upon Old Testament imagery; witness, for example, the monographs by K. Nielsen (1989), M. Brettler (1989), P. W. Macky (1990), and J. Galambush (1991). Despite their advances, however, much work remains to be done on figurative uses of language and their functions within particular literary contexts.

Myriad definitions of metaphor and theories of metaphorical construal appear in the philosophical literature.[24] In *Metaphors and Religious Language*, J. M. Soskice groups metaphor theories under three headings: "those that see metaphor as a decorative way of saying what could be said literally [substitution theories]; those that see metaphor as original not in what it says but in the affective impact it has [emotive theories]; and those that see metaphor as a unique cognitive vehicle enabling one to say things that can be said in no other way" [incremental theories] (1985:24). She then locates her own, "interanimation" theory beneath the third heading:

> Our own preferred theory of metaphor . . . should regard metaphor neither as a simple substitution for literal speech nor as strictly emotive. Metaphor should be treated as fully cognitive and capable of saying that which may be said in no other way. It should explain how metaphor gives us "two ideas for one", yet do so without lapsing into a comparison theory. These are basics. Ideally, a theory of metaphor should go even further and discuss . . . the hearer's reception of it, how the hearer decides that the speaker is speaking metaphorically rather than nonsensically, and so on. (44)

Soskice's own definition of metaphor as "that figure of speech whereby we speak about one thing in terms which are seen to be suggestive of another" (1985:15) builds, as she acknowledges, upon I. A. Richards's famous remarks about how metaphors create meaning: "when we use a metaphor," Richards wrote, "we have two thoughts of different things active together and supported by a single word, or phrase, whose meaning is a resultant of their interaction" (1938:93). Richards went on to distinguish between the "tenor," or underlying subject of a metaphor, and the "vehicle," or complete utterance conveying that subject.

Philosopher M. Black also acknowledges a debt to Richards for his own well-known "interaction" theory of metaphor. Simply stated, Black's theory holds that a metaphor consists of a principal subject and a subsidiary one. Its cognitive content results from "interaction" between those two subjects or, more precisely, between their associated commonplaces. So, for example, in the metaphor, "man is a wolf," associations with the principal subject, "man," and the subsidiary subject, "wolf," interact to produce cognitive meaning: "the wolf-metaphor suppresses some details, emphasizes others—in short, *organizes* our view of man" (1962:41). (Here, Black's language requires greater precision, for *associations do not interact by themselves*; rather, they are brought into relationship with each other by hearers or readers who encounter the metaphor within a specific context and from a distinctive cultural perspective.) He further claims that in any metaphor, some words are used metaphorically, whereas others are not (1962:27). A word used metaphorically forms the "focus" in a literal "frame" (the rest of the sentence); and because of its new context, it bears fresh meaning.

Black's theory has commended itself to more than a few biblical scholars. This is scarcely surprising, since his treatment of a previously-neglected subject from the perspective of modern analytic philosophy endowed metaphors with new status as irreplaceable expressions of cognitive meaning. Soskice shows, however, that Black has misconstrued Richards on the two interrelated points identified above. First, he errs in stating that every metaphor contains two subjects. To the contrary, a metaphor possesses one (underlying) subject, the tenor conveyed by its vehicle.[25] Second, Black erroneously asserts that in metaphor, "*some* words are used metaphorically while the remainder are used nonmetaphorically" (1962:27). Here, Black breaks from Richards's insistence that we arrive at a metaphor's meaning "only through the interplay of the interpretive possibilities of the whole utterance" (1936:55). Consider the following example:

> A stubborn and unconquerable flame
> Creeps in his veins and drinks the streams of life.

In these lines, Soskice observes, the tenor—a burning fever—is communicated through the interanimation of words in the vehicle as a whole (45). Note that in these lines, the tenor is nowhere explicitly stated—further evidence against Black's assertion that two distinct subjects are present in any metaphor.

Because she so lucidly identifies traps in Black's theoretical discussions, we are surprised to see Soskice falling into them on occasion. Aware that Black's heavy reliance upon "A is a B" type tropes has helped perpetuate his claim that two subjects are present in any metaphor, for example, she turns to metaphors consisting of a noun plus an attributive adjective:

> Richards has no need for two explicit subjects. He can say of "giddy brink" that the tenor is the brink and the vehicle giddiness, and the associations one has with giddiness. Of "writhing script", he can say that the script is the tenor and the vehicle is writhing, and the associations we have with writhing. (47)

For the sake of consistency, however, Soskice should say that the vehicle (i.e., the entire utterance) illumines the tenor (e.g., a particular style of penmanship).

Because of potential pitfalls, I abandon Richards's elegant "tenor" and "vehicle" terminology for the admittedly more cumbersome language employed by J. David Sapir in "The Anatomy of Metaphor" (1977:5). Sapir speaks of a metaphor's "topic" (i.e., "what we are talking about or referring to when we use the metaphor"), its "continuous term(s)" (those implying the topic; in Soskice's example, the topic of the metaphor implies the continuous term "script" and vice versa) and its "discontinuous term(s)," e.g., "writhing." Distinguishing among these three features permits our analysis a greater degree of precision.

The bulk of our theoretical discussion appropriately has focused upon metaphor, since it takes pride of place among the tropes. But other types of figurative language also appear in relevant Isaian texts, principal among them the simile. Like M. Black, many literary critics deny simile the impact of metaphor, since a simile's simple comparison cannot rival metaphor's richer interactive meaning. Soskice counters, however, that "the most interesting similes" are functionally the equivalent of metaphors; the presence of "like" [or "as"] is but "an aspect of superficial grammar" (1985:59). By "most interesting similes," Soskice refers to "modelling similes," i.e., those which, like metaphor, "use a subject that is reasonably well known to us to explain or provide schematization for a state of affairs which is beyond our full grasp." "Illustrative similes," by contrast, simply point to certain similarities between two entities. The former function well, she notes, if one "wishes to produce an exploratory schema," the latter when precision is the goal (60).

Yet another difference between some similes (and metaphors) and others is significant: the presence or absence of explicit secondary predicates. The phrase "secondary predicate" refers to "the complex of concepts, assumptions and ideas that, correctly or incorrectly, but usually, is linked to the secondary subject and can be derived from it." But while *implicit* secondary predicates do not specify those associations crucial for a given simile's (or metaphor's) construal, *explicit* secondary predicates do. Return, for example, to our travailing woman simile ("Like a travailing woman I shall shout, I shall gasp and pant"). There, terms of the explicit secondary predicate— "shout," "gasp," and "pant"—direct the reader to precisely those aspects of a travailing woman's behavior that illumine God's power and impending acts (42:14-17; K. Darr 1987a).

Other tropes significant for our study include synecdoche and metonymy on one hand, catachresis and neologism on the other. Synecdoche and metonymy share a crucial characteristic in that both involve the replacement of one word or phrase with another drawn from a single semantic or perceptual domain.[26] (Recall that metaphors, by contrast, draw from two different domains, such that "we speak about one thing in terms which are seen to be suggestive of another" [Soskice 1985:15].) Synecdoche involves replacement within a *hierarchical* classification: "an initial term replaces another that is either more general or more particular than itself" (Sapir 1977:13). Sapir cites, by way of example, two sets of synecdochical replacements for "tree": on the one hand, replacement by its parts (the anatomical mode), branches, leaves, trunk, roots, etc; on the other hand, replacement by varieties (the taxonomic mode), poplar, oak, willow, birch, etc. Metonomy, by contrast, usually involves the substitution of one cause for another (19): "the causal pairs: cause-effect, container-contained, act-agent, etc. are effective precisely because they, in their abstractness, suggest a complete entity. By substituting one of the two causes in a context that calls for the other, a totality is implied that would otherwise not be suggested" (20-21). When we substitute Homer (agent) for *Iliad* (act), for example, "we extend the world of the poem (*Iliad*) not only to its author but also to his other work (the *Odyssey*) and his times" (21).

Finally, both catachresis and neologism fill lexical gaps. The former involves assigning a new meaning to an existing word; the latter, the creation of an entirely new word. Such figures are, of course, more difficult to recognize in an ancient and imperfectly understood language than in one's native tongue. As an example, consider Lam 1:8-9 and 17, where a *hapax legomenon* (a word occurring only once), *nîdah*, suggests both the "mockery" (*shq*) in verse 7b and the *niddah* (menstruous woman) of verses 8-9 and 17.

Identifying Associated Commonplaces

Knowledge of culturally-defined associated commonplaces is essential for construing figurative language. Encountering a contemporary "A is a B" metaphor like "time is money," for example, competent North American readers are able mentally to sift through associations with both the continuous term, "time," and the discontinuous term, "money," to arrive at the metaphor's topic (e.g., unlike U. S. currency, time is not associated with green paper rectangles or round pieces of metal, but it can be "spent" or "wasted"; and its use or misuse has economic consequences).

How can we recover the complex associations surrounding a trope's terms in the world of ancient Israel? Unlike modern anthropologists doing fieldwork in extant cultures not their own, biblical scholars cannot ask ancient Israelites to explain their figurative uses of language. We have only texts, biblical and extra-biblical, to assist us. Our task is hindered by incomplete or unrecoverable data. We benefit, however, from the biblical authors' penchant for traditional imagery.[27]

Many contemporary literary critics judge metaphors in the same way they judge fish dinners: the fresher the better. But ancient Israel's authors appear not to have shared their preference for novel tropes. To the contrary, the artful use of familiar imagery demonstrated an author's knowledge of his or her tradition, imbued fresh verses with the authority accrued to earlier compositions containing the same or similar imagery, and helped audiences interpret new works. This is not to suggest that the biblical authors never coined fresh metaphors. But alongside (what at least appears to be) innovative imagery, one finds numerous recurring tropes possessing what P. Wheelwright, in his discussion of certain *symbols*, has called "ancestral vitality" (1962:105).[28] Such images enriched new contexts by bringing with them meanings and associations borne in earlier sources. Hence, the prophets' repeated embrace of traditional imagery aids our interpretation of their diverse child and female tropes, because it enables us to examine references to these two groups in various literary contexts, thereby gaining some sense of their normal range of associated commonplaces.

Needless to say, we must investigate ancient Israel's tropes, including its so-called "root metaphors," with care, lest we too facilely assume that the insights gleaned enable us to grasp the "essence" of Israel's society and culture. Cultures are, Crocker reminds us, too filled with "contradictions, ambiguities, and befuddlements" to be captured by even their most popular and fully-formulated tropes (1977:66). With that caution in place, however, study of metaphors and models can shed light not only on Israel's literary conventions, but also on its experiences and attitudes, its "world view." Against assertions that historical and literary methods are antithetical, therefore, we note that recovering, as best we can, ancient Israel's complex webs of socially- and culturally-conditioned associations with a particular trope's terms is a "history-recovering" task, yet one essential to our literary approach.[29]

Figurative Language and Strategic Speech

Earlier, I noted that J. A. Darr's reader-oriented method includes the critical premise that "literature functions rhetorically." I added, moreover, that while all communication draws addresser and addressee together (Cohen), figurative uses of language invite communication of a special sort. W. Booth observes (1977:173):

> the receiver's process of interpretation is itself part of what is communicated; the activity of interpretation, performed at the speaker's command, produces a "bonding" which is part of the "meaning." Thus the act of interpreting metaphor will always be more intense ("other things being equal") than engagement with whatever we take to be non- metaphoric (for some, what is *literal*; for others, what is *normal*).

The present study provides numerous opportunities to discuss and illustrate Darr's claim. For example, a variety of tropes and other textual strategies encourage Isaiah's readers to align themselves with "those in [Zion] who repent" (1:27), while distancing themselves from leaders persisting in Israel's history of rebellion. What is the goal of such strategies? To persuade readers to recognize the folly of obduracy, repent of their sins, embrace obedience to Yahweh's Torah, and await both the ultimate punishment of sinners, and the new creation on Yahweh's horizon.

In this chapter, however, let me offer only a few preliminary remarks. First, figurative language accomplishes both informative and performative functions (K. Nielsen 1989:56-67). By "informative," I refer to imagery's ability to communicate ideas, data, perspectives, etc., to its audience; by "performative," I mean that aspect of imagery intended to elicit participation on the part of readers or hearers. Neither function replaces the other; to the contrary, successful tropes fulfill both simultaneously.

Second, persuasion is rhetoric's most embracing motive. Listening to a speaker, C. Crocker observes, the question becomes "What is he trying to get [the addressee] to do, and which of his own ends might be served by such action?" (1977:37). Certainly, Israel's prophets were largely about the business of persuading their audiences to different points of view, new perspectives on their world. In "Of Broken Pots, Fluttering Birds and Visions in the Night," J. C. Exum elaborates upon this foremost motive of tropes:

> literary tropes and rhetorical figures . . . are not just embellishments but rather mediums of persuasion. They are forceful ways of making a point; they center attention and involve the listener in making essential connections necessary for interpretation. Too often in biblical studies, however, in our intense pursuit of the theological message we tend to neglect its medium, as if form were some kind of container from which the message can be extracted. (1981:331)

Third, in discussing the rhetorical, and especially persuasive, nature of tropes, our essentially reader-oriented method necessarily includes the author. After all, the author or speaker conceives the topic and constructs the trope that abets his or her motives and strategies for "selecting enemies and allies, for socializing losses, for warding off [the] evil eye, for purification, propitiation, and desanctification, consolation and vengeance, admonition and exhortation, implicit commands or instructions of one sort or another" (Burke 1957:262). Of course, the *reader* plays an essential role in the communication; that role includes filling the gaps that are particularly a property of figurative speech (Hrushovski 1984:13), as well as other functions identified thus far. Nevertheless, authors may seek, through certain tropes, to present themselves, or their relationships to an audience, in strategic ways. Or, they may express an attitude toward some "external" context that "entitles" it, predisposing the audience to a particular perception, rather than to other perceptions (Crocker 1977:37-38). Whatever their goals, their tropes must persuade persons of "the *truth* of [their] position":

> Most often . . . this truth is not presented as a known fact, but through a semantic movement or transformation of meaning, as a "revelation" or new comprehension about the nature of things. No additional, previously unknown elements are added to the listener's knowledge of the empirical characteristics of things; rather, he is led to see their *natures* through their *relationships*. (Crocker 1977:42)

Finally, determining a trope's meaning and judging its deftness requires that we take *context* seriously:

> what any metaphor *says* or *means* or *does* will always be to some degree alterable by altering its context. Every metaphor . . . could be made to communicate various shades of meaning; each of them could even be made, by employing the easy turns of irony, to say the reverse of what it seems to say. . . . It follows that whether any metaphor is judged to be *good* is inescapably dependent on its context: what surrounds it in the text, spoken or written, and who speaks it to whom for what purpose. (Booth 1977:173-74)

I reject formalist theories that define metaphors as a phenomenon of word meaning, while bracketing out context. K. Harries correctly reminds us that certain isolated metaphors may, by "tensions and collisions . . . continue to call us beyond the[ir] literal meaning[s]" (1977:71).[30] Nevertheless, context remains crucial to metaphorical construal. Consider, for example, Hezekiah's proverb in Isa 37:3b, the object of our attention in Chapter 6. In a different literary context, his statement ("Babes are positioned for birth, but there is no strength to deliver"; author's translation), might be understood as the aggrieved king's dramatic, somewhat stylized, but literal report of childbirth complications in the royal harem. Given its Isaian context

(Sennacherib's threatened siege against Jerusalem), however, readers will almost certainly interpret the phrase metaphorically—more specifically, as a metaphorical proverb. As Soskice observes: "it is true that a particular sentence may bear two construals, a literal one and a metaphorical one. But this only points to the ambiguity of the sentence prior to full consideration of its context" (1985:85).

CONCLUSION

In this chapter, I have set out both a methodological approach to Isaiah, and my theoretical understanding of how we can construe figurative uses of language in that ancient Israelite text. By concentrating upon the reader (a heuristic device), the text, and the extratext, I have structured the following investigation of how female and child imagery contributes to our reader's sequential construal of Isaiah as a coherent literary work. Moreover, my discussion of how metaphors and related tropes "mean," and toward what ends, considers seriously the text's intent to persuade readers to new ways of perceiving their world. For sequential readers, Isaiah's vision is not glimpsed all at once (though Isaiah 1 presages the path it will follow). Only by moving within and through that vision can they discover fully the purpose of a divine plan that—like the word of our God—"is established forever" (Isa 40:8b).

2

CHILD IMAGERY
AND THE RHETORIC
OF REBELLION

The significance of the prophet Isaiah's children—their number, names, and functions as "signs and portents in Israel from the Lord of Hosts" (Isa 8:18), has long been a topic of debate. Seldom do scholars comment upon references to offspring beyond Isaiah's memoir (6:1–8:18), however, though they abound in oracles of judgment and salvation alike.

References to Shear-jashub, Immanuel, and Maher-shalal-hash-baz tell us little of stereotypical associations with progeny in ancient Israelite society. Their significance lies in their (essentially passive) contributions to the prophet's ministry—Isaiah's penchant for giving them "message" names and linking future events with their developmental milestones[1]—rather than in their ability strategically to quicken associated thoughts and feelings. Elsewhere, however, literal and figurative references to children reveal a number of ancient Israel's conventional ideas about babies, youths, and adult progeny, frequently inviting readers to perceive the bonds joining Yahweh and Israel as familial ties.

The Hebrew Bible testifies to Israel's belief that progeny are life's greatest blessing. Birth announcements (S. Parker 1988; 1989:63–70) were met with joy, and the Israelites knew the pleasures of child-rearing. But offspring brought other benefits as well: social stability; enhanced status and security; an increased labor pool; and potentially beneficial alliances forged through marriages. Both males and females assisted their families in the fields, among the flocks, in trades, and at home.

Within Israel's patrilineal society, of course, sons were especially crucial for preserving a family's name and social status,[2] and for the orderly transfer of family land across the generations. Not surprisingly, then, many of the Hebrew Bible's associations with children, especially sons, are quite positive. In Ps 127:3-5, for example, we read:

> Sons are the provision of the Lord;
>> the fruit of the womb, his reward.
> Like arrows in the hand of a warrior
>> are sons born to a man in his youth.
> Happy is the man who fills his quiver with them. (*Tanakh*)

But parents in Israel's ancient Near Eastern world knew that cheek by jowl with childhood's beauty and freshness, innocence, honesty, and vulnerability went its lack of self-restraint, inexperience, rebelliousness, and seemingly endless energy (Isa 40:30 notwithstanding). Not surprisingly, then, negative associations with children also appear in Scripture. Finally, some of the physical and psychological limitations naturally associated with minors could, when attributed to adults, become decidedly pejorative.

In this chapter, we shall first identify ancient Israelite associations with children astir in Isaiah—limited knowledge, competence, and self-discipline; weakness and vulnerability; lovability; hope for familial longevity; disrespectful behavior; and rebelliousness. But we shall also discern, as best we can, the informative and performative functions of references to children within their immediate and broader literary contexts. Our questions are these: how do figurative references to children with their attending associations contribute to their oracular settings? How do they contribute to a sequential reading of Isaiah 1–66? In particular, how does the recurring metaphor of Israel as God's (and Jerusalem's) rebellious children function, change, and reach its (proleptically announced) resolution?

STEREOTYPICAL ASSOCIATIONS WITH CHILDREN

Isaiah contains references to offspring of all ages—nurslings, youths, fully-grown adults. Naturally, ancient Israel's associations with children could vary, depending upon their ages, stages, and gender. Limited knowledge and competence were associated with young children, for example, but not with adult offspring. Familial models and metaphors, by contrast, could quicken thoughts of the blood, social, and emotive bonds joining members of family units, regardless of their ages.

Limited Knowledge and Competence

When Isa 10:19 threatens that in the aftermath of Yahweh's consuming wrath, Assyria's remaining trees "shall be so few that a boy [na'ar] can record them," no criticism of minors is intended. The author simply presumes that the competencies of young children (including knowledge of their "one-two-three's") are limited. The same stereotypical association underlies Isa 11:8, where infants unknowingly play over a viper's hole, but are spared the deadly consequences of their actions because they live in the paradisiacal age to come (cf. Judg 8:20; 1 Kgs 3:7).

Because of their limited experience, ancient Israel's children required training in all areas of life. The bulk of such training probably took place in the domestic sphere, as adult family members (male and female) instructed minors in the skills, behaviors, and values necessary for successful life. But we do not know whether, or to what extent, education also occurred in more formal settings (Crenshaw 1985:601-15). The book of Proverbs contains extensive instructions designed to help Israel's youth master a wide variety of experiences. Deuteronomy 6:7 requires that parental instruction include Yahweh's laws and rules;[3] and Hezekiah's prayer (Isa 38:10-20) refers to fathers teaching their children of God's gracious acts on Israel's behalf (vs. 19).

While their recognized need for secular and religious instruction was no criticism of the young, however, certain of Isaiah's figurative references to children play upon their limited knowledge to threaten or insult adults. Isaiah 3:1-5, for example, predicts the exile of Judah's religious, military, and civil leaders, threatening that no competent replacements will be left in the land:

> And I will make boys their princes,
>> and babes shall rule over them. (vs. 4; see also Jer 4:22)

The MT of Isa 3:12 pairs infants and women in order to highlight the incompetence, ignorance, and irresponsibility of Jerusalem's current leaders:

48

> My people—children are their oppressors,
>> and women rule over them.[4]
> O my people, your leaders mislead you,
>> and confuse the course of your paths.

S. Ackerman (1992:164) interprets this text to mean that in a future period of political and social chaos, women will assume actual government and religious offices. But the poem claims that current leaders are "women" and pairs women with children. Isaiah 3:4, 12 are best understood, therefore, as examples of reversal. The poet presumes his audience's familiarity with the routine circumstances he contrasts: under normal circumstances, babes and women do not rule, and children are not oppressors (Dobbs-Allsopp 1993:14-39).

Another famous and much-debated text utilizes repetition and wordplay to suggest how certain drunken, gluttonous priests and prophets respond with indignation to a scolding in tones normally reserved for undisciplined toddlers:

> To whom would he give instruction?
> To whom expound a message?
> To those newly weaned from milk,
> Just taken away from the breast?
> That same mutter upon mutter,
> Murmur upon murmur,
> Now here, now there! (28:9-10; *Tanakh*)[5]

Behind the rhetorical questions of verse 9 lies the presumption that newly-weaned children must be taught how to behave in public.[6] The suggestion that certain *adults* required such training, however, clearly offended those priests and prophets occupying prominent positions within Jerusalem's royal cult.

Weakness and Vulnerability

If certain texts in Isaiah scold Jerusalem's leaders for behaving like little children, or threaten that the nation's future leaders will be as incompentent as babies, others anticipate a future, edenic age in which children will perform quite extraordinary acts of leadership:

> The wolf shall live with the lamb,
>> the leopard shall lie down with the kid,
> the calf and the lion and the fatling together,
>> and a little child shall lead them. (Isa 11:6)

49

This well-known text achieves its rhetorical power, in part, through the striking juxtaposition of ravenous predators and very young animals—lambs and kids that are the easiest of prey. At the head of the menagerie is a little child [*na'ar qaton*], whose natural defenses and experience are scant. The image of paradise returned reveals Israel's stereotypical notions of extreme youth's weakness, vulnerability (cf. Isa 11:8), and innocence.

Infancy and childhood were perilous stages of life that many in Israel's world did not survive. Childbirth complications, disease, accidents, warfare, and periods of famine or other natural disasters contributed to a high infant mortality rate.[7] Isaiah 65, yet another depiction of a paradisiacal future, promises both an end to infant mortality and an extended human lifespan:

> No more shall there be in it
> > an infant that lives but a few days,
> > or an old person who does not live out a lifetime;
> for one who dies at a hundred years will be considered a youth,
> > and one who falls short of a hundred will be considered
> > accursed. (65:20; see also vs. 23)

Lacking the physical strength, practical knowledge, and experience required to feed, clothe, and shelter themselves, anticipate danger, and elude attackers, young children required adult nurture and protection. Without such care, they easily fell victim to natural calamities or intentional assaults (Lev 26:21-22; Deut 28:41). Numerous biblical texts witness to battle-related atrocities committed against minors whose protectors had been wounded, captured, or killed (e.g., Deut 28:41; 2 Kgs 8:12; Jer 9:19-20; Lam 2:11-12). Isaiah 13:15-18, part of a description of the chaotic conditions that will pertain on the Day of Yahweh, depicts the fate awaiting Babylon's defenseless infants and their mothers:

> All who remain shall be pierced through,
> All who are caught / Shall fall by the sword.
> And their babes shall be dashed to pieces in their sight,
> Their homes shall be plundered, / And their wives shall be raped.
> "Behold, I stir up the Medes against them,
> Who do not value silver / Or delight in gold.
> Their bows shall shatter the young;
> They shall show no pity to infants,
> They shall not spare the children." (*Tanakh*)

According to Isa 9:16 (ET 17) the inhabitants of Israel's Northern Kingdom, and especially their leaders, are so perverse that in the approaching battle, Yahweh will not even take pity on their vulnerable orphans and widows.

Quite apart from wartime atrocities, however, fatherless children risked falling victim to greedy, unscrupulous people within their own communities. Israel's prophetic literature, including Isaiah, repeatedly censures the wealthy leadership class for exploiting the marginalized, vulnerable, and poor in their midst—fatherless children, widows, immigrants. Kings (and, by extension, their administrators) were enjoined to emulate divine support for helpless members of society (see, e.g., Prov 29:14). But particularly during times of social upheaval, children and others lacking the protection of adult Israelite males were vulnerable to attempts at land appropriation (Isa 5:8), enslavement (2 Kgs 4:1), and perverted juridical processes (Jer 5:27-28):

> Your rulers [NRSV princes] are rebels
> and companions of thieves.
> Everyone loves a bribe / and runs after gifts.
> They do not defend the orphan,
> and the widow's cause does not come before them.
> (Isa 1:23; see also Isa 1:16-17; 10:1-2; Amos 2:6; 8:6)

Here, "orphans" and "widows" function meristically to designate all of society's least powerful citizenry; and Jerusalem's rulers are accused of greedily exploiting their most vulnerable subjects.

Lovability and Familial Longevity

The horrific depictions of violence against children lodged in passages like Isa 13:13-17 derive their rhetorical power not only from the contrast between military savagery and children's weakness and vulnerability, but also from the fact that ancient progeny, no less than modern, were precious to their parents and constituted a family's only hope for a future beyond the lifespans of its adult members.[8] The similes in Zech 12:10 suggest that the sorrow following the death of an only child is life's most bitter grief, and so can convey a sense of the profound sorrow attending other situations: "they shall mourn for him, as one mourns for an only child, and weep bitterly over him, as one weeps over a firstborn."

In 2 Sam 14:7, the wise woman of Tekoa pretends that her pleas to David are on behalf of her son who, though guilty of fratricide, is nonetheless her sole hope for the family's survival.

These two associations with offspring—profound love and familial (and more broadly, national) longevity—frequently appear in Isaian oracles of weal and woe alike. In some texts, one or the other association predominates. Isaiah 49:14-18, for example, foregrounds children as objects of parental love, first by lifting up a mother's unwavering devotion to her nursing infant (which is nonetheless exceeded by Yahweh's devotion to Israel), and then by urging Jerusalem to bejewel herself with the precious children who are returning home.

In Isa 48:18-19, by contrast, stock hyperbolic phrases emphasize the importance of progeny for (in this case, Israel's) ongoing existence:

> If only you would heed My commands!
> Then your prosperity would be like a river,
> Your triumph like the waves of the sea.
> Your offspring would be as many as the sand,
> Their issue as many as its grains.
> Their name would never be cut off
> Or obliterated from before Me. (*Tanakh*; see also Isa 59:21)

The same association undergirds Isa 56:4-5, where Yahweh promises that righteous eunuchs, though childless (note the image of the withered family tree in verse 3; Coogan 1990:139), will nevertheless secure for themselves "a name better than sons or daughters . . . an everlasting name."

In many texts, however, these two associations are inextricably linked. The birth announcement in Isa 9:1-6, for example, bespeaks both the great joy accompanying the birth of a child (in this case, likely a prince),[9] and hope for unending peace and justice when this little child grows to lead the nation:

> His authority shall grow continually,
>   and there shall be endless peace
> for the throne of David and his kingdom.
>   He will establish and uphold it
> with justice and with righteousness
>   from this time onward and forevermore.[10]

In grim contrast to rejoicing over new life and hope for a peaceful and just future, the city of Sidon bewails both her dead children, and her own hopeless situation: "I am as one who has never labored, never given birth, never raised youths or reared maidens" (Isa 23:4). Pampered Lady Babylon likewise will be bereaved of children and husband, despite her use of a sorceress's skills (Isaiah 47).[11] A childless widow, she will be thrust into the most precarious social situation. Her future will be bleak indeed.

Particularly in chapters 40–66, references to the status and condition of Zion's children give readers a sense of the nation's deep sorrow on the one hand, and its imminent joy on the other. Mother Jerusalem has already endured the childlessness threatening her rivals, Sidon and Babylon. Isa 51:20 forces upon her a pitiful description of her offspring's plight:

> Your sons lie in a swoon
> At the corner of every street—
> Like an antelope caught in a net—
> Drunk with the wrath of the Lord,
> With the rebuke of your God. (Tanakh)

But numerous texts proleptically announce the joyous return of Zion's and Yahweh's sons and daughters—their precious ones, and her hope. Certain of these texts not only depict the returning diaspora as Jerusalem's offspring, but also heighten the scenario's impact by depicting them as little children—vulnerable, innocent infants and toddlers who must be carried and suckled.[12] Readers of Isa 49:22-23a relish a reversal in which the earth's mighty rulers serve as child-care providers and wetnurses for Zion's little ones. Gender-matched parallelism (Watson 1984:123-28) functions meristically to stress the completeness of the anticipated homecoming:

> Thus says the Lord God:
> I will soon lift up my hand to the nations,
>   and raise my signal to the peoples;
> and they shall bring your sons [m.] in their bosom [m.],
>   and your daughters [f.] shall be carried on their shoulders [f.].
> Kings shall be your foster fathers,
>   and their queens your nursing mothers.
> With their faces to the ground they shall bow down to you,
>   and lick the dust of your feet. (Isa 49:22-23)

Jerusalem's children will be so numerous that they will grumble, complaining to their mother that her quarters cannot adequately shelter them all (Isa 49:20-21; see also Isa 54:1-3).

But a bit of churlishness only enhances the joy suffusing these anticipations of a mother and child reunion.

Homecoming imagery is not the only means by which Isaiah describes Jerusalem's repopulation. Other texts promise that she will bear additional children, raising them in the marvelous age to come. These infants, miraculously born before the onset of labor pains and the recipients of Mother Jerusalem's nurture, care, and comfort, will enjoy the paradisiacal life denied the sons of Eve, whose births occurred only after their parents' expulsion from the garden of Eden.[13]

Disrespectful Behavior

Symptomatic of the social upheaval attending Judah's loss of experienced leadership (Isa 3:1-4), a youthful bully abuses his elder:

> The people will be oppressed,
>> everyone by another / and everyone by a neighbor;
> the youth will be insolent to the elder,
>> and the base to the honorable. (Isa 3:5)

This text, like the story of Elisha's run-in with the bad boys of Bethel, acknowledges that uncontrolled youths have a propensity toward disrespectful behavior. How could ancient Israelite parents secure their children's respect and obedience?

Rebelliousness

Rebelliousness, our final Isaian association with children, figures prominently in the remainder of this chapter. In order appropriately to contextualize that discussion, we must emphasize that ancient Israelite society placed great value upon filial obedience and devotion. In the Decalogue the apodictic imperative, "Honor your father and your mother" (Exod 20:12), was further reinforced by a motivation clause offering long life in the promised land as a reward for compliance (Harrelson 1980:92-105; Crenshaw 1981: 82-83). Elsewhere, Israel's proverbs admonished offspring to follow parental advice:

> Hear, my child, your father's instruction,
>> and do not reject your mother's teaching;
> for they are a fair garland for your head,
>> and pendants for your neck. (Prov. 1:8-9; see also 6:20)

Even beyond their adolescent years, children were expected to honor, obey, and provide for their parents:[14]

> Listen to your father who begot you;
>> and do not despise your mother when she is old. (23:22)

But despite parental instruction, discipline, and affection, ancient Israel's children could become rebellious and a source of grief. The sages suggested dire threats (Prov 30:17) and corporal punishment to control recalcitrance: "Blows that wound cleanse away evil," they advised; "beatings make clean the innermost parts" (Prov 20:30). Parents justified such thrashings by claiming that they, like Yahweh, punished out of love:

> My child, do not despise the Lord's discipline
>> or be weary of his reproof,
> for the Lord reproves the one he loves,
>> as a father the son in whom he delights. (Prov 3:11-12)

When such measures failed to rehabilitate a rebellious child, disgrace and dishonor threatened the family:

> Those who do violence to their father
>> and chase away their mother
> are children who cause shame
> and bring reproach. (Prov 19:26)

Deuteronomy 21:18-21 prescribes actions for parents who, having exhausted all other methods of controlling a defiant, intemperate child, must seek community assistance in the final resolution of a familial crisis:

> If a man has a wayward [sôrer] and defiant [môreh] son, who does not heed his father or mother and does not obey them even after they discipline him, his father and mother shall take hold of him and bring him out to the elders of his town at the public place of his community. They shall say to the elders of his town, "This son of ours is disloyal and defiant [sôrer ûmoreh]; he does not heed us. He is a glutton and a drunkard." Thereupon the men of his town shall stone him to death.
>> (Tanakh)[15]

These harsh words, and others as well (e.g., Exod 21:15; Lev 20:9; Deut 27:16), leave little doubt that in ancient Israelite society, stereotypical associations with unbridled offspring were negative indeed. In the following pages, we shall return to the familial crisis legislated in Deut 21:18-21.

ISAIAH'S VISION AND THE
RHETORIC OF REBELLION

Isaiah 1: "Oh, Rebellious Children"

More than once, Isaiah 1 charges Yahweh's children with re-bellion. This "first impression" of Israel, derived from no less reliable a source than Yahweh, decisively colors the reader's view of God's people, and especially of their leaders. Moreover, because the language of rebellion is present as the reader moves from accusation (vss. 1-2) to exhortation (vs. 5), from ad-monition (vss. 18-20) to condemnation (vs. 23), and finally to judgment (vs. 28), it contributes to his sense of the chapter's coherence.

Readers encounter the metaphor of Israel as God's rebel-lious offspring in the book's very first oracle, an accusation:

Hear, O heavens, and listen, O earth; / for the Lord has spoken:
I reared children [*banîm*, sons] and brought them up,
   but they have rebelled against me [*pase'û bî*].
The ox knows its owner, / and the donkey its masters' crib;
but Israel does not know,
   my people do not understand. (Isa 1:2-3)

The metaphor continues in verse 4, part of a prophetic admoni-tion (vss. 4-9), with the epithets "offspring who do evil" (*zera' mere'îm*) and "children who deal corruptly" (*banîm mashî-tîm*).[16] In these verses, of course, grown children, rather than infants or little boys and girls, are decried. As we have seen, however, referring to chronologically mature persons as children could serve strategic ends. In this initial oracle, readers are invited to perceive Yahweh as a parent who has provided Israel's sustenance throughout its life. In other words, the familial blood bond uniting fathers and their children becomes the metaphorical lens through which the reader perceives the relationship between Yahweh and Israel. And in light of the nature of that bond, with its mutual concerns and responsibili-ties (once the child has grown to maturity), Israel's rebellion and incomprehension appear all the more heinous.

That the reader of Isaiah first glimpses God's people through the lens of rebellious child imagery merits special attention, for the opening part of a literary work is especially persuasive and programmatic for readers (Sternberg 1978:93-96). Moreover, metaphorical depictions of Israel as God's rebellious children will recur in subsequent chapters, functioning as key elements in what we shall call Isaiah's "rhetoric of rebellion." In the remainder of this chapter, we examine those texts, not only to identify the metaphor's meanings and functions within each oracular setting, but also to trace how the reader construes this larger, recurring rebellion theme.

Isaiah contains no literal descriptions of rebellious Israelite minors, save for the youthful bully whose disrespectful actions are symptomatic of social chaos (Isa 3:4). As we have just discovered, however, its initial oracle depicts the people of Israel as rebellious, corrupt offspring who—baldly stated—lack the sense of livestock. They have "turned their backs" (vs. 4; *Tanakh*) on their divine parent; and they continue to rebel (*sarah*), despite repeated beatings (vs. 5a). Yahweh therefore assumes the role of the thoroughly vexed parents in Deuteronomy 21, assembling witnesses—there, the town's elders; here, the heavens and the earth—to hear the charges against them: God's children practice evil and deal corruptly; they have forsaken and despised their father; and their rebellion persists even in the face of corporal punishment that leaves them bruised and bleeding (vss. 5b-6). Not only they, but also their homes, land, and cities have been decimated as a result of their corruption (vss. 7-8). So severe is the situation that only a "few survivors" remain (vs. 9):

> If the Lord of hosts / had not left us a few survivors,[17]
> we would have been like Sodom, / and become like Gomorrah.[18]

Cultic acts alone cannot compensate for the people's defiling, oppressive deeds. To the contrary, their endless but insincere sacrifices and prayers are offensive to Yahweh, who sorely desires that the community cleanse itself of evil and oppression. Note the piling up of imperatives:

> Wash yourselves; make yourselves clean;
>> remove the evil of your doings
>> from before my eyes;
> cease to do evil, / learn to do good;
> seek justice, / rescue the oppressed,
> defend the orphan, / plead for the widow. (Isa 3:16-17)

Even in the face of such serious offenses, Yahweh hopes for a change in his children's ways. And in an offer of parental forebearance, the people are given a choice:

> If you are willing and obedient,
>> you shall eat the good of the land;
> but if you refuse and rebel [*ûmerîtem*],
>> you shall be devoured by the sword;
>> for the mouth of the Lord has spoken. (Isa 3:19)

Be willing and obedient and eat (*'kl*), or refuse and rebel and be eaten (*'kl*). The root *mrh*, twice present in Deuteronomy's ultimate "cure" for wayward offspring, did not appear in Isaiah's first characterization of Israel as rebellious children (1:2-5). But here in verse 20, it recalls the accusation lodged in those opening verses.

The following lament over Zion's depraved status charges rebellion once more: the city's princes (that is, her powerful leaders) are *sôrerîm*, "rebels" and cronies of thieves who love a bribe, but won't be bothered to care for orphans and widows (1:23). Under such conditions, Yahweh concludes, only a great purge can restore the once-faithful city. Note the pivot pattern and reversed gender parallelism (trans. by Watson 1984:221):

> Zion [f.] by justice [m.] shall be redeemed,
>> and those [m.] in her who repent, by right [f.].
> But rebels [*pose'îm*; see 1:2] and sinners shall be
>> destroyed together,
>> and those who forsake the Lord shall be consumed.
>> (Isa 1:27-28)

These two verses presage the course that the rebellion motif will take in the remainder of Isaiah. As we shall see in Chapters 4 and 5 below, they also are crucial for the reader's understanding of Lady Zion's fate.

In the remainder of this chapter, we shall note how various rhetorical strategies seek to persuade readers to align themselves with "those in [Zion] who repent" (1:27), while distancing themselves from those rebels and sinners who "forsake the Lord" (1:28). Vocabulary varies; we have begun to develop a sort of argot of rebellion, including forms of *ps'* (twice), *sur*, *mrh*, and *srr*. And each of these terms will reappear in subsequent contexts where rebelliousness threatens the familial ties joining Yahweh and Israel. Forms of *ps'* (BDB: "rebel, transgress"), in particular, will prove significant for the reader's construal of Isaiah's "rhetoric of rebellion." Unlike *srr, ps'* is not especially linked with the attitudes and actions of offspring (be they minors or fully-grown). Rather, it often describes national revolts (with *be,* "against"), and rebellion or "transgression" against God. Nevertheless, *ps'* is associated from the very outset of the book with the metaphor of Israel as God's rebellious children. Moreover, its use in contexts of political and theological obduracy relates to our theme, since Isaian oracles containing child imagery often charge rebellion against Yahweh, denounce political alliances, and depict the nations functioning as God's "instruments." More generally, however, a child metaphor alone does not determine whether or not a particular text belongs to the "rhetoric of rebellion." The appearance of *ps'* and/or the other vocabulary of rebellion potentially signals that rhetorical theme, even if child imagery is not an explicit feature of each and every pertinent text.

Isaiah 1, then, levels charges against Israel and describes the consequences of persistent obduracy. The nation's history of rebellion against its father is illustrated with particular perniciousness by its leaders. Sans repentance, their end will be like the snap! crackle! pop! of dried tinder meeting a spark (vs. 31). But with its familial metaphors and urgings toward reconciliation, Isaiah 1 holds out hope as well.

Isaiah 3:8: "Babes Shall Rule Over Them"

Only twenty-two verses later, a leadership crisis threatens to leave Jerusalem and Judah in the hands of "children" and vulnerable to anarchy (3:1-5). Again, the entire national population is charged with rebelliousness:

> For Jerusalem has stumbled / and Judah has fallen,
> because their speech and their deeds are against the Lord,
> defying [*lamrôt*] his glorious presence. (3:8)

The personification of "stumbled" Jerusalem and "fallen" Judah contributes to the poetic image of a body politic that is out of control.

The reappearance in Isaiah 3 of certain words, speech formulae, and themes encountered already in Isaiah 1 reinforces their importance for readers: once again, Israel's perverted leaders (cf. 1:21-31) are accused of rebellion (3:8, from the root *mrh*; cf. 1:18-20); both chapters employ courtroom formulae (3:13-15; cf. 1:2-3, 18-20); and both contain child imagery, although the associations of limited knowledge and experience in 3:4, 12 differ from the charges of deliberate rebellion lodged against Yahweh's (adult) children in 1:2-5a, 20, 23, and 28. Finally, both chapters contain references to Sodom. In 1:9, the city signifies utter destruction, while in 1:10 and 3:9, emphasis falls upon its extreme iniquity.

Read sequentially, then, Isaiah 1–3 argues that Yahweh's rebellious children, including their oppressive rulers, are offered the opportunity to repent of their defiance and injustice. Those who accept that offer and become obedient will partake of Judah and Jerusalem's future salvation (1:27; 2:1-4); those who do not, persisting in their defiance and sinfulness, will surely be destroyed (1:28). Indeed, even now (*kî hinneh*, 3:1) the purging of Judah's leadership is begun, and social chaos threatens.

Isaiah 30: "O Rebellious Children"

Although Isaiah 4–29 contain a variety of accusations against the inhabitants of Northern Israel and Judah, rebellious child metaphors do not reappear until chapter 30, an indictment of Judean policy makers whose recourse to Egyptian aid is decidedly at odds with Yahweh's plan for Israel.[19] Immediately preceding verses (29:22-24) have foretold a time when Jacob, beholding his children, will sanctify God's name. But as 30:1-5 makes clear, that time has not yet arrived. The epithet "rebellious children" (*banîm sôrerîm*) reminds readers of charges already lodged in Isaiah 1 and 3, including the reference in 1:23 to Israel's roguish (*sôrerîm*) rulers:

> O rebellious children [*banîm sôrerîm*], says the Lord,
> who carry out a plan, but not mine;
> who make an alliance, but against my will,
>   adding sin to sin; (30:1)

The rebuke is followed by God's command that these words be inscribed lest Israel forget its rejection of Yahweh's instruction. For readers, 30:8-9 echo and underscore the scroll's initial characterization of God's people:

Go, write it down on a tablet / And inscribe it in a record,
That it may be with them for future days, / A witness forever.
For it is a rebellious people ['am merî],
    faithless children [banîm kehasîm],
Children who refused to heed / The instruction of the Lord.

(Isa 30:8-9; Tanakh)

Here, associations identified thus far—children's limited knowledge and experience, their need for instruction, and rebelliousness—converge to convey a sense of reckless filial obduracy on the one hand, and parental exasperation on the other.

Summary

What, to this point, do readers surmise about Yahweh's rebellious children, including especially their childish (i.e., foolish and destructive) leaders? Taken together, the texts examined depict unrepentant Israel as the very personification of the odious son of Deut 21:18-21. The latter is wayward (sôrer, Deut 21:18a); so is Israel (sôrerîm, Isa 1:23; banîm sôrerîm, Isa 30:1a). He is defiant (môreh, Deut 21:18, 20); Israel is rebellious as well (lamrôt, Isa 3:8; 'am merî, Isa 30:9a; hem pase'û bî, Isa 1:2b). Moreover, as sequential readers of Isaiah know, Israel's leaders share the odious son's excessive appetites for food and alcohol (Deut 21:20b; Isa 5:11-13, 22; 22:13; 28:1-4, 7-8 [against Ephraim's rulers]). Finally, neither rebel repents, even in the face of repeated corporal punishment (Deut 21:18b; Isa 1:5a). If, as Deut 21:21 states, the disobedient son's offenses justify capital punishment, then Israel is no less deserving of death.

ISAIAH 40–55: "I HAVE SWEPT AWAY YOUR TRANSGRESSIONS LIKE A CLOUD"

Rebellious child imagery does not reappear until Isa 48:8-11. Readers arriving here have passed from Isaiah 1–39 into chapters widely identified as the product of so-called Deutero-Isaiah. For our reader, whose progress through Isaiah focuses particularly upon child and female imagery, the transition from Isa 39:8 to 40:1 is not the severe "jolt" that modern commentators, presupposing a shift in authorship, time, and geographical locale, emphasize.[20] By that point in the scroll he is quite accustomed to rapid changes of subject and tone. Yet there are

61

numerous differences between chapters 1–39 on the one hand, and 40–55 on the other; and our reader becomes increasingly aware of them. He will discover, for example, that chapters 40–55 extend forgiveness to all Israel, including—one presumes —those most guilty of the offenses bristling from texts like Isaiah 30. Indeed, we shall argue that Isaiah 40–55 constitute a prolonged "grace note" within the larger scroll. To be sure, many of its passages do not downplay the extremity of Israel's rebelliousness. To the contrary, their accusations can *exceed* in severity those appearing in Isaiah 1–39. But they insist nonetheless that despite its past transgressions, Yahweh's care and involvement with Israel persist.

How are readers persuaded that the destruction merited by Israel is not the end of its relationship with God? What of the servant's reconciling role? Will the reader regard him as synonymous with Israel? If not, what is his relationship to God's rebellious offspring? Finally, how do our familial models and metaphors invite readers to perceive the ties binding Israel and its God in Isaiah 40–55? Our reader knows that family bonds often withstand what might otherwise appear unbearable burdens. The harshness of Deut 21:18-21 notwithstanding, ancient parents—like their modern-day counterparts—could continue to love even the most recalcitrant of children.[21] One recalls, for example, David's heartbroken response to the news that Absalom, the son who had sought not only his throne, but also his life, was dead (2 Sam 18:33).

When passages in the Deutero-Isaian corpus speak of God's willingness to remain in relationship with Israel, or encourage Israel to remain in relationship with its God, they do not always foreground divine love or family ties as the motivation for those choices. Nevertheless, the familial models of Isaiah 40–55—not only father/rebellious child metaphors, but also the husband/wife metaphors to which we shall turn in Chapters 4 and 5—are aptly suited to convey a sense of the pain, anger, and shame that Israel, Yahweh, its divine father, and Jerusalem, its mother, have experienced, and also to express how it is possible that those relationships can survive and be healed in the aftermath of calamity.

"FROM BIRTH YOU WERE CALLED A REBEL"

Our next four texts share the theme of rebellion. Two of the four do not contain rebellious child metaphors *per se*. Yet each is integral to our larger Isaian "rhetoric of rebellion." Recall that for the sequential reader, the presence of vocabulary associated with Isaiah's argot of rebellion suffices to signal our theme, even as passages containing explicit child imagery reenforce the rebellious child metaphor introduced already in Isaiah 1.

Isaiah 43:25-27 and 44:21-22

Isaiah 43:25-27 follows a recital of Israel's offenses culminating with Yahweh's complaint:

> But you have burdened me with your sins;
>> you have wearied me with your iniquities. (vs. 24b)

In the following verses, however, God promises to "blot out" the long history of disobedience that justifies Israel's demise:

> I, I am He
>> who blots out your transgressions [*pesa'êka*] for my own sake,
>> and I will not remember your sins.
> Accuse me, let us go to trial;
>> set forth your case, so that you may be proved right.[22]
> Your first ancestor sinned,
>> and your intermediaries rebelled against me [*pase'û bî*].[23]
> Therefore I profaned the princes of the sanctuary,
>> I delivered Jacob to utter destruction,
>> and Israel to reviling. (Isa 43:25-28)

These verses also remind the reader of Isaiah 1 with its rhetoric of rebellion: both texts contain forms of *ps'*; both issue invitations to resolve the dispute between Yahweh and Israel in language associated with juridical settings; both offer alternatives to punishment; and both single out Israel's leaders for special reproach. Yet there is a striking difference between these two texts that is of crucial importance to our larger analysis of rebellion in Isaiah: 1:18-20, 27-28 held out redemption for those who repented of their transgressions and embraced obedience, but threatened the utter destruction of those who persistently refused to repent. Isaiah 43:25-28, on the other hand, looks back on well-deserved destruction (vs. 28), but freely offers expiation to transgressors (vs. 25)—not because they have repented, or because they can justify their actions, but rather "for my [God's] own sake." Said differently, a shift in perspective has appeared in the Deutero-Isaian corpus. Earlier texts proclaimed the fate of rebels and sinners: refusal to repent meant fiery destruction. In our present text, by contrast, all Israel is characterized as historically rebellious (in agreement with Isa 1:2-3), but all are offered forgiveness.

This same shift from the tenor of earlier chapters is reflected in Isa 44:21-22, where God encourages all Israel's return with promises of forgiveness and reconciliation motivated by the intimate Creator/created link uniting Yahweh and Jacob/Israel:

> Remember these things,[24] O Jacob,
>   and Israel, for you are my servant;
> I formed you, you are my servant;
>   O Israel, you will not be forgotten by me.
> I have swept away your rebellions [pesa'êka] like a cloud,
>   and your sins like mist;
> Return to me, for I have redeemed you.

This text also is part of Isaiah's rhetoric of rebellion, though God's people are here called "servant," rather than son. In this context, the epithet clearly refers to all Israel. Will its referent remain the same, or change as readers move further into Isaiah's vision?

Isaiah 46:8 and 48:8-11

In two persuasive passages, Yahweh describes Israel as "rebels." Despite all that God has done for *and* against Israel, the people must be convinced of their God's power and purpose:

> Remember this and consider,
>   recall it to mind, you transgressors [pôse'îm],
> remember the former things of old;
>   for I am God, and there is no other;
>   I am God, and there is no one like me.

The second text, 48:8-11, contains rebellious child imagery. In language strikingly harsh and reminiscent of certain parts of Ezekiel (e.g., Ezekiel 16 and 20), Yahweh's charges that, despite their long-lived relationship (vss. 1-2), obstinant Israel would have ascribed knowledge of "the former things" to its idols, had not the prophets proclaimed them Yahweh's doing. Now, God promises to tell Israel new things, things so unheard of that the people cannot claim to have learned them from some other source. Note that this text goes beyond the accusation lodged in Isa 1:2-3: both texts stress Israel's lack of understanding (1:3; 48:8); both use a form of the root *ps'* to describe its defiance (1:2; 48:8); and both contain smelting imagery. But while Isa 1:2 suggested that Israel rebelled only after its upbringing was completed, this text traces its obduracy back to Israel's earliest emergence as a people:

> You have never heard, you have never known,
>   from of old your ear has not been opened.
> For I knew that you would deal very treacherously,
>   and that from birth you were called a rebel [*ps'*]. . . .
> See, I have refined you, but not like silver;
>   I have tested you in the furnace of adversity.[25]
> For my own sake, for my own sake, I do it,
>   for why should my name be profaned?
> My glory I will not give to another. (48:8-11)

Here God does not assume the role of a patient parent, extending forgiveness to even the most odious offspring. To the contrary, Israel has been forced to endure a trip to the "furnace of adversity." Yet out of concern for the divine reputation, Yahweh has refrained from utterly destroying these life-long rebels.

Isaiah 50:1

In Isa 50:1, the people of Israel appear as the children of their father, Yahweh, and their mother, Jerusalem. In preceding verses, God has promised personified Jerusalem that mighty nations will soon be forced to return her sons and daughters. The rhetorical questions in verse 24 presuppose a negative response. But that response is immediately countered by a divine refutation. Note how Yahweh's role in Israel's plight has been recast: instead of acting as its punisher and destroyer (e.g., 43:28), the Lord delivers Zion's children, saving them from the "mighty" and the "tyrant":

> Can the prey be taken from the mighty,
>   or the captives of a tyrant[26] be rescued?
> But thus says the Lord:
> Even the captives of the mighty shall be taken,
>   and the prey of the tyrant be rescued;

for I will contend with those who contend with you,
    and I will save your children. (49:24-25)

How have Jerusalem's children become the captives of tyrants? Yahweh defends the former divine role in their plight, acknowledging that both they and their mother have been separated from him, but blaming the children for their alienation (50:1):

Where is your mother's bill of divorce
    with which I put her away?
Or which of my creditors is it
    to whom I have sold you?
No, because of your sins you were sold,
    and for your transgressions [ps'] your mother was put away.

Here is the pointed claim that the disobedient children are responsible not only for their own suffering, but also for Zion's rejection.[27] The rhetorical questions in verse 1a constitute Yahweh's denial that his separations from spouse and offspring are permanent. Zion has indeed been "sent away," but her dismissal was not caused by some misdeed on her part. Since she is blameless and no formal statement of divorce (*seper kerîtût*) exists, Yahweh can reclaim her as his wife (Whybray 1975:149). Moreover, his children were sold off for their sins, and not because their father was forced into a last-ditch attempt to repay his creditors. Why, the very idea that God could incur debts is preposterous! Hence, Yahweh has both the power and the means to reclaim his children from the Babylonian tyrant.

In a society where care for one's elderly parents was a crucial obligation, the strategy motivating mother/child imagery in Isa 50:1 seems clear. Personified Jerusalem appears the helpless, hapless mother who birthed and nurtured her children, only to suffer rejection and alienation from her husband on account of their sins. Cast as rebellious children whose irresponsible acts have caused their mother both pain and shame, the people appear all the more heinous.

"The Lord God has Opened My Ear, and I was not Rebellious"

An extended discussion of the so-called "servant songs" of Isaiah 40–55 would lead us far afield of child imagery and the rhetoric of rebellion in Isaiah. Yet both the third (50:4-11) and the fourth (52:13–53:12) songs contain vocabulary that, by this point in the scroll, is a well-established part of our argot of rebellion. Reading these passages *only* as part of the "servant songs" corpus can obscure their potential significance.

Unlike Israel, the servant does not rebel against God. To the contrary, he remains receptive to God's word, despite despicable treatment from those he seeks to teach. The clear distinction between the servant who does not rebel, and Israel, a rebel from birth (48:8-11), mitigates against our reader simply equating the servant (in 50:4-11) with Israel, or at least with the nation as a whole:

> Morning by morning he wakens—wakens my ear
>   to listen as those who are taught.
> The Lord God has opened my ear,
>   and I was not rebellious [*we'anokî lo' marîtî*],
>   I did not turn backward.
> I gave my back to those who struck me,
>   and my cheeks to those who pulled out the beard;
> I did not hide my face
>   from insult and spitting. (50:4b-6)

Similarly, Isa 52:13–53:12 distinguishes between the innocent servant (Isa 53:9) and guilty rebels. Forms of the root *ps'* appear four times (vss. 5, 8, 12 [twice]) in this poem; and in each case, they refer to the transgressions of those on whose behalf the servant has suffered:

> But he was wounded for our transgressions [*ps'*],
>   crushed for our iniquities;
> upon him was the punishment that made us whole,
>   and by his bruises [*ûbahaburatô*] we are healed. (53:5)

The sequential reader interprets this "song" in light of the text itself, prior Isaian texts (including programmatic references to children who rebel [*ps'*], to beatings, bruises [*habbûrah*], and bleeding wounds [Isaiah 1]), and also the extratext, including notions of vicarious suffering. The punishment due Israel so long as it persisted in its rebelliousness (ch. 1) has instead been borne by the obedient servant. In subsequent chapters, the single servant will become a plurality of servants[28] who, though by no means historically blameless, have sincerely repented of their past transgressions, live in obedience to Yahweh's instruction, and anticipate the complete fulfillment of

Isaiah's vision. Who are they, and how can they endure the oppressive acts and cultic offenses of those who, despite both the lessons of history and the servant's efforts on their behalf, continually refuse to "turn from rebellion" (Isa 59:20)?

Summary

Within Isaiah 40–55, earlier charges against Israel, God's rebellious children, are not refuted. No less than the wayward son of Deuteronomy 21, Israel has behaved in ways that justify the death penalty. Indeed, Isa 48:8 goes beyond Isaiah 1 and 30 by labelling Israel—all of it—a rebel from birth.

Careful examination reveals that the rebellious child metaphors of Isaiah 40–55 do not function primarily to quicken the reader's sense of persisting family ties. To be sure, familial imagery is well-suited to arguments that certain ineffable relationships can survive the most painful experiences. Many Deutero-Isaian texts draw their rhetorical verve from the human desire to be reconciled with one's estranged family, to embrace again one's children. In the texts we have examined, however, rebellious child metaphors function to emphasize human irresponsibility and guilt. That, too, is an important part of the rhetoric of Isaiah 40–55, which seeks not only to reassure readers of Yahweh's ongoing love, devotion, and forgiveness, but also *to explain and justify Israel's suffering at Yahweh's hand.*

These observations do not disqualify our earlier claim that Isaiah 40–55 constitute a grace interval in Isaiah. Human culpability notwithstanding, Yahweh willingly extends forgiveness to his children (albeit for reasons that include concern for the divine reputation), despite their rebellious natures. There is a way beyond the ultimate penalty proclaimed in earlier chapters: God is willing to foreswear its utter destruction, if only Israel accepts forgiveness and steps out in faith. Will Yahweh's offer to dispel transgressions "like a cloud" suffice for all Israel, irrespective of its response? Or, when all is said and done, must the outcome announced already in Isa 1:27-28 prevail?

Unlike Yahweh's obdurate children, the servant does not rebel against God. To the contrary, he is utterly obedient. The identity of the servant remains ambiguous in chapters 40–55. In some contexts he appears to be Israel; in others, he clearly cannot represent the people as a whole. Will he reappear in subsequent texts, his identity and purpose clear? Can he ultimately atone for the transgressions of others?

ISAIAH 56–66: "SURELY YOU ARE OUR FATHER"

Chapter-by-chapter analysis of Isaiah 56–66 is crucial to the reader's understanding of Isaiah's rhetoric of rebellion, including its rebellious child metaphors. Chapters 1–39 contained Yahweh's initial articulation of the dilemma: no less than the odious son in Deut 21:18-21, God's children—and especially their leaders—deserve to die. Chapters 40–55, while maintaining that charge, nonetheless extended forgiveness and reconciliation to a pan-Israelite audience. Now, in Isaiah 56–66, the theme of Yahweh's disobedient leaders becomes increasingly prominent even as it moves toward (anticipated) resolution.

Isaiah 56–57: "Are You Not Children of Rebellion?"

Fresh on the heels of the joyous scene in Isa 55:12-13, Isaiah 56 begins with an imperative and a promise: do what is just and right, including sabbath observance, for God's salvation and deliverance are imminent (vss. 1-2). Proselytes must be permitted to take their place among Yahweh's ingathered people, childless eunuchs will be given an everlasting name; and both groups are welcomed as fully-functioning members of Israel's cultic life (vss. 3-8).

With the chiastic tricolon of Isa 56:9, however, the tone shifts dramatically:[29] wild animals are summoned (see also Jer 12:8-9) to devour Israel's oppressive, intemperate leaders. Yes, Israel's latest generation of leaders, the class so frequently threatened and condemned in Isaiah 1–39, continues to transgress, despite the forgiveness proffered in Isaiah 40–55: witness their self-indulgence and excessive appetites for food and booze (Isa 56:11-12; see also Isa 28:1-4, 7-8). In Isa 57:1-2, the diatribe against these "dogs" gives way to a lament bemoaning how the righteous suffer at their hands. But it resumes in verses 3-4 as the leaders are summoned and charged. Note that in this text, the image is not of Yahweh's children rebelling against their divine parent, but rather of progeny whose parentage renders them *inherently* heinous:

> But as for you, come here, you children of a sorceress,
> you offspring of an adulterer[30] and a whore.[31]
> Whom are you mocking?
>> Against whom do you open your mouth wide
>> and stick out your tongue?[32]
> Are you not children of rebellion [*yildê pesa'*; NRSV: transgression],
> the offspring of deceit [*zera' saqer*]. (57:3-4)

Here, the leaders are condemned with phrases similar in tone to the contemporary, vulgar "son of a bitch"; in both the ancient and modern slurs, the intent is to insult one's foes by charging that their progenitors are in some sense deviant.[33] From so poisonous a pedigree no good issue can come. Depicted metaphorically as the birth products of transgression and deceit, these community leaders epitomize the proverbial "like mother, like daughter" of Ezek 16:44. True to their horrid natures, they participate in disgraceful forms of worship, including the ritual slaughter of helpless children (Isa 57:5).[34]

Isaiah 40–55 certainly was not without its contentious elements: God's sometimes harsh justifications of the penalty Israel has endured; the polemical choice of Cyrus as God's anointed; the ridicule and condemnation of idolators; the physical and psychological abuse inflicted upon the servant. But this shocking text returns readers to a theme—the singling out of Israel's leadership for special rebuke—that, though integral to Isaiah 1–39, was conspicuously absent from Isaiah 40–55, with its pan-Israelite offers of forgiveness.

How does the reader understand the reappearance of references to an oppressive Israelite leadership? In order to answer this question, we must remember what was said in Chapter 1 about Isaiah's unfolding vision and our reader's place in it. He knows when Isaiah prophesied, and he knows that some of his prophecies came to pass prior to Isaiah's death. Others were fufilled in subsequent centuries, still others are awaiting fulfillment (e.g., the ultimate redemption of those in Zion who repent). Until that day arrives, however, he lives under circumstances falling far short of God's promises. Having "drunk to the dregs the bowl of staggering" (Isa 51:17), Israel's corrupt leadership classes continue to sin, refusing the forgiveness Yahweh has proffered (e.g., Isa 55:6-7). Despite the punishments that have fallen upon God's people, despite promises of reconciliation freely extended (Isaiah 40–55), despite even the claim that the servant has willingly borne the punishment for Israel's past transgressions, the leaders of our reader's day remain as blind, undiscerning (56:10), oppressive (57:1-2), and idolatrous (57:6-13) as their ancestors.

Yet suddenly, the message of Isaiah 40–55 reasserts itself: Yahweh's highway *shall* be built (57:14), and the dilemma of Israel's persistent rebelliousness resolved when God heals transgressors. References to persistent wickedness in the face of corporal punishment and to the need for healing both evoke and address the painful accusations of Isa 1:2-6:

> Because of their wicked covetousness I was angry;
> > I struck them, I hid and was angry;
> > but they kept turning back to their own ways.
> I have seen their ways, but I will heal them;
> > I will lead them and repay them with comfort. (57:17-18)

God's promises might appear to resolve the ongoing problem of Israel's disobedience. But the text does not end there, of course. The chapter's last words, a counterweight to Yahweh's promise of peace, likens the wicked to a troubled sea, constantly tossing, churning up mire, never at peace. Some commentators suggest that Isaiah 57:20-21 refers to sinners *outside* Israel. It is unlikely, however, that readers—even on the basis of the healing proffered in 57:16-19—will simply dismiss verse 21 as having no import for Israel's own evildoers. By this point in the scroll, they know all too well that wickedness can persist despite every divine offer and act of reconciliation.

Isaiah 58–59: Accusation and Confession

Isaiah 58–59 are pivotal texts for our reader's construal of Isaiah's rhetoric of rebellion. Intimately linked and reminiscent of Isaiah 1, these two chapters constitute a precise, if proleptic and as yet incomplete, dramatic enactment of events and outcomes first presaged in the initial chapter of Isaiah's vision.

Isaiah 58: "Announce to My People Their Rebellion"

Isaiah 58 begins with Yahweh's imperatives:

> Shout out, do not hold back!
> > Lift up your voice like a trumpet!

> Announce to my people their rebellion [ps'],
> to the house of Jacob their sins. (vs. 1)[35]

The following dialogue (vss. 2-5) condemns those whose ostensible righteousness, based upon impeccable attention to fasting and other prescribed cultic obligations, is betrayed by their self-serving motivations and acts of violence. Readers recall Yahweh's inaugural claim that "my people" (1:3) have "rebelled against me" (1:2), and their leaders' insincere cultic practices, oppression, and acts of violence (1:10-23). Moreover, just as accusation was followed by invitation and the possibility of reconciliation in Isaiah 1, so here condemnation is not the final word. Instead, rhetorical questions (58:6-7) coupled with conditional clauses (vss. 9b-10, 13) spell out God's moral mandate, while interspersed verses (vss. 8-9a, 11-12, 14) disclose, in language reminiscent of Isaiah 40–55, the rich rewards awaiting those who obey Yahweh's demands. Healing remains possible, but the people must make a choice.

To whom are these words of condemnation, instruction, and invitation directed? The opening verse commands that its rebellion be announced to "my people," that is, to all Israel (though second person masculine singular suffixes would seem to address Israel individual by individual). Isaiah 1:2-3 also lodged the charge of rebellion against "Israel"/"my people" as a whole; and readers recall other pan-Israelite accusations (e.g., "you were called a rebel from birth"; 48:8 [Tanakh]). In Isaiah, Israel's history is unquestionably a history of rebellion; and none save the servant of Isa 50:4-11 can claim utter obedience. And yet, already in Isaiah 1 the nation's religious and administrative leaders were singled out for special censure. Repeatedly in Isaiah 1–39 and again in 56:9–57:13, generations of leadership have been charged with rebellious, self-serving, and violent acts. So while Isa 58:1 accuses all of God's people of rebellion, both the technical cultic terminology of verses 2-6 and the claim that those indicted wield power (vss. 3-4) suggest that Israel's leadership—especially its cultic heads—again are particularly the focus of Yahweh's sharp critique (Hanson 1975:108-11).

What is Israel's response to Yahweh's demands for justice, offers of healing, and promises of salvation? Judging from the rejoinder in Isa 59:1-3, it appears that some of the accused, at least, wonder if *divine* impotence, rather than *human* recalcitrance, explains the delay of Yahweh's salvation. Note how the following verses encourage readers to align themselves with the speakers, while rejecting "our" opponents, perpertrators of evil and the cause of our distress:

> See, the Lord's hand is not too short to save,
>   nor his ear too dull to hear.
> Rather, your iniquities have been barriers
>   between you and your God . . .
> For your hands are defiled with blood,
>   and your fingers with iniquity [cf. 1:15];
> your lips have spoken lies,
>   your tongue mutters wickedness. (59:1-3)

Subsequent verses graphically elaborate upon the sins that "you" (shifting to "they" in vss. 4-8) have committed: lying, perverting justice, bloodshed, and destruction. Faced with the clear choices articulated in Isa 58:6-14, those addressed in 59:3-8 have nevertheless persisted in their iniquities. As a consequence, "we" suffer on account of their sins:

> We grope like the blind along a wall,
>   groping like those who have no eyes;
> we stumble at noon as in the twilight,
>   among the vigorous as though we were dead.
> We all growl like bears;
>   like doves we moan mournfully.
> We wait for justice, but there is none;
>   for salvation, but it is far from us. (Isa 59:10-11)

Isaiah 59: "Rebellion, Faithlessness to the Lord, and Turning Away from Our God"

Then, in the midst of lamentation, these first person plural speakers do what the nation as a whole, and especially its leaders, have persistently refused to do: in a strategically-placed (see below) and pivotal text that is replete with Isaiah's argot of rebellion, *they sincerely confess Israel's sins*:

> For our many sins [ps‘] are before You,
> Our guilt testifies against us.
> We are aware of our sins [ps‘],
> And we know well our iniquities:
> Rebellion [ps‘], faithlessness [(we)kahes][36] to the Lord,
> And turning away from our God,
> Planning fraud and treachery [sarah],[37]

> Conceiving lies [*dibrê saqer*] and bringing them forth from the
> heart. (Isa 59:12-13; *Tanakh*)[38]

With these words, the lamenters (and the reader) acknowledge
that Isaiah's first charges against Israel are true and just. The
nation addressed in that initial oracle may have lacked the
discernment of oxen and even of asses, but these penitents fully
recognize Israel's history of culpability before God (vss. 12-13).

What is Yahweh's response to this sincere confession that a
dearth of justice and its effects (vss. 14-15a) are the consequence of Israel's historic rebellion against its God? Verses
15b-20 function to reassure the lamenters that redemption lies
beyond repentence. Yahweh, the divine warrior, prepares to
battle his enemies; and when the battles have been won to the
west and to the east (59:19), God will turn toward Jerusalem:

> And he will come to Zion as Redeemer,
>> to those in Jacob who turn from transgression [*ps'*],
>>> says the Lord. (59:20)

The announcement of Israel's rebellion (*ps'*) to "my people" in
Isaiah 58 may have evoked doubts about Yahweh's ability to
deliver in some quarters (59:1). But for others within the community, it has elicited this sincere act of confession. To them,
Yahweh comes as Redeemer. Isaiah 59:20 echoes Isa 1:27:

> Zion shall be redeemed by justice,
>> and those in her who repent, by righteousness.

But what of those whose responses are disbelief, violence,
injustice, and blaming God? With the notice of Yahweh's preparations for battle, readers also recall the fate of Israel's
persistent rebels and sinners, proclaimed already in Isa 1:28:

> But rebels and sinners shall be destroyed together,
>> and those who forsake the Lord shall be consumed.

Isaiah 60–62: "Arise, Shine, for Your Light has Come"

It is precisely to those penitents who hear the announcement of
Israel's rebellion and respond with wholehearted confession that
the words of Isaiah 60–62 speak. True, Zion is the addressee, as
the shift from third person masculine plural and second person
masculine singular grammatical forms (59:21) to second person
feminine singular grammatical forms (Isaiah 60) makes clear. The
sequential reader is prepared for the shift, however, by the parallel-

ing of "Zion" and "those in Jacob who turn from transgression" in 59:20. On the "other side" of their confession, the penitents embodied in personified Jerusalem are promised glorious restoration:

> Arise, shine; for your light has come,
>   and the glory of the Lord has risen upon you.
> For darkness shall cover the earth,
>   and thick darkness the peoples;
> but the Lord will arise upon you,
>   and his glory will appear over you.
> Nations shall come to your light,
>   and kings to the brightness of your dawn. (Isa 60:1-3)

As we shall see in Chapters 4 and 5, addressing these penitents as personified Jerusalem allows the poet to tap the rich ancestral vitality of traditions describing Jerusalem as Yahweh's wife/children, and to present the reunion of Yahweh, Jerusalem, and her inhabitants as a *family* reunion. Yahweh's promises to Zion/the penitents include the humiliation of all her oppressors. The author of Isa 60:14, for example, relishes an image of the children of Zion's enemies doing obeisance at her feet. References to kings and nations in surrounding verses strongly suggest that Israel's foreign oppressors are primarily in view. By now, however, readers know that the penitents/personified Zion have internal, as well as external foes; and the latter are surely among those who will bow down before her.

Under a new and righteous leadership, Zion's mourning will cease and she will bask in everlasting light (60:17b-20). Despite that promise, however, the single voice raised in Isa 61:1 must acknowledge that mourning persists in Jerusalem (vss. 2-3). That voice, reminiscent of the first person speech of the earlier "servant songs," briefly abandons the address to personified Jerusalem, speaking directly to those in Zion who mourn, and promising them an everlasting covenant (see 59:21), salvation, and the riches of nations. "For Zion's sake," the speaker avows (and the reader right along with him), "I will not keep silent" (Isa 62:1). With verse 2, however, the speaker resumes direct address to personified Jerusalem, proclaiming her coming vindication and approaching (re)marriage to Yahweh. Moreover, Zion's sentinels are instructed continually to remind God of the as-yet-unfulfilled promises to Jerusalem:

> Upon your walls, O Jerusalem, / I have posted sentinels;
> all day and all night / they shall never be silent.
> You who remind the Lord, / take no rest,
> and give him no rest
>> until he establishes Jerusalem
>> and makes it renowned throughout the earth. (62:6-7)

According to the NRSV annotation for these verses, the sentinels' (prophets') purpose is "to remind Jerusalem of her imminent salvation, the certainty of which the Lord's oath (vss. 8-9) underscores." But the text says the opposite, i.e., that the sentinels are to remind *Yahweh* of the divine oath to bring about Jerusalem's imminent salvation. The end of Isaiah 62 returns readers to the image of the Lord's highway and promises marvelous new names for both the people of Israel and Jerusalem, names that reflect their transformation. But the oppressors are still oppressing, and the mourners still mourn. The posted sentinels are a tacit acknowledgment that the proclaimed salvation is, for the moment, pure prolepsis functioning as (self-)evidence of the very reality it anticipates. If the reader is disposed steadfastly to believe that Yahweh is Yahweh, the omniscient and omnipotent deity whose powers and plan have filled the vistas of Isaiah's vision, then the "evidence" compels; and he is emboldened to go on believing God's promises, e.g., "I am Yahweh; in its time I will accomplish it quickly" (60:22b). But the dissonance between promise and present reality persists. The quick cut back to the divine warrior (Isa 63:1-6) whose preparations for battle were described in Isa 59:15b-19, and the vivid descriptions of his appearance, soaked as he is with the blood of enemy nations, function further to reassure readers that Yahweh's plan for Israel and the nations is moving forward.

Isaiah 63:7–64:11: "You, O Lord, are Our Father, Our Redeemer from of Old is Your Name"

Claus Westermann lauds Isa 63:7–64:11, calling it "probably the most powerful psalm of communal lamentation in the Bible" (1969:392). Flowing out of the extravagant promises and painful undercurrents of Isaiah 60–62, potentially dammed in by the claim that the Divine Warrior's redemptive work has, in fact, already begun (63:1-6), the lament swells to a torrent of suffering, frustration, and despair. Its outpourings are not altogether chaotic, however. To the contrary, the lamenters lift up their filial status in strategic ways, the better to move Yahweh to pity and action on their behalf:[39]

> I will recount the gracious deeds [hsd] of the Lord,
>   the praiseworthy acts of the Lord,
> because of all that the Lord has done for us,
>   and the great favor to the house of Israel
> that he has shown them according to his mercy,
>   according to the abundance of his steadfast love [hsd].
> For he said, "Surely they are my people,
>   children who will not deal falsely" [banîm lo' yesaqqerû];
> and he became their savior / in all their distress.
> It was no messenger or angel / but his presence that saved them;
> in his love and in his pity he redeemed them;
>   he lifted them up and carried them all the days of old. (63:7-9)

As the historical retrospect continues, the penitents confess that Yahweh's early confidence in filial devotion and loyalty (vs. 8) was misplaced. The children so lovingly protected and reared grew up to become rebels; and their transgressions had a profound effect upon God's behavior: the once-loving parent became Israel's foe:

> But they rebelled [marû]
>   and grieved his holy spirit;
> therefore he became their enemy;
>   he himself fought against them. (63:10b)

Despite this horrific turn of events, memories of God's past gracious acts—the exodus and miraculous escape at the Red Sea—embolden the lamenters to plead for renewed love and powerful divine intervention. For the first time in Isaiah, Yahweh's historically rebellious children—the penitents of 59:12-13 who continue to suffer—address God directly as "father":

> Look down from heaven and see,
>   from your holy and glorious habitation.
> Where are your zeal and your might?
>   The yearning of your heart and your compassion?
>   They are withheld from me.
> For you are our father,
>   though Abraham does not know us
>   and Israel does not acknowledge us;
> you, O Lord, are our father;
>   our Redeemer from of old is your name. (63:15-16)

Commentators disagree about the significance of references to Abraham and Israel (vs. 16). Do the lamenters contrast Israel's forebears, long dead and incapable of responding to their present plight, with Yahweh, their eternal father? Or do the names "Abraham" and "Israel" refer to the lamenting community's opponents?[40] For our reader, the second of these options certainly comports well with what he has learned thus far about the people's oppressive leadership. Regardless of how one resolves this complex issue, verse 16 is striking for its twofold insistence that Yahweh is Israel's father, though their relationship has been compromised by a history of human sin and consequent divine abandonment. Repentant Israel pleads with God to relent, to reclaim as his own the children who long for their father's love and protection, but who have become "as a people You never ruled, to which Your name was never attached" (vs. 19a; *Tanakh*).[41]

Following a fervent prayer for Yahweh's presence (63:19b–64:3) and a description of the lamenters' dilemma, guilt, and alienation from God (vss. 4-6), their cry, "You are our Father," reappears. C. Westermann rightly notes that "in 63.16 the accent falls on God's being a Father, but here in 64.7 (8) it is on the fact that the speakers are children"(1969:397). Of course, what is emphasized in Isa 63:16 is not simply that the speakers are children, but specifically that they are *Yahweh's* children.

The implications of this strong familial bond are driven home by the immediately following potter/clay metaphor:

> Yet, O Lord, you are our Father;
> > we are the clay, and you are our potter;
> > we are all the work of your hand.
> Do not be exceedingly angry, O Lord,
> > and do not remember iniquity forever. (vss. 7-8; ET 8-9)

This trope appears elsewhere in Israel's prophetic literature (e.g., Jeremiah 18) and readers of Isa 63:7–64:11 have already encountered an oracle juxtaposing familial and potter/clay metaphors.[42] In 45:9-10, creatures with the audacity to question their creators' wisdom and authority were chastised: Isa 45:9 insists that God controls the shape of the clay, Israel.

Central to these potter/clay metaphors is the potter's (Yahweh's) absolute control over the clay. Less emphasized, but present nonetheless, is the concomitant notion of the clay's

(Israel's) malleability, and hence of the potter's responsibility for the form it assumes. Both ideas are integral to the metaphor (though in any given trope one or the other can be foregrounded to a greater degree); and both function strategically within the context of the lament in Isa 63:7–64:11. On the one hand, the penitents acknowledge Yahweh's authority, power, and justice, confessing Israel's history of rebellion (Isa 63:10). On the other hand, they remind God, via the potter/clay metaphor, that the father/child relationship entails responsibility for *both* parties. Insisting that "we are all *the work of your hands*" (Isa 64:7; ET vs. 8), the lamenting community not only stresses the intimate link uniting God and people, but also plays upon that sense of parental responsibility to—and for—one's offspring that can persist long after children have passed from their progenitors' control. If such a strategic use of familial imagery strikes us as bold, we should remember that this lament, a daring statement of suffering, frustration, and despair, does not shrink from exploiting a variety of rhetorical strategies in hopes of restoring God's love, mercy, and responsiveness to Israel. In Isa 64:11 also, the supplicants seek to evoke parental guilt *and* compassion ("Will you keep silent, and punish us so severely?" [Isa 64:11; ET 12]). Elsewhere, they charge God with turning away from them (Isa 64:6 [7]) and with hardening their hearts ("Why, O Lord, do you make us stray from your ways and harden our heart, so that we do not fear you?" [Isa 63:17]).

From the extremities of their distress, the penitents beg for intercession, their lament deeply rooted in Yahweh's familial ties and shared experiences with Israel.[43] What will be God's response to their plea?

> After all this, will you restrain yourself, O Lord?
> Will you keep silent,[44] and punish us so severely?
> (Isa 64:11 [12])

Isaiah 65: "So I will Do for My Servants' Sake and Not Destroy Them All"

God's first response is a disclaimer—a refutation of Israel's charge that its father has turned a deaf ear to his children. To the contrary, Yahweh claims repeatedly to have taken the initiative to reunite with his rebellious offspring, but they have refused *every* overture (Isa 65:1-2). The following catalogue of offenses (vss. 3-5) is an imaginative exercise in the extremities of abomination, while the quotation, "Keep to yourself, do not come near me, for I am too holy for you" (Isa 65:5), places Israel's cultic leaders squarely in the squalor.

Yahweh vows vengeance. But punishment will not be inflicted upon the entire nation. Isaiah 65:8-14 spells out the crucial distinction between "you who forsake the Lord" on the one hand, and "my servants" (i.e., those penitents who have sincerely confessed Israel's history of rebelliousness [59:12-13] and await God's redemption) on the other:

> My servants shall eat, / but you shall be hungry;
> my servants shall drink, / but you shall be thirsty;
> my servants shall rejoice, / but you shall be put to shame;
> my servants shall sing for gladness of heart,
> > but you shall cry out for pain of heart,
> > and shall wail for anguish of spirit.

Isaiah 66: "It is They Who Shall be Put to Shame"

The climactic fulfilment of Yahweh's restoration promises to Zion/those in Jacob who repent, presaged in Isa 1:27, is proleptically described in the book's conclusion. But Isaiah 66 describes more than Zion's redemption (see further below, Chapter 6). It also addresses the fate of those who persist in their disobedience despite every chastising wound, every purging punishment, every offer of forgiveness, everything.

The chapter begins with Yahweh scornfully dismissing an earthly temple (66:1-29), recalling the negative response to David's suggestion that a temple be built in Jerusalem (2 Sam 7:5-7). Readers may temporarily find the reference to temple builders obscure. But the following verses dispel any doubt about their identity: they are those cultic officials who oppress the righteous (56:9–57:13). Verses 3-4, a catalog of cultic offenses recalling Isa 65:3-5, cite the most horrid of pagan rituals, and equate them with the religious rites of Zion's opponents.[45] The diatribe against those committing cultic atrocities (66:1-2a, 3-4) was interrupted in verse 2b by a consoling address to "the humble and contrite in spirit, who trembles at my word." Verse 5 returns to these humble ones, reassuring them that their current adversaries will be punished:

Hear the word of the Lord,
>   you who tremble at his word:
Your own people who hate you
>   and reject you for my name's sake
have said, "Let the Lord be glorified,
>   so that we may see your joy";
>   but it is they who shall be put to shame.

Here is further, explicit confirmation of the reader's judgment that other Jews, and not just foreigners, are the enemy: these foes mock the servants, because their hopes for divine intervention are as yet unrealized. On the heels of the prophetic word of assurance ("but it is they who shall be put to shame"), however, appears yet another theophanic vision of the Divine Warrior—in Jerusalem at last, and ready to defeat transgressors:

Listen, an uproar from the city!
>   A voice from the temple!
The voice of the Lord,
>   dealing retribution to his enemies!

The description of the divine warrior's battle is interrupted, in a sense, by a quite different tone (vss. 7-14).[46] It resumes, however (vss. 15-16), further detailing the Divine Warrior's approach:

For the Lord will come in fire,
>   and his chariots like the whirlwind,
to pay back his anger in fury,
>   and his rebuke in flames of fire.
For by fire will the Lord execute judgment,
>   and by his sword, on all flesh;
>   and those slain by the Lord shall be many.

When all is said and done, and Yahweh's new heavens and new earth have been unfurled (Isa 65:17-25; 66:22-23), those who have "rebelled against me" (*happose'îm bî*) will indeed be destroyed (66:24), just as promised in Isaiah's inaugural chapter. And the survivors of the Divine Warrior's final battle, Yahweh's repentant, obedient children, will go out and gawk at their smoldering corpses.

Summary

What is the sequential reader's construal of Isaiah 56–66 when these chapters are read in light of all that precedes them, and with special focus upon rebellious child imagery and the larger rhetoric of rebellion in Isaiah? Isa 56:1-8 demands justice and righteousness from a thoroughly inclusive community, but also promises imminent salvation and deliverance. Isa 56:9–57:13 reintroduces the theme of Israel's corrupt leaders, accusing them of crimes—drunken self-indulgence, oppression, illicit reliance on other deities or international relations—familiar from Isaiah 1–39. This diatribe is followed by a reaffirmation (in the spirit of Isaiah 40–55) of God's intention both to be with the "contrite and humble in spirit" (vs. 15), and to heal the wicked who have persisted in their sins. Isaiah 58 announces Israel's rebellion and sin, but also invites reconciliation.

Chapter 59 responds to a charge of divine impotence from disbelieving quarters, shifting the blame for salvation's delay squarely upon those whose hands are defiled with blood (59:3; so also the leaders condemned in 1:15), and who thwart justice (vss. 4-8; so also the leaders condemned in 1:17, 23), to "our" hurt (59:9-12). Such are the critical conditions that elicit from the lamenters a confession of the nature and magnitude of the community's historic rebellions against God and their consequences (59:12-15). The significance of that confession is signalled by Yahweh's response to it: the divine warrior prepares for battle, anticipating both world-wide victory and fulfillment of the promise articulated already in Isa 1:27.

Chapters 60–62 encourage the lamenters, addressed as "Zion"/"those in Jacob who turn from transgression" (59:20), with both promises of glorious restoration and assurances that God is constantly reminded of those promises. A second divine warrior passage (63:1-6) functions further to reassure the oppressed that the divine plan is moving forward, as God's vengeance over enemy nations is (proleptically) proclaimed.

In a great communal lament, the oppressed again confess Israel's history of rebellion, strategically entreating their father's help (63:7–64:12). God responds first by denying the charge of neglect: Israel, and not its deity, has been silent and rebellious. Yet, for the sake of "my servants," Yahweh announces the imminent creation of "a new heavens and a new earth" (65:17). Isaiah 66 describes Zion's miraculous renewal (as we shall see in our Chapter 6), but also the divine warrior's arrival in Jerusalem, ready to slay "those who have rebelled against me" (Isa 66:24).

CONCLUSION

From its earliest oracles through post-exilic contributions to the emerging scroll, from its first accusation against rebel Israel to the announcement of their demise (chapter 66), Isaiah's vision abounds with references to children—young and old, innocent and obdurate. And just as the prophet's own offspring furthered his ministry, however passively, through their conceptions, births, names, and developmental milestones, so literal and especially figurative references to children function strategically to persuade readers to a perspectival realignment, an assent to the depiction of reality that the text presents: God's relationship with Israel is as enduring, as complex, and as powerful as the familial blood bond binding parents and children across generations (as well as across what we would call "generation gaps"). As such, it can survive even the most painful, wrath-invoking, and shameful circumstances. Jerusalem's intemperate, oppressive rulers are spoiled, headstrong children who stand sorely in need of harsh discipline. Present suffering notwithstanding, God offers repentant Israel a world so edenic, so devoid of natural calamity and human strife, that even its curious toddlers cannot get into trouble.

As we have seen, rebellious child metaphors are recurring and important elements within Isaiah's larger rhetoric of rebellion, for they tap ancient Israelite society's extremely negative attitudes toward disobedient offspring, communicating with unrivaled poignancy both the pathos and the joy experienced by all members of God's family. Readers are informed straight off (Isaiah 1) that the people of Yahweh, including especially their leaders, are rebellious children who, despite God's tenacity, forebearance, and love (especially Isaiah 40–55) are doomed to destruction unless they repent of their transgressions (Isaiah 1–39 and especially 56–66). Repeated charges interspersed with offers of forgiveness and healing urge both nation and reader to turn away from Israel's history of rebellion. First person plural confessions and laments, as well as words of consolation and promise addressed to "you," align readers with that element within rebel Israel that confesses its sins, repents of its past, and embraces obedience. Second and third person accusations function to distinguish "us" from "you" (also "they") who persistently refuse to obey.

The servant who suffered for Israel's rebellions becomes a plurality of servants in Isaiah 56–66. Despite the trials they endure, these servants are committed to emulating his obedience. They do not, however, endure mistreatment *on behalf of* rebels and sinners. The judgment of Isa 1:28 stands: persistent transgressors will die.

Through its pervasive rhetoric of rebellion, then, Isaiah beckons Israel and its readers from a history of disobedience against God to obedience and an edenic life lying immediately on God's horizon. But it also insists that those who refuse Yahweh's invitation to repentance will be utterly destroyed. Readers of Isaiah's vision are urged to decide whether to clamor among Jerusalem's reunited and newborn children, or smolder among the corpses of those choosing not to repent (Isa 66:24).

3

THE WAYS
WOMEN ARE:
ASSOCIATIONS
WITH FEMALES

n Isaiah, literal references to women are rare. This is scarcely surprising for, as C. Meyers observes, "relatively little attention or mention is given in the Bible to women's lives or concerns, except insofar as they are part of 'all Israel,' which is the over-riding focus of the biblical authors" (1989:267). When women actually do appear in Isaiah, they remain anonymous; and their attitudes and activities—whether judged negatively or positive-ly—are presented as commonplace.[1] The two (or one) women mentioned in Isaiah's memoir, for example, contributed to the prophet's ministry by means of their reproductive capacities. They (or she) bear sons—the ancient Near Eastern woman's most important function—but neither is named.[2]

Both literal and figurative references to women divulge a number of ancient Israel's (sometimes conflictive) associations with females. Certain sociological studies suggest that women's social roles and standing may have shifted during strategic stages in Israel's history—the pre-monarchical period, the exile, the post-exilic years (Meyers 1988; Camp 1985). Nonetheless, figurative references to women throughout Isaiah show few signs of innovation. Only in a handful of texts do female meta-phors and other tropes bear meanings and convey messages otherwise unattested in our Hebrew Bibles.

In Chapter 2, we both identified certain of ancient Israel's associations with children and traced an important Isaian

theme, Israel's rebellion against Yahweh. In this chapter, however, we must limit our focus to identifying Isaiah's numerous
and complex associations with women: subordination and
dependence; vulnerability; haughtiness and vanity; submissiveness; limited knowledge and competence; familial and conjugal
love; fertility and reproduction; maternal devotion, compassion,
and nurture; bereavement with its rituals of mourning and
lament; and women's sexuality as a source of danger and
shame (menstrual pollution, prostitution, and adultery). Tracing
a second major Isaian theme, the roles of cities and nations in
Yahweh's plan, must be postponed until Chapters 4 and 5.

RECOVERING STEREOTYPICAL ASSOCIATIONS

As noted above, there is a crucial distinction between recovering ancient Israelite society's stereotypical associations with
women, and reconstructing the actual lives of Israelite women
living at various periods in Israel and Judah's histories. Then,
no less than now, one cannot simply equate widespread ideas
about women and children with the realities of their lives. In our
own society, for example, stereotypical ideas about these groups
abound—"dumb blondes," "terrible twos"—though they bear
no resemblance to the intellectual powers of blonds, or to the
behavior patterns of any given toddler. So also Isaian associations with women may not accurately reflect the behaviors, attitudes, experiences, competencies, etc., of women living during
the centuries when Isaiah was created. Moreover, stereotypical
ideas about women surely varied depending upon their ages,
marital status, social locations, and economic resources. Hence
we must attend to how such factors influence the associations
that references to women and female imagery evoke.

Subordination and Dependence

In ancient Israelite society most women, like minors, depended
upon free, adult Israelite males for physical protection, social
status, legal standing, and economic support. Their dependency
derived, in part, from their comparatively lesser physical
strength. But brawn alone cannot fully explain women's dependency in ancient Israelite society. Sociological, as well as physiological, forces subordinated women to men.

Two characteristics of Israel's society contributed to conventions concerning women's subordination and dependence. First, that society was hierarchical during most, if not all, of its history, exhibiting, as P. Bird (1989a:289-90) puts it, "a relatively sharp sexual division of labor and differentiation of roles marked by significant asymmetry of power and prestige." She identifies the implications of asymmetrical social divisions for women:

[This asymmetry] has been commonly linked to a distinction between public and domestic spheres in which women are identified with the tasks of nurture and home maintenance, whatever their activities outside the home (which are often economically significant), and men are identified primarily by activities outside or beyond the home, including agricultural production, craft specialization, commerce, and government. To the public realm of male activity and male control belong most, if not all, of the extra-familial or trans-familial activities and institutions, including political, legal and religious institutions. As a consequence of this distinction of realms, women are to some degree always outsiders (treated as marginal or as intruders) in the institutions and activities of the public sphere, even when they may have regular and essential duties there.[3]

Even in the domestic sphere where women's experience and skills presumably exceeded those of most males, final authority resided with husbands and fathers (Bird 1989a:290).[4]

If we fail adequately to recognize the asymmetry of power and authority in ancient Israelite society, we risk misconstruing the data "by interpreting complementarity of roles, especially when accompanied by expressions of honor, as evidence of equality" (Bird:1989a:291).[5] On the other hand, it is important to distinguish between what people say they do, and what they actually do. In everyday situations, women may have exercised considerable informal power and authority within both public and private spheres on account of their special talents, influence with men, and teaching roles within the home.[6]

Second, an honor/shame value system was integral to ancient Israel's patrilineal society, as G. A. Yee observes:

The values of honor and shame were particularly divided along gender lines. The male embodied the positive value of honor in his manliness, courage, his ability to provide for his family and defend their honor, and his assertion of sexual masculinity. The female embodied the positive value of shame in her concern for her reputation. This concern manifested itself in her meekness and timidity, her deference and submission to male authority, her passiveness, and her sexual purity. A man failing to exhibit courage or defend the family honor, or a woman failing to remain sexually pure, would equally be rendered *shameless* and therefore *get shamed* by the community. Both genders would have failed to consider their personal reputations and that of their household; they would not *have had shame*. However, the individual causes of their *shamelessness* differed according to their gender. (1992:198)

Israel's women depended upon their fathers, and then their husbands, for life's staples; and Israelite husbands were obligated to provide their wives with food and clothing.[7] As Isa 4:1 makes clear, however, female dependency involved more than just the staples of physical survival. At the conclusion of a scathing indictment and dire predictions, a hyperbolic account of war's ravages describes the fate awaiting Zion's women:

> Seven women shall take hold of one man in that day, saying,
> "We will eat our own bread and wear our own clothes;
> just let us be called by your name; / take away our disgrace."

Widowed and alone, these women willingly waive their marital rights in exchange for the physical and legal protection, social status, and potential pregnancy that a male spouse provides.

Weakness and Vulnerability

Like their modern-day counterparts, the women of ancient Israel's world were vulnerable to violence. According to Middle Assyrian laws, for example, "married women . . . could be struck or mutilated by their husbands at will" (Frymer- Kensky 1992a:80). Moreover, females faced the danger of rape by family members, acquaintances, and strangers. Biblical texts refer to rape by military foes (Isa 13:16; Zech 14:2; Lam 5:11), an act intended to shame not only the woman, but also the male family members who were unable to protect her (2 Sam 12:11).[8] In the wake of defeat, women, like their children, could either be killed on the spot or sold into slavery.[9] Israelite storytellers delighted in tales of how women outwitted Israel's enemies (e.g., Jael in Judg 4:17-22; the Wise Woman of Abel of Beth-maacah in 2 Sam 20: 16-22). But for most women, the reality of contact with foes was undoubtedly the stuff of tragedy, not triumphalistic legend.

Without the physical and legal protection of adult males, Israelite women—especially poor women—could fall victim to oppression by members of their own communities.[10] According to Prov 15:25, Yahweh protects widows' rights:

> The Lord tears down the house of the proud,
> but maintains the widow's boundaries.

But the prophets' repeated harangues against the rich and powerful for their oppression of the poor and vulnerable—including widows, orphans, and immigrants—suggest that actual conditions belied the proverb's assertion. In Isaiah, such charges intensify the reader's repugnance toward those rebellious and self-indulgent Jerusalemite leaders who stand accused of exploitation for personal gain (Isa 1:16-17, 23; 10:1-2).

Haughtiness

Israel's sages commended humility, rather than pride, to all persons (Prov 18:12). They warned their students of the dangers attending pride and haughtiness:

> Pride goes before destruction,
> and a haughty spirit [gobah ruah] before a fall. (Prov 16:18)

Readers are warned about the consequences of haughtiness already in Isa 2:11-17, a passage framed (vss. 11, 17) by the humbling of humanity and concomitant exaltation of Yahweh:

> The haughty eyes ['ênê gabhût] of people shall be brought low,
> and the pride of everyone shall be humbled;
> and the Lord alone will be exalted / in that day.
> For the Lord of hosts has a day
> against all that is proud and lofty,
> against all that is lifted up and high;[11]
> against all the cedars of Lebanon, / lofty and lifted up;
> and against all the oaks of Bashan . . .
> The haughtiness of people [gabhût ha'adam] shall be humbled,
> and the pride of everyone shall be brought low;
> and the Lord alone will be exalted on that day.

In subsequent chapters, readers will be reminded of the folly of pride (5:15-16). Note the echo of 2:11, 17, but here with a play on gbh: the "eyes of the haughty [gbh]" people will be brought low, but Yahweh of Hosts will be exalted [gbh]); and also in 10:33-34 (against Assyria).

In Isa 3:16—4:1, human haughtiness is given a female face and form. Jerusalem's daughters (i.e., her female inhabitants) personify the pride already roundly condemned in Isa 2:11-17:

> Because the daughters of Zion are haughty [gabehû]
>   and walk with outstretched necks,
>   glancing wantonly with their eyes,
>   mincing along as they go, / tinkling with their feet;
> the Lord will afflict with scabs
>   the heads of the daughters of Zion,
> and the Lord will lay bare their secret parts.[12] (3:16-17)

Thus, only verses after the poem about the fate awaiting the haughty (2:11-17), readers are invited to envision in great detail the affliction of the haughty daughters of Zion, who glance wantonly with their eyes (3:16).[13] Yahweh replaces their vanity and affectations with scabs, exposing them to the roving eyes of onlookers, so that the once-wanton "lookers" are humiliated, objects of shameless stares. Following a list of clothing and adornments stripped from these women (vss. 18-23), verse 24 contrasts present affluence with future poverty and disgrace. Verses 25 and 26, with their second person feminine singular grammatical forms, slip almost seamlessly into an address to personified Zion; note "her gates" (vs. 26). Isaiah 4:1 returns, however, to desperate women, now described as seizing a single man in hopes of marriage.

For readers of Isa 3:16—4:1, then, Yahweh's threat against all who/that are haughty (2:11-17) is graphically realized in the stripping and degradation of a specific group, the daughters of Zion. Introduced as vain and wanton, they are disgraced and left to bargain for the status, protection, and prospects for a future that only a man can provide.

Submissiveness

During a time of national and personal crisis, the women of Isa 4:1 are by no means passive. Though in their desperation, they offer to forego even those necessities of life that husbands were required to supply their wives, they nonetheless are described as seizing (hzq) any available male—scarcely submissive behavior. Female submissiveness appears, nevertheless, as a congruous feature of Israel's social structure. Frymer-Kensky acknowledges as much in comments that, ironically, are intended to *blunt* the notion that ancient Israelite women were expected to be submissive (1992a:128-29):

> The superior position of husbands was never justified or explained in the Bible (as it was elsewhere) by claims to innate male superiority or a "natural" female desire to obey. Male dominance was assumed: it was part of the social order of the world that the Bible did not question. . . . In the primeval history of Genesis, there is a "historical" explanation of male dominance and hierarchy. . . . The divine declaration to Eve in Genesis 3:15, "your desire is for your husband and he rules you" is part of the divine legitimation of the difficult but unquestioned conditions of human existence: work, pain, hierarchy, and death. This divine warrant validates the status quo. It is a reification of the social order that people already have before them, and is tantamount to saying "it is so because it is so."

We may grant Frymer-Kensky's point that from a biblical perspective, there is nothing about *femaleness per se* that inevitably leads to *submissiveness*. But that does not obviate the fact that ancient Israel's asymmetrical social structure and honor/shame value system created expectations for, and positively reinforced, female submissiveness to the male head of household. We are *not* suggesting that the women of ancient Israel's world were so submissive as to be unable to exert their wills, or to conceptualize and implement strategies for achieving goals, but simply that female submissiveness was a valued, if not always realized, attitude. The following proverbs, which may not themselves reflect actual conditions, at least suggest that persistent obduracy and argument (nagging) were no more regarded as virtues in women than they were in children:

> A stupid child is ruin to a father,
>   and a wife's quarreling is a continual dripping of rain.
>
> It is better to live in a desert land
>   than with a contentious and fretful wife.
>   (Prov 19:13 and 21:19[14]; cf. 27:15-16)[15]

Moreover, texts recovered from Israel's neighbors reveal that female submissiveness was prized elsewhere in Israel's world. H. Fischer (1989:7) quotes one of the rare cases where a husband praises his deceased wife in an Egyptian tomb chapel inscription: "she did not utter a statement that repelled my heart; she did not transgress while she was young in life." "In short," Fischer says, "she was submissive and virtuous." A collection of Mesopotamian moral instructions likewise reveal the idealization of female submissiveness (Lambert 1960:102-3; see Rollin 1983:39):

> Do not marry a prostitute whose husbands are legion,
> An *istaritu* who is dedicated to a god,
> A *kulmasitu* whose favours are many.
> In your trouble she will not support you,
> In your dispute she will be a mocker,
> There is no reverence or submissiveness with her.
> Even if she dominate your house, get her out,
> For she has directed her attention elsewhere.

Note that in this text, the sexual activities of the prostitute are not really at issue. Rather, prostitutes (and the other categories of women referred to as well) are disparaged precisely on account of their lack of submissiveness.

As we shall see when we turn to the so-called "ladies' lots" in Isaiah (Chapters 4 and 5), Yahweh's plan for Israel and the nations requires the submissiveness of all the earth's haughty and rebellious "women" (cities), including those involved in prostitution! Only in a few texts do readers relish female defiance, a bit of youthful pluck.

Limited Knowledge and Competence

In Chapter 2, we noted that the MT of Isa 3:12 pairs women and children in a charge that Jerusalem's leaders are grossly incompetent. This text stands at odds with myriad biblical references to the wisdom, creativity, and daring exhibited by many women characters.[16] Clearly, however, Isaiah 3:12 speaks of public leadership roles that are wholly part of the "man's world." To label as "women" (and "children") the men who currently fill those roles is both to belittle them, and to state baldly their utter incompetence.

A second, enigmatic text contains a reference to wood-gathering females whose activity may either *result* from the people's lack of understanding, or be *illustrative* of it, or both:

> For the fortified city is solitary,
> a habitation deserted and forsaken, like the wilderness;
> the calves graze there,

there they lie down, and strip its[17] branches.
When its boughs are dry, they are broken;
women come and make a fire of them.
For this is a people without understanding;
therefore he that made them will not have compassion on them,
he that formed them will show them no favor. (27:10-11)

Images of animals feeding or living among the ruins of destroyed cities (vs. 10) are commonplace in the Hebrew Bible (e.g., Isa 13:21-22; 17:2; 32:14; Jer 9:11; 10:22; Lam 5:18). But the reference to wood-gathering women (vs. 11) is rare, as O. Kaiser notes: "The idea of women following the grazing cattle to break off the dry branches for firewood is an original one. The attentive may have perceived a hidden allegory in this. But on the surface nothing more is stated [than] that these women will be the only persons to visit the ruins" (1974:230).

How do first-time readers construe Isaiah 27, including its references to broken boughs and branches, and female gatherers of wood? I suggest that they are able to understand Isa 27:10-11 adequately because the image of gathering firewood and water is "a common literary topos" (Dobbs-Allsopp 1993: 74). The fact that women are the gatherers in our text might reasonably be taken as indicative of the toll warfare takes on men's lives. As we shall see, however, these verses assume an additional, *ironic* significance when read by someone familiar with Isaiah as a whole.

Isaiah 27 is plagued by text-critical problems, the identity of the now-desolate "fortified city" of verses 10-11 seems obscure, and the relationship between verses is not immediately obvious. Recently, however, M. Sweeney (1987:51-66) has constructed a compelling argument for viewing the chapter as a redactional unity. He views Isaiah 27 as a later theological reinterpretation of not only Isa 5:1-7 (the original "song of the vineyard"), but also Isaiah 1 and 17. Like Isa 5:1-7, Isaiah 27 addresses all Israel, including Judah. Like Isaiah 1 and 17, it depicts punishment leading to eventual restoration. Hence, Isaiah 27 is concerned with the future redemption of Israel.

Sweeney does not question the women's appearance in verse 11. He does, however, contrast the luxuriant vine imagery in 27:6 with the dry branch imagery in Isa 1:29-31 (1987:56): because of their religious practices, Israel's idolators will become like kindling and desiccated vegetation (ch. 1); on "that day" when Jacob/Israel has chosen to make peace with God, it will blossom like a well-watered vineyard (ch. 27). The import of 1: 29-31 for understanding Isaiah 27, however, goes beyond contrasting imagery. These verses, along with other references to flora in Isaiah's vision, shed light on the significance of the desiccated branches and boughs.

In Isaiah, literal and figurative references to plants function in at least four important ways: 1) to depict human hubris; 2) to drive home the devastating effects of Yahweh's punitive wrath upon sinful peoples; 3) to describe sites where illicit religious rites occur;[18] and 4) to signify divine blessing and prosperity. Already in Isaiah 1, in learning that Jerusalem's rulers (the persistently rebellious sinners within her) who participate in pagan practices beneath trees and in gardens (vs. 29) will become like withered oaks and shriveled gardens and burn like tinder (vss. 30-31), our reader encounters two of the three negative associations with plants just listed. In subsequent chapters additional charges, including condemnations of "fertility gardens," reenforce the reader's associations of plants with idolatry. Moreover, towering trees symbolize human arrogance, burning plant imagery illumines the rapid spread of wickedness, and images of desolate cities—reduced to grazing land for livestock and living quarters for desert critters—illustrate the enormity of divine punishment. In contrast to such texts, however, readers encounter proleptic descriptions (= promises) that those who repent of Israel's history of rebelliousness shall be called "oaks of righteousness, the planting of the Lord, to display his glory" (Isa 61:3), while Jerusalem's desert-like environs will soon become like the garden of the Lord.

For first-time readers of Isaiah 27, the eradication of idolatry in Israel (vs. 9, and note especially the reference to 'aserim, sacred trees or poles, in the same verse) is crucial to the rehabilitation of Jerusalem and its inhabitants. On account of their sins, both land and populace languish. A future, thriving existence is possible if the people choose faithfully to accept Yahweh's provision. And as verses 6, 12-13 demonstrate, Israel's reconciliation with Yahweh and the restoration of Jerusalem are anticipated outcomes. At present, however, conditions are the very antithesis of the "garden of God." On account of the past idolatries of its inhabitants, Jerusalem's environs resemble a wilderness (fulfilling the threat already issued in Isaiah's call to prophecy [6:11-13]) whose only value lies in the dried-up branches and boughs that can be gathered for firewood.

But for second-time readers and critics peering through the "objective lens," there is great irony in this juxtaposition of the abolishment of idolatry, women gathering dry branches for firewood, and the immediately following (and syntactically connected) claim, "for this is a people without understanding." They recall yet another Isaian text linking idolatry, the procurement and burning of wood, and charges of incomprehension. Isa 44:9-20 mocks the foolishness of an idol maker who selects a choice log, uses half for fuel to cook his supper, but then carves the other half into an image before which he bows:

> He prays to it and says, "Save me, for you are my god!" They do not know, nor do they comprehend; for their eyes are shut, so that they cannot see, and their minds as well, so that they cannot understand. (Isa 44:17-18)

Like these idol-making men, the wood-gathering women—uncomprehending members of an imperceptive people—gather and burn branches from the gardens and trees that both hosted and epitomized Israel's idolatries. Yet they fail to perceive either the folly of their past rituals, or the deep irony of gathering as fuel for the fire (cf. 1:31) dry branches from the vegetal settings whence their leaders sought fertility. So construed, the actions of the wood-gathering women are *illustrative* of, and not simply the *result* of, the people's lack of understanding.

Objects of Familial and Conjugal Love

Among Isaiah's references to females, readers encounter familial images that convey a sense of parental affection for daughters, and of husbands' love for their wives.[19] The homecoming imagery of Isaiah 40–55, for example, includes explicit references to the return of cherished daughters as well as sons (Isa 43:5; 49:22; see also 60:4). In Isa 62:4-5, Zion is promised Yahweh's devotion with the language of conjugal love that elsewhere finds its fullest expression in the Song of Songs. Such references reveal that in ancient Israelite society, the emotive ties joining parents to children, as well as husbands and wives, were powerful and complex, admitting both tender nurture and severe discipline, immense love and explosive rage.

Daughters

In Chapter 2, we observed the importance of sons for a family's name and social status, and especially for the orderly transfer of family land down through the generations. Biblical annunciation scenes and birth announcements were, we noted, reserved for male infants; and evidence suggests that if a destitute family were forced to sell children into slavery, the females were the first to go (Bird 1992). The vulnerability of daughters within Israel's social hierarchy is a commonplace. Certain narratives, for example, show fathers handing their daughters over to strangers for violent sexual abuse (Gen 19:8; Judg 19:24).

Still, certain texts suggest that daughters had a place in the ancient Near Eastern family. Job's second set of offspring includes not only seven sons, but also three daughters; and the same ideal complement of sons and daughters is attested in other ancient Near Eastern texts.[20] In the Song of Songs, a male suitor refers to a mother's loving pride in her daughter, his beloved:

There are sixty queens and eighty concubines,
and maidens without number.
My dove, my perfect one, is the only one,
the darling of her mother,
flawless to her that bore her. (6:8-9a)

In the suitor's admittedly hyperbolic speech, we nonetheless glimpse a mother's pride in her daughter's beauty. The tragedy of Jephthah's daughter (Judges 11) seems an odd text to cite in support of the claim that parents loved their daughters. But while modern interpreters are justly outraged by her death (where is the divine intervention of Gen 22:12?), the narrative's pathos depends upon the presupposition that Jephthah (who blames the victim in Judg 11:35) loves his daughter and only sorrowfully fulfils his vow.

Both Follis (1987) and Frymer-Kensky (1992a:126, 168-75) have identified a spectrum of commonly-held associations astir in texts where Zion, or some other city, is called "daughter."[21] Addressing a city as daughter could, in some contexts, function to emphasize that city's beauty, stability, civility, and culture.

Often, such language betrays tender feelings of love and devotion. In other contexts, however, daughter imagery appears in expressions of wrath, functioning either to encourage readers' assent to the justice of "her" current or impending plight (Isaiah 47), or to evoke a sense of pity, pathos, and horror.

Wives

Marriage, in ancient Israel, was a crucial legal and economic transaction with important implications for a family's continuity, status, and day-to-day existence. But it was also, as E. J. Adler (1989:66-67) notes, an artificial bond:

> As opposed to the natural and biological ties of siblings, or parents and children, that of man and wife is artificial, created and defined by the customs of a given community. The legal codes of the Bible and Mesopotamia reflect this peculiarity of marriage with their numerous statutes regulating and defining this more frail institution.[22]

J. Galambush compares marriage in ancient Israelite society to vassaldom (1992:33):

> Israelite marriage was, like vassaldom, a relationship of mutual obligation between two parties, one (the husband) superior and the other (the wife) inferior in terms of their legal status.[23] As in a treaty agreement, the husband was required to protect the wife . . . , and the wife was to obey the husband, and to refrain from sexual relationships with other men. The husband, like the suzerain, was free of any such obligation of exclusivity.

One could add that just as love is part of intimate marital relations, so also "love" language appears in the Amarna letters and in certain ancient Near Eastern treaties to express the vassal's obligation to the suzerain (Moran 1963:77-87). But as E. W. Nicholson has wryly remarked, "vassals did not as a rule 'love' those who conquered, subdued and dominated them"; in the language of treaties, vassals "loved" their suzerains through acts of obedience and faithfulness (1986:80).[24] Married women were expected to do no less. But as many biblical texts attest, there could be more to marriage than male provision and female faithfulness and obedience:[25] "love" could be mutual. In Isaiah, emotive elements frequently are foregrounded in Yahweh's speeches to Jerusalem, depicted metaphorically as his wife. Such metaphors structure the reader's perceptions of the complex and enduring relationship shared by Yahweh and Jerusalem, and sometimes threatened by the actions of *both* parties.

Fertility

In ancient Israelite society, a woman's status was largely determined by her reproductive capacity. If she bore many children, especially boys, her social standing increased.[26] The birth and survival of offspring allowed her to exercise some authority (over her children; see Bird 1974), and helped to insure security in old age. Infertile women could be objects of shame and reproach; according to 1 Sam 1:1-11, even a husband's preferential love could not ease the pain of childlessness. Barrenness was regarded as an act of God (Gen 16:2; 30:2), a sign of divine displeasure or punishment (Gen 20:18; 2 Sam 6:23).[27] It is altogether likely, therefore, that biblical depictions of women yearning for children, especially boys, are largely accurate.[28] "Recent writing has questioned the existence of a 'maternal instinct' that drives women to have babies, and has focused instead on the patterns of early socialization that create nurturing women and a desire to mother," Frymer-Kensky writes. "But there can be no doubt that in a society in which women's role is defined by motherhood and her status depends on it, barren wives can be expected to feel anxious and unsatisfied" (1992a:125). Biblical narratives attest to barren women's pain (Gen 30:1) and to the strength of the mother/child relationship (Judg 5:28-39).[29]

But while Israelite women had much to gain from bearing children, they had a great deal to lose, as well. Even normal deliveries were often preceded by lengthy, excruciating labor. Many pregnancies ended in miscarriage or stillbirth. Maternal death was an all too frequent consequence of conception (e.g., Gen 35:16-19).[30] Severe hemorrhaging took many women's lives; a breech birth, or some other complication, could result in the deaths of both child and mother.[31] An Akkadian incantation describes the imperiled infant's plight (Lambert 1969:32):

> The woman in childbirth has pangs at delivery,
> At delivery she has pangs, the babe is stuck fast,
> The babe is stuck fast. The bolt is secure—
> to bring life to an end,
> The door is made fast—against the suckling kid. . . .

In an Assyrian elegy for a woman who has died in childbirth, the author assumes the persona of the deceased woman and voices her sorrow (Whiting 1989:37-39; see Reiner 1985:85-93):

5 On the day I bore fruit, how happy I was!
6 Happy was I, happy my husband
7 On the day of my labour pains, my face was overcast;
   on the day I gave birth, my eyes were clouded.
9 My hands were opened (in supplication),
   as I prayed to Belet-ili:
   You are the mother of those who give birth, save my life!
11 When Belet-ili[32] heard this, she veiled her face: You [.....],
   why do you keep praying to me?

r. 4 [Ever since] those days, [when] I was with my husband,
   [as] I lived with him, who was my lover,
   death slunk stealthily into my bedroom.
7 It brought me out of my home, it separated me from my love,
   and set my feet toward a land from which I shall not return.

Archaeologists have recovered texts containing ancient Near Eastern rituals designed to protect pregnant women from witchcraft (Rollin 1983:40; Reiner 1966:93), and to elicit divine assistance during delivery.[33] Prayers were directed to deities like the Hittite goddess ^{D}NIN.TU, "mother of all procreation and birth, the power that moulded the child in the womb" (Pringle 1983:135), and the Sumerian goddess Ninhursag (Frymer-Kensky 1992a:49). Midwives, and in some instances male priests, performed rituals and recited incantations intended to purify the birth environment, ease labor, prepare the birthstool, insure a speedy delivery, and cleanse the infant (Pringle 1983:140; Frymer-Kensky 1992a:49). Rites were undertaken to protect both mother and child—vulnerable in a state of impurity—against attacks by hostile powers such as Lamastu, demon of puerperal fever (Van Dijk 1985:26).

Did Israel's midwives perform analogous rituals to protect and assist mother and child? The Bible does not answer this question, and archaeology has not recovered any pertinent texts. We know that for Israel's priests, childbirth rendered women unclean.[34] But for the most part, the biblical authors were content simply to affirm that Yahweh fashioned the fetus and brought it to birth.[35] One can plausibly conjecture that labor, delivery, and the survival of both mother and infant were matters of crucial concern to all Israelites, and the special focus of women's religious reflection and rituals.[36] The canonical authors, however, either did not know (or think to preserve) religious practices associated with childbirth, or had no occasion to refer to such, or else deliberately suppressed them.[37]

Labor and Birth Imagery

When the biblical authors employed labor and childbirth *imagery*—that is, when they drew from the essential and everyday, but also liminal experiences of labor and delivery to structure and illumine other, less well-known realities—they made use of both positive and negative associations.

The Anguish of Labor. Israel and other ancient Near Eastern nations did not downplay the severity of birth pangs. Note, for example, the following Sumerian proverb (Gordon 1959:516):

> A sick person is (relatively) well;
> it is the woman in childbirth who is ill!
> (And) a sick woman in childbirth is the worst of all!

The Hittite term for a woman in labor was "the one who keeps on wailing" (*wiwiskitallas*; Pringle 1983:137). The Hebrew verb *hîl* often denoted the anguished writhing accompanying labor.

In myths, too, references to labor emphasized its pain. According to one Sumerian myth, the moon god Sin fell in love with a cow, Gi-Sin ("slave girl of Sin"); and, assuming the form of a bull, came down to earth to mate with her.[38] Gi-Sin conceived and in due course went into labor. But her pain was so prolonged and severe that Sin dispatched two mother goddesses equipped with "the water of birth pangs" (amniotic fluid) and oil to assist in the birth. The calf was delivered safely, and the presence and practices of these mother goddesses became the paradigm for human midwifery and its rituals.[39] Another myth tells how Etana, the legendary king of Kish, mounted an eagle and flew to the heavens in search of an herb to relieve his wife's pangs, only to crash back down to earth. As a result of his failure all females, including goddesses, continue to suffer pain in childbirth (see I. Seibert 1974:29). In the well-known biblical story of Adam and Eve, Gen 3:16a explains the extremity of labor pangs as Eve's lot for refusing to obey God: "And to the woman [the Lord God] said, 'I will make most severe your pangs in childbearing; in pain shall you bear children.'"[40]

Apart from such references, whether mythic or mundane, to *actual* labor pains, the literature of Israel and its neighbors refers *figuratively* to travailing women. In the 13th-century Hittite prayer of Queen Puduhepa to the Sun-goddess of Arinna, for example (Fontaine 1987:98), the royal supplicant first quotes a proverb ("Among men there is a saying: 'To a woman in travail the god yields her wish'"), and then applies it to herself ("[Since] I, Pudu-hepa, am a woman in travail [and since] I have devoted myself to thy son, yield to me, Sun-goddess of Arinna, my lady!"). From the context, it seems highly unlikely that Puduhepa was actually pregnant and in labor. Rather, she voices the cultural belief that deities are particularly attentive to the petitions of laboring women, and correlates herself with the proverbial woman in travail in an attempt to secure a prompt and positive response to her request (108-112).

The Travailing Woman Simile. The Akkadian epic of Gilgamesh describes the gods' terrified reaction to a great flood:

> The gods were frightened by the deluge,
> And, shrinking back, they ascended to the heaven of Anu.
> The gods cowered like dogs
> > Crouched against the outer wall.
> Ishtar cried out like a woman in travail,
> The sweet-voiced mistress of the [gods] moans aloud:
> "The olden days are alas turned to clay,
> Because I bespoke evil in the assembly of the gods."[41]

In this text, as in Queen Puduhepa's prayer, actual labor is not involved. Here, however, the reference to travail does not function to increase the chances of a favorable response to a petition. Rather, Ishtar's behavior is likened to that of a woman in travail in order to convey a sense of profound anguish.

Turning to the Hebrew Bible, we discover that travailing woman similes appear rather frequently, and—with but one exception, found in Isaiah—convey precisely the same meaning as in the Gilgamesh Epic. That is, they describe the demeanor of persons who are not actually giving birth to anything, either literally or figuratively, but who are in some sense *acting* as if they were. Psalm 48:5-7 [ET 4-6], for example, employs the simile to describe the panic-stricken reactions of foreign rulers when they catch sight of Jerusalem, God's inviolable city. In Jer 6:23-24, the simile serves to depict the anguish and dismay of Jerusalem's inhabitants as enemy warriors draw near. These texts, and others that could be cited as well, reveal that in Israel (and elsewhere in its ancient Near Eastern world), the travailing woman simile was stereotypically employed to describe the psychological anguish and physiological reactions of persons facing impending doom, or anticipating the destruction of others.[42] With its associations of trembling bodies, anguished cries, panic-stricken faces, and incapacitating agony sprung from terror, the simile reveals ancient Israelite society's recognition both of women's intense pain in childbirth, and of the aptness of labor imagery for conveying a sense of "the anguish of the times" (B. Anderson 1978:468).

Travailing Woman Similes in Isaiah. Readers of Isaiah first encounter the travailing woman simile in Isa 13:6-8, part of an oracle against Babylon (13:1-22) that is first among the scroll's collected oracles against foreign nations (13:1–23:18). They arrive at these oracles fresh on the heels of marvelous promises that Israel will assume pride of place among the nations and be avenged against its foes, "re-membered" and vindicated by God's power (Isaiah 11–12). That the oracles against foreign nations begin with the destruction of Babylon is propitious, for—as the reader knows—that nation was responsible for the destruction of Jerusalem (including the Solomonic temple) and collapse of the Davidic monarchy, and so represents Israel's quintessential foe. Geographically specific scenes combine with descriptions of cosmic upheaval to portray the terrifying events that will transpire on the Day of Yahweh:

> Wail, for the day of the Lord is near;
> it will come like destruction from the Almighty!
> Therefore all hands will be feeble,
> and every human heart will melt, / and they will be dismayed.
> Pangs and agony will seize them;
> they will be in anguish like a woman in labor [*kayyôledah*].
> They will look aghast at one another;
> their faces will be aflame. (Isa 13:6-8)

With its descriptions of physiological and psychological anguish, the travailing woman simile functions here precisely as in other biblical contexts cited thus far. There is no suggestion, of course, that the persons whose behavior the simile illumines are actually on the brink of giving birth—either literally or figuratively—to anything.[43] Rather, the anguish of those anticipating military atrocities is perceived through the image of a woman in labor.

Commentators disagree about whose suffering is described in these verses, some insisting that verses 7-8 depict the Judeans' response to advancing Babylonian troops, others concluding that it is the Babylonians themselves who are panic-stricken. Whatever the oracle's earliest setting and meaning, however, it will almost certainly be construed by the reader as descriptive of the beginning (and what an auspicious beginning it is!) of the fulfilment of God's promises to carry out the divine plan for Israel and the nations (articulated already in Isa 1:27-28 and explicitly embracing the nations, as well as Jerusalem, already in 2:1-4).

A second travailing woman simile appears in Isa 21:1-10, the difficult "oracle concerning the wilderness of the sea" (21:1). Again, it functions (ironically) to describe the anguished response of the speaker (from the reader's perspective, the prophet Isaiah) to overwelming military might:

Therefore my loins are filled with anguish;
pangs have seized me,
like the pangs of a woman in labor [kesîrê yôledah];
I am bowed down so that I cannot hear,
I am dismayed so that I cannot see.
My mind reels, horror has appalled me;
the twilight I longed for
has been turned for me into trembling. (vss. 3-4)

Thus far in Isaiah, the travailing woman simile has functioned in a conventional way to convey the extremities of despair. The behavior has moved inward from Israel's external enemies to the prophet Isaiah himself, but without any change in meaning (though the prophet's use of it in 21:3-4 incorporates the recurring Isaian themes of deafness and blindness. Readers who are already familiar with this (apparently wellestablished) trope may scarcely linger over it in the two contexts examined thus far. The third appearance of the travailing woman simile in Isaiah is certain to capture their attention, however, for it illustrates the process of defamiliarization discussed in Chapter 1: who, after all, would anticipate that a simile conventionally employed to describe profound anguish and incapacitating terror could be used to describe the demeanor of Israel's God? Has Yahweh also fallen victim to paralyzing anguish? Verses just prior to our third text suggest quite the opposite: the Lord has unrivaled control over world events:

> I am Yahweh, that is my name;
>> my glory I give to no other, / nor my praise to idols.
> See, the former things have come to pass,
>> and new things I now declare;
>> before they spring forth, / I tell you of them. (42:8-9)

Like Isa 13:7-8 and 21:3-4, the travailing woman simile appearing in the following unit is surrounded by military imagery.[44] Introduced by a (new) victory song and description of Yahweh going forth "like a warrior," it is followed by Yahweh's self-proclaimed intention to lead the redeemed on an exodus-like victory march (my transl.):

> Sing to Yahweh a new song,
> his praise from the end of the earth! . . .
> Yahweh goes forth like a warrior,
> like a seasoned combatant he stirs up zeal;
> He shouts, yea, he raises a war cry;
> he shows himself mighty against his foes.
> "I have long kept silent;
> I have been mute; I have restrained myself.
> Like a travailing woman [kayyôledah] I will blow;[45]
> I will both gasp and pant.
> I will desiccate mountains and hills,
> and all their vegetation I will wither;
> I will change rivers into islands, / and dry up pools. . . .
> These are the things I will do, / and I will not desist.
> They shall be turned back, utterly put to shame,
> those who trust in graven images;
> who say to molten images, / 'You are our gods!'"

In one respect, the travailing woman simile in verse 14 is like the others examined thus far: it describes extreme and agitated behavior, rather than signaling the imminent appearance or "birth" of some new entity, be it a new world, or a new people (Darr 1987a:567-71). In other respects, however, its usage here is unique: only here, in all of Hebrew Scripture, does it describe the behavior of Yahweh. Conventionally an expression of human *reaction*, it here signals divine *initiative*; elsewhere associated with physiological and psychological manifestations of panic,[46] it here focuses attention upon what emanates from the mouth of God. The ways in which Yahweh's behavior resembles that of a travailing women are clearly stated (recall Kjärgaard's explicit secondary predicate): Yahweh does not experience feeble hands, pangs, and anguished loins. Rather, like a travailing woman, Yahweh blows and gasps and pants, desiccating vegetation and drying up pools of water in preparation for the redemption of God's people. The pronounced auditory character of the travailing woman simile links it to the preceding image of Yahweh going forth like a warrior, shouting a battle cry. And, of course, both images are introduced by the joyous roar of a new song of praise to Yahweh (vss. 10-12).

In the midst of rhetorically charged oracles—material designed to convince the reader that God's word to Jerusalem is a word of comfort, that transgressions can be forgiven, that idols are worthless, and that the world is moving toward the fulfilment of a plan that God formed long ago and is fully able to accomplish—a twist on an old cliché mimetically makes its point: *events are not always as they seem*. Images of human terror and anguish can be transformed into images of unparalleled power, just as the earth's mighty rulers can, in an instant, be "blown away" by God's slightest breath (40:24). One searches in vain for a better example of how enlivening previously-suppressed associations with an established trope revives its power to transform the reader's perception of reality.

Birth Imagery and Creative Acts

Birth imagery appears in a number of Isaian texts and toward a variety of ends: to illumine the otherwise obscure origins of certain entities; to shame and castigate sinners; to stress the intimate link uniting bearer and borne; and to signify prosperity and divine blessing. In what follows, we shall examine texts in Isaiah, and elsewhere in the Hebrew Bible, containing childbirth imagery. Our findings are pertinent not only to the present context, but also to our discussions in Chapters 4, 5, and 6 of additional Isaian texts containing childbirth imagery.

The Creation of Natural Phenomena. Unlike its neighbors, ancient Israel did not, so far as we know, speculate about the genesis of its deity. While the Mesopotamian *Enuma Elish* told of Marduk's birth to Ea, his father and Damkina, his mother, the Hebrew Bible contains no such stories about Yahweh.[47] Neither does it link the creation of what we would term natural phenomena to sexual intercourse between deities, or between deities and human beings or animals.[48] Israel's Egyptian neighbors might speak of Geb and Nut (earth and sky, respectively) as the offspring of Shu (air) and Tefnut (moisture). But in its canonical literature, Israel does not explain creation as the outcome of intercourse between Yahweh and a goddess or other female entity. For the most part, the Hebrew Bible depicts God creating through the spoken word (Genesis 1), or through the physical manipulation of materials (Gen 2:7, 19, 21-22). In addition, poetic texts tell how Yahweh spread out the heavens and fixed the boundaries of the sea (Ps 104:1-9), or describe creation as the outcome of God's primordial battle with Rahab or Leviathan, the mythic sea monsters (e.g., Ps 74:13-17).

A handful of extant texts, however, describe creative acts using language elsewhere employed to describe childbirth.[49] Psalm 90:2, for example, uses parturition imagery to illumine Yahweh's creation of the earth:

> Before the mountains were birthed (*yulladû*),[50]
>> before You brought forth the earth and the world,
>> from eternity to eternity You are God. (*Tanakh*)

The word translated "were birthed" is a third masculine (passive) form of the verb *yalad*. The activity conveyed by this verb is not gender specific. It can refer to the masculine act of begetting (as in the famous "begat" passages that confound so many would-be readers of Genesis). But it also denotes the female act of bringing forth offspring.[51] The verb *hîl*, however, rendered "brought forth" in *Tanakh*, is gender specific. In literary contexts where reproduction is involved (be it literal or figurative), this verb refers only to anguished writhing.[52]

In this text, then, creation appears the product of divine labor, a travail that is not without suffering. Subsequent verses do not develop the female imagery more fully, and masculine verb forms are used thoughout to refer to Israel's deity. Nevertheless, the image of God laboring to bring forth mountains and world is a profound and often-overlooked image of God's intimate involvement in creation.

The author of Job 38 also chose childbirth imagery to illumine ineffable origins. In a remarkable passage, Yahweh speaks of Sea, the monstrous adversary of Baal in Canaanite mythology, appearing as a babe emerging from the womb of the primordial deep,[53] located beneath the earth. Yahweh swaddles him with clouds and sets his boundaries. The rhetorical purpose of such imagery is clear: this is no violent chaos monster, no threat to Yahweh, but a harmless infant over whom God exercises total control.

Later in the same chapter, with irony, God questions Job about the origins of rain, dew, ice, and frost, moving from an image of male begetting to one of female birthing:

Has the rain a father,
  or who has begotten [hôlîd] the drops of dew?
From whose womb did the ice come forth,
  and who has given birth [yeladô] to the hoarfrost of
    heaven? (Job 38:28-29)

Job is silenced, for these questions point to knowledge lying beyond human ken. However, the poet's insemination and childbirth imagery invites readers to glimpse the genesis of natural phenomena in terms that are suggestive of sexual reproduction—a means of creation that, though no less mysterious, is nonetheless part of everyday life. Are the answers to these questions simply that rain has no father, nor dew a mother? Or is God challenging Job to acknowledge that Yahweh sired the rain, and ice proceeds from the divine womb?[54]

The Creation of a People. Deuteronomy 32:1-43, the so-called "song of Moses," contains various images for God. In verse 6, for example, the author asks, "Is not he your father, who created you, who made you and established you?" Five verses later, Yahweh is likened to an eagle, tending its young and bearing them up on its wings. At the end of the song, the deity is depicted as a warrior bent on bloody revenge (vss. 41-43).

In verse 18, the poet refers to God as "the rock," a familiar metaphor. But he also makes use of birth imagery (my transl.):

The Rock that begot you [yeladeka] you neglected,
  you forgot the God

who labored in anguish with you [*meholeleka*].

As in Ps 90:2, the natal verbs are *yalad* and *hîl*.[55] Both forms are masculine, and yet the second verb, and perhaps the first as well, refers to female behavior in childbirth. Why has the author chosen to depict Israel's creation in this way?[56] Understanding this strategic use of birthing imagery begins when we remember that Israel knew well the powerful link uniting mother and child:

> Can a woman forget her nursing child,
> or show no compassion for the child of her womb?
> Even these may forget,
> yet I will not forget you. (Isa 49:15)

Initially part of its mother's own body, a baby was brought forth only after great effort and pain on her part. Once born, the helpless infant depended upon her nurturing care.[57] In Deut 32:18, then, natal imagery serves to highlight Yahweh's intimate connection with Israel, the anguish endured by the deity on its behalf, and God's sustaining care. From such a perspective, the people's subsequent abandonment of their God, already described in verses 15-17, appears all the more heinous.

As noted in Chapter 2, Isaiah employs birth and homecoming imagery to describe Israel's return. In ancient Israelite society, there could be no more positive image of Jerusalem than that of a faithful wife bearing sons for her husband. This imagery, reflecting the greatest of Israel's family values, becomes one way of conveying a sense of the marvelous future awaiting the people of God.

Birthing Abstract Entities. Elsewhere, childbirth imagery highlights the intimate connection between bearer and borne, but for a purpose quite different than in Deut 32:18. In a stinging indictment of adversaries, Isa 59:4 (see also vs. 13) charges:

> No one sues justly / Or pleads honestly;
> They rely on emptiness and speak falsehood,
> Conceiving [*harô*] wrong and begetting [*hôlêd*] evil. (*Tanakh*)

Tanakh translates *hôlêd* (the Hiphil infinitive absolute of *yalad*) as "begetting" precisely because it is a Hiphil, rather than a Qal, form. This translation certainly is plausible, but as BDB notes, "bearing" may be a better translation of *hôlêd* in this context, because its parallel term, the Qal infinitive absolute *harô* (from *harah*, meaning "to conceive, become pregnant") refers to women's reproductive activity. Following BDB, the text seems to say that dishonest enemies conceive wrong and give birth to evil, the female imagery progressing sequentially from the beginning of pregnancy to its end. If one follows *Tanakh*, however, then the line shifts from an image of female conception to an image of male begetting (forming a meristic pair?). In either case, the point is that these wicked people themselves generate evil to which they are inextricably linked, the latter very much the product of the former (a point made also by the proverbial "like mother, like daughter" of Ezek 16:44).

Psalm 7 likewise uses birth imagery to describe the activities of sinners (vss. 15-17; ET 14-16):

> See how they conceive [*yehabbel*][58] evil,
>   and are pregnant with [*harah*] mischief,
>   and bring forth [*yalad*] lies.[59]
> They make a pit, digging it out,
>   and fall into the hole that they have made.
> Their mischief returns upon their own heads,
>   and on their own heads their violence descends.

Similarly, Eliphaz reminds Job of the fate awaiting the wicked:

> For the company of the godless is barren,
>   and fire consumes the tents of bribery.
> They conceive [*haroh*] mischief and bring forth [*yalod*] evil,
> And their womb [NRSV: heart] prepares [*takîn*] deceit. (20:34-35)

In these two texts, context suggests that not only do the wicked produce wickedness, but also the mischief conceived and borne by evildoers redounds upon themselves.

Summary

In Israel's ancient Near Eastern world, references to labor were employed figuratively to awaken sympathy (Queen Puduhepa's prayer), and to illumine experiences of anguish (the travailing woman simile). The Bible's travailing woman similes stereotypically convey a sense of profound human anguish. In Isa 42: 10-17, by contrast, the simile was transformed into a fresh expression of power through the suppression of conventional associations and the foregrounding of others (defamiliarization). References to childbirth—an ineffable experience, but one integral to ongoing human (and animal) existence—function to describe the genesis of certain creative acts and new realities ("bringing forth" imagery). The occasional presence of the verb *hîl* reminds readers of the anguish associated with childbirth. But the products of labor—be they mountains, nations, or mischief—clearly are important as well. Parturition imagery serves a variety of purposes, among them to illumine Yahweh's mysterious acts of creation, to shame and castigate those entities brought to birth which are troublesome or recalcitrant, to stress the intimate link between bearer and borne, and to signal Yahweh's blessing and Israel's concomitant prosperity.

Maternal Devotion, Nurture, and Compassion

Among the most positive associations with women appearing in the book of Isaiah, and elsewhere in the Hebrew Bible, are maternal devotion, nurture, and compassion.[60] To be sure, fathers also exhibited such qualities. Psalm 103:13, for example, likens Yahweh's compassion to that of a father. But while both parents loved and cared for their children, the maternal role is especially prominent in certain biblical narratives and poems. According to 1 Kgs 3:16-28, the maternal compassion exhibited by a prostitute sufficed to convince Solomon of her identity as the living infant's true mother. Maternal devotion compelled Rizpah to protect the impaled bodies of her two deceased sons from marauding birds and wild animals (2 Sam 21:7-14). So strong were motherhood's associations with love and care that the obverse, maternal cannibalism, served to express the ultimate horror threatened by Yahweh in some texts (e.g., Deut 28:51-57) and bewailed in others (e.g., Lam 2:19-20; 4:10).[61]

In Isaiah, traditional maternal attributes are twice held up as exemplars, the most fitting human analogies for attributes of God. In Isa 49:14-15, quoted above, God responds to Zion's charges of abandonment by claiming a steadfast devotion and compassion for Jerusalem exceeding even that of a nursing mother for her child.[62] In the second text, Yahweh promises Jerusalem's inhabitants a divine comfort best illumined by the simile, "as a mother comforts her child" (Isa 66:13), thereby evoking powerful associations: the intimacy of the mother-child relationship, profound security, innocence, and ignorance of death (Harris 1990:230). We shall return to this text in Chapter 6.

Bereavement and Mourning

Our previous discussions of women's vulnerability, of the high value placed upon offspring, especially sons, of familial and conjugal love, and of maternal devotion, inform our understanding of the psychological, economic, social, and legal implications of bereavement. The loss of one's father or husband could, in the absence of some other adult male provider, imperil a woman's future. The deaths of cherished children threatened her as well, since adult offspring were expected to care for their widowed mother's physical needs.

Among the Bible's most poignant passages are depictions of women weeping over their deceased children. Many of these women, however, are not living, human females. Jeremiah 31:15-22, for example, begins with the audial and visual image of the ancestress Rachel, mother of Joseph and Benjamin, grieving over the loss of her children, Israel's northern tribes:

> A voice is heard in Ramah, / lamentation and bitter weeping.
> Rachel is weeping for her children;
> she refuses to be comforted for her children,
> because they are no more. (Jer 31:15)

In Lam 1:16, daughter Zion weeps for the children she has lost to exile and death:

> For these things I weep; / my eyes flow with tears;
> for a comforter is far from me, / one to revive my courage;
> my children are desolate, / for the enemy has prevailed.

In both texts, familial metaphor heightens rhetorical impact. Commentators note that in ancient Israelite society, mourning rituals were especially, though not exclusively, the responsibility of females, including specialists called "keening" or "mourning women" (meqônenôt; Jer 9:16). In these texts, however, Rachel and Zion are bereaved mothers, not professional mourners.

E. Jacob hazards that "the predominance of women [mourners] may be explained by their greater emotivity and sensitivity"; be that as it may, he also acknowledges that the performance of keening and other mourning rituals required technical skills and training.[63] Female mourners are called "singing women" (hassarôt) in 2 Chr 35:25 (see also the reference to hassarîm, "singing men," in the same verse) and "skilled women" in Jer 9:19-20 (ET 20-21). In the latter text, women are commanded: "teach to

your daughters a dirge, / and each to her neighbor a lament."
In his lament over Saul and Jonathan, David enjoins the
"daughters of Israel" to weep over their fallen king, while Ezek
32:16 claims that the "women of the nations" will chant over
Egypt the lament of 32:1-15. Clearly, then, women had a significant role to play in ritual mourning within ancient Israelite
society. Whether such activities were regarded as *religious* rites
is, of course, a much more difficult question to answer (Lesko
1989:299-302).

Isaiah contains references to both human women and personified cities engaged in mourning rituals. Isaiah 32:9-14
criticizes the complacency of certain female participants in the
fall vintage festival.[64] It threatens, moreover, that within a
year, their complacency will be replaced by mourning rituals
occasioned by calamity.

> Tremble, you women who are at ease,
> shudder, you complacent ones;
> strip, and make yourselves bare,
> and put sackcloth on your loins.
> Beat your breasts for the pleasant fields,
> for the fruitful vine,
> for the soil of my people
> growing up in thorns and briers;
> yes, for all the joyous houses
> in the jubilant city. (32:11-13)

Isaiah 3:24 also refers to women wearing sackcloth; and its
reference to shorn heads is reminiscent of passages that cite cut-
ting the hair as part of ritual mourning (e.g., Isa 15:2; Jer 7:29;
16:6; 41:5 [the beard]; 47:5; 48:37; Mic 1:16; the practice is denied priests in Lev 21:5 and proscribed for all Israel in Deut 14:1).
But Isa 3:17-24 is not about the physical mortifications self-inflicted
by mourners. Rather, it describes the degradations forced upon
captives by their captors. Only in verses 25-26, where second
person feminine singular forms signal a subtle shift in subject
from the women of Jerusalem to Lady Zion herself, do we encounter a woman performing mourning rituals *per se*:

> Your men shall fall by the sword
> and your warriors in battle,
> And her gates shall lament and mourn;
> despoiled,[65] she shall sit upon the ground.

Sitting on the ground (yet another ritual act of mourning: Lam 2:10, Ezek 26:16; see the discussion of Isaiah 47 in Chapter 5), Lady Zion mourns the deaths of her warriors—her children, and the husbands of the once-haughty women who endure physical abuse and humiliation at the hands of their enemies.

Woman's Sexuality as a Source of Danger

Menstruation

Even the most modest, submissive, and faithful women were, on account of their menstrual periods, regarded by (at least some) biblical authors as both defiled and defiling on a recurring basis.[66] Within the Pentateuch, priestly legislation seeks to subject women to certain regulations in order to maintain the purity of Israel's priesthood, and of the nation's men in general.

Following Mary Douglas (*Purity and Danger*), J. R. Wegner carefully distinguishes between

> priestly concepts of purity and impurity on the one hand (misleadingly rendered in most Bible translations as "clean" and "unclean"), and popular understandings of "cleanliness" and "dirt" on the other. . . . [Douglas's] analysis showed that pollution "occurs" when bodily processes, insufficiently understood in primitive societies, are perceived as disturbing the harmony of the cosmos. (1992:39)

But this distinction between cultic impurity and dirtiness, though valid and important for a discussion of the Leviticus legislation, does not hold for metaphorical references to menstruation and menstrual blood in certain poetic texts. In Lam 1:8-9, 17, for example, menstruation metaphors and word plays invite readers to a particular perception of the defiling effects of Jerusalem's sin:

> Jerusalem sinned grievously,
>   so she has become a defilement [*nîdah*];
> all who honored her despise her,
>   for they have seen her indecency;
> she herself groans, / and retreats.
> Her uncleanness [*tum'atah*] was in her skirts;
>   she took no thought of her end [NRSV: future];
> her downfall was appalling / with none to comfort her.
> "O Lord, look at my affliction,
>   for the enemy has triumphed!" (1:8-9)[67]

On account of her sin, Jerusalem is depicted as a defiled woman whose menstrual blood soils her skirts (so also B. B. Kaiser 1987:174-76). More than simply a morally neutral state of ritual impurity is evoked by this language. To the contrary, the poem's imagery presents Jerusalem as both defiled and disgraced. When, in verse 17, she is described as having become a "filthy thing" (niddah) in the midst of Jacob's foes (so NRSV, but "menstruant" or "defiled woman" appears more appropriate to the context), one again is struck by the negative associations with such defilement.[68]

Associations with polluting menstrual blood also are active in Isa 4:4, part of a salvation announcement that includes a final purification of those daughters of Zion who were first addressed in 3:16, and whose undoing was described in intervening verses. Isaiah 3:16–4:1 clearly depicts the humiliation of Jerusalem's haughty female inhabitants; and the reader will recognize in the reference to the "daughters of Zion" (4:4) Yahweh's final solution to their sins. Whoever remains in Zion will be holy, for Yahweh will have washed away (though, the text further specifies, by means of a "wind of judgment") their "filth." Yet this notice of the purging of Zion's female inhabitants is coupled with an additional notice that Yahweh will cleanse the bloodstains of Jerusalem from her midst. Here is a more inclusive address that mitigates against understanding Isa 4:4 as a description of the future purging of females alone:

> On that day the branch of the Lord shall be beautiful and glorious, and the fruit of the land shall be the pride and glory of the survivors of Israel. Whoever is left in Zion and remains in Jerusalem will be called holy, everyone who has been recorded for life in Jerusalem, once the Lord has washed away the filth of the daughters of Zion and cleansed the bloodstains of Jerusalem from her [NRSV: its] midst by a spirit of judgment and by a spirit of burning. (Isa 4:2-4)

So'ah, translated "filth," most often refers to excrement (e.g., 2 Kgs 18:27 = Isa 36:12 [both qere]). In Isa 28:8, however, it refers to the vomit of drunkards, so its broader meaning may be odious bodily excretions of any sort. The reference to Jerusalem's bloodstains (demê yerûsalaim) suggests slaughter, the violent shedding of blood, but also menstrual blood (again, see Lev 20:18). Hence, the confluence of females and female imagery, bodily excretions, and blood stains in Isa 4:2-4 stirs negative associations with menstrual pollution (so also Sweeney 1988:159).

In certain poetic texts, then, references to, or associations with, female menstrual blood function to convey a sense of filth and loathsomeness. Though priestly legislation may view menstrual impurity from a morally neutral perspective, associations with menstruation in certain biblical poems function to intensify one's sense of sin's defilement.

Sexual Intercourse Outside of Marriage

In ancient Israelite society, males—whether married or unmarried—were not legally forbidden sexual intercourse with an unmarried woman (e.g., a widow, divorcée, or single adult), so long as her reproductive capacity was not the property of another male (normally her father or, in the case of a levirate widow, her father-in-law). Israel's legal texts proscribe neither prostitution, nor consorting with a prostitute (although Deut 23:18 forbids bringing a prostitute's wages to the temple in payment of a vow). But married women were forbidden sexual intercourse with anyone save their husbands (according to Deut 22:22, the legal penalty for adultery was death for both offenders), and unmarried women whose reproductive capacities were not legally theirs to control were not permitted to have sexual intercourse with either married or unmarried men.[69]

Prostitution. We know that prostitution was part of Israel's world, because references to prostitutes appear in both biblical and extra-biblical literature. From these references we gain some understanding of how and why women were forced into prostitution, and we discern certain stereotypical associations with the profession and its practitioners (Hebrew *zônah* or *'issah zônah*, "prostitute").

Ancient Near Eastern women became prostitutes for reasons as old as the profession itself. "Then, as throughout history," R. Harris observes (1989:149), "girls became prostitutes as a result of poverty, war, and male violence. They came from the ranks of the poor, captives of war, and foreigners" (see also Rollin 1983:38-39). The link between poverty and prostitution is apparent in a Sumerian text, "The Cursing of Agade," where the prostitute and the (male) pauper appear as paired terms:

> May your pauper drown the child who seeks money for him,
> May your prostitute hang herself at the entrance
>   to her brothel. . . . (Bird 1992)

Here, P. Bird notes, are examples of "gender determined ways in which the poor make a living. The poor man (if this text, which is very difficult, is rightly interpreted) makes his living begging in some manner by using a foundling child; the poor woman by using her own body, the only thing she possesses with which she can gain a living."

Female slaves living in the Late Babylonian period could be forced into prostitution for their owner's economic benefit (Kuhrt 1989:232-33). Not all prostitutes were poor and/or slaves, however. Harris notes the presence in Mesopotamia of high-priced courtesans, as well as simple streetwalkers (1989: 149). We should not assume that expensive prostitutes were free to keep their earnings. Those who worked for pimps may have realized little economic gain. Still, not all prostitutes would have been destitute; and "those who were self-employed and free agents might accumulate enough in fees to be free of any ties to a man." (149). That some prostitutes were able to feed, clothe, and shelter themselves and other family members adequately is suggested by a text from the Late Babylonian Period concerning the adoption of a prostitute's son by her brother. Though the text is difficult, it apparently stipulates that the boy remain with his mother, who presumably was able to meet his physical needs (Kuhrt 1989:235-36).

Both biblical and extra-biblical evidence suggests that while prostitution was not illegal (Harris 1989:149), social attitudes concerning its practitioners were at best ambiguous, and at worst decidedly negative (Bird 1989b). On the one hand, both prostitutes and tavernkeepers were "important in the leisure activities of Mesopotamian men" (Harris 1990:222); and their presence undoubtedly was tolerated, even encouraged, in many public arenas frequented by males (Glassner 1989:74; Bird 1989:87). Moreover, the social status of legally and economically independent prostitutes may have differed from that of their poorer or enslaved counterparts (Kuhrt 1989:232-33). On the other hand, prostitutes were "'abnormal' in that they stood outside the routine of home and family"; and independent prostitutes who were not under the direct control of any man were likely regarded as "dangerous" and "bound to inspire fear" (238).[70] Recall the Mesopotamian moral instructions that warned against marriage to prostitutes on account of their lack of submissiveness:

> In your trouble she will not support you,
> In your dispute she will be a mocker.
> There is no reverence or submissiveness with her.
> Even if she dominate your house, get her out,
> For she has directed her attention elsewhere.

In the Gilgamesh Epic (VII, iii:10ff.), Enkidu pronounces the prostitute's destiny: she is "one debarred from any family-life, subject to physical abuse from drunkards, living alone in the recesses of the city-walls, poorly clothed, barefoot, and a prey to all insults" (Kuhrt 1989:236). One can reasonably doubt that all prostitutes endured such mistreatment and misery. Yet Enkidu's words reveal negative social associations surrounding these women.[71] Later in the Gilgamesh Epic (VII, iv:1-10; Speiser 1969:86-87), Enkidu relents and predicts a less harsh fate for prostitutes. But his words betray society's fear that they threaten the security even of women who have ideally fulfilled their reproductive responsibilities: "[on thy account] shall be forsaken the mother (though) a mother of seven" (Kuhrt 1989:238).

Certain treaty curses likewise suggest the prostitute's low social status. In the treaty between Ashurnirari V of Assyria and Mati'ilu of Arpad, an imprecation against the signatory's men seems to "go one better" than the also-attested curse that warriors will become women by threatening that they will become prostitutes:

> If Mati'ilu sins against this treaty with Ashurnirari . . . may Mati'ilu become a prostitute, his soldiers women, may they receive [a gift] in the square of their cities (i.e., publicly) like any prostitute. (Weidner 1969:533; see also Wiseman 1969:540)

In a world where the prospect of soldiers becoming, acting, or being treated like women was ominous enough, the—in a sense double—threat that they would become women of low status, enduring public payment (and concomitant humiliation) for their services would have been even more appalling.

Apprehensions concerning professional prostitutes also appear in the Hebrew Bible. True, Tamar is not condemned by the biblical narrator for posing as a prostitute in order to shame her father-in-law into fulfilling his obligation to her (Genesis 28); and Rahab, the Jericho harlot who betrayed her city, is, from the biblical perspective, a heroine (Joshua 2). But unsavory associations with prostitutes also are apparent: the sages included them among those "out of bounds" women whose seductive ways threatened to destroy young men's lives (see, e.g., Prov 6:26a; 23:27-28),[72] while the use of harlotry imagery to describe illicit female sexual activity or religious infidelity betrays its nefarious cultural associations (see below). Hence, J. Galambush (1992:29) may be correct when she states that "the prostitute is the one woman whose extramarital sex is not condemned as fornication or unchastity *in the legal sense* [emphasis mine], presumably because it violates the rights of no man." But P. Bird probably comes closer to ancient Near Eastern (including Israelite) "public opinion" when she concludes that "the distinction between [illicit] fornication and prostitution was essentially a legal one and . . . popular opinion regarded the behavior as essentially the same" (1989:82).

To summarize: though legally tolerated in Israel's ancient Near Eastern world, prostitutes were perceived as potential threats to family security and as "wanton women." Negative associations with prostitution functioned to warn young women against becoming (or acting in ways suggestive of) prostitutes, to threaten men with the ridicule and disgrace ostensibly endured by such women (e.g., the treaty curses of Ashurnirari V), and to discourage sexual activity outside socially-sanctioned marital relationships.

Biblical narratives with prostitutes among their characters may not be the best source for uncovering ancient Israel's most negative associations with prostitution. In such narratives, as in the Gilgamesh Epic, they could play important, positive roles in advancing the plot (Harris 1990:222-23). As noted, however, Israel's proverbial literature reveals the sages' concern that consorting with prostitutes threatened the futures of their (male) students. Figurative references to harlotry function to encourage negative perceptions of both illicit female sexual activity, and of Israel's faithlessness to its God. In such (mostly prophetic) texts, as we shall see, the rhetorical impact of adultery metaphors is further intensified by figurative references to harlotry.

Adultery. The specter of female sexual infidelity threatened the very foundations of ancient Israel's patrilineal society. Expressed most gravely, a married woman's undetected liaison with a man other than her husband could result in a family's inheritance falling to an illegitimate heir. Sirach 23:22-23, though late, likely reflects an ancient view:

> So it is with a woman who leaves her husband
>> and presents him with an heir by another man.
> For first of all, she has disobeyed the law of the Most High;
>> second, she has committed an offense against her husband;
> and third, through her fornication she has committed adultery
>> and brought forth children by another man.

But the promiscuous wife, daughter, or levirate widow was, in any event, guilty of willfully dispensing sexual and reproductive capacities that were not hers to control, moving her husband or father (-in-law) to unbridled anger, and imperiling his family's honor.[73] If woman is the "essential thread" joining the pieces of patriarchy's social fabric, she also "indicates the seams where the fabric is subject to tears" (Newsom 1989:155).

In the book of Proverbs, Israel's youths are urged to reserve their own sexuality for their wives:

> Drink water from your own cistern,
>> flowing water from your own well.
> Should your springs be scattered abroad,
>> streams of water in the streets?
> Let them be for yourself alone,
>> and not for sharing with strangers. (Prov 5:15-17)

As we have seen, the sages warned their young male students against "out-of-bounds" women, insisting that the seductive words of, e.g., prostitutes, foreigners, and foolish women, concealed perilous consequences: dishonor, disease, poverty, indeed, a trip to death's door (Prov 2:18-19; 5:5). But the married seductress posed a particularly pernicious threat, since her actions—the most serious of sexual offenses—quickened the jealous rage of her cuckolded husband.[74] In Proverbs 6, for example, the sages conceded a distinction between consorting with the prostitute who separates you from your money, and an adulterous liaison that imperils your life:

> for a prostitute's fee is only a loaf of bread,
>> but the wife of another stalks a man's very life.

> Can fire be carried in the bosom
>> without burning one's clothes?
> Or can one walk on hot coals
>> without scorching the feet?
> So is he who sleeps with his neighbor's wife;
>> no one who touches her will go unpunished.
>> (Prov 6:20-21, 23-29)

Because ancient Israel's proverbial literature reflects the sages' primary concern for the welfare and safety of their young male students, its focus is fixed upon the dangers posed by seductive women and their avenging males, rather than upon the consequences of illicit sexual activity for the women themselves. Elsewhere in the Hebrew Bible, however, we find references to penalties (e.g., stoning,[75] burning [see Gen 38:24]) inflicted upon adulteresses—both actual women, and entities personified as females.[76] To be sure, one cannot simply assume that the Bible's laws, narratives, and poems accurately reflect ancient Israelite legal and social practices, or that those practices remained static throughout the periods covered in the Hebrew Bible. Though certain Pentateuchal law codes demand the deaths of both offending parties in an adulterous liaison (Lev 20:10, Deut 22:22),[77] for example, some scholars have argued, on the basis of biblical and extrabiblical evidence, that the male whose rights were violated had some say concerning the offending parties' fates.[78] In poetic (mostly prophetic) texts, figurative descriptions of penalties for female faithlessness (e.g., divorce [Hos 2:4; Jer 3:8], public stripping [whether preliminary to sexual assault, or indicative of the withdrawal of support from her husband's family, and compensation for the male's loss of honor],[79] and mutilation[80]) may or may not accurately reflect actual practices (Adler 1989:43-57). What such texts do reveal, however, are both extremely negative social associations with adultery (McKeating 1979:69), and the intention not only to inflict physical and psychological suffering upon the woman, but also to return upon her the shame and dishonor that she has brought upon the offended man and his family (Deut 22:21; Lev 21:9; see Yee 1992:105-6).

In describing illicit female sexual activity, the biblical authors frequently used not only the literally precise term *n'p*, "to commit adultery," but also the term *znh*, "to commit fornication, be a harlot." Galambush (1992:28-29) calls the use of *znh* to describe the illicit sexual activity of a woman *who is not actually a prostitute* a "first level" metaphorical use of *znh*. A "second level" metaphorical use of *znh*, derived from the first, functions to structure one's understanding of Israel's worship of gods other than Yahweh:

> The male Israelite's worship of other gods is understood as parallel to a woman's illicit sexual activity, because in each case the offender has transferred the exclusive rights of the one in authority (at the second level, Yahweh, rather than husband or father) to a second, competing party (the other god). Unlike the first level metaphor, the second level metaphor is applied to cultic activity and does not ordinarily entail any literal sexual activity. The subject of the verb *znh* as a second level metaphor is always male or of mixed gender, since it is the Israelite male whose cultic activity (like the female's sexual activity) is legally circumscribed. (30-31)

Recent critics agree on the rhetorical strategy motivating metaphorical uses of prostitution terminology in both first and second level metaphors: "the use of *znh* rather than *n'p* serves to emphasize promiscuity rather than infidelity, 'wantonness' rather than violation of marriage contract or covenant," P. Bird observes. "The connotations [are] of repeated, habitual, or characteristic behavior. . . . The metaphorical use of *znh* invokes two familiar and linguistically identified images of dishonor in Israelite culture, the common prostitute and the promiscuous daughter or wife" (1989:80, 89). E. J. Adler also points to the greater rhetorical punch of *znh*: while *n'p* is a technical, legal term for extramarital sexual activity by both men and women, *znh* (in its literal and first-level metaphorical usages) refers to illicit sex by females alone. Moreover, *znh* implies iterative activity, identifies its motive (economic gain), and brings to the continuous term the discontinuous term's associations of treachery and callousness (1989:311-14).[81]

Although Isaiah's vision contains no literal references to prostitutes, prostitution charges and imagery appear in several oracles addressed to personified Jerusalem and other "ladies," the personified capital cities of Israel's foes. As we shall see in Chapters 4 and 5, Isaiah both adopts and adapts these conventional tropes.

CONCLUSION

At the beginning of this Chapter, we noted that Israel's hierarchical and asymmetical social divisions, as well as the honor/shame values embedded in its patrilineal culture, had crucial and wide-ranging implications both for the lives of Israelite women, and for stereotypical associations with females. Prized especially for their reproductive abilities, women were expected to remain sexually inactive before marriage and to refrain from all illicit sexual activity throughout their lives. They were, moreover, valued for submissiveness and modesty, and for competence in "women's work"—including the singing and dancing likely associated with the vintage festival, and the ritualized mourning that followed death and calamity. Like its ancient Near Eastern neighbors, Israel presupposed the inferior legal and social status of women.

Numerous biblical texts, including many Isaian texts, employ images of mothers, wives, and daughters to convey a sense of the love, passion, jealousy, anger, shame, and pride believed to be as integral to the relations binding God and Israel as they were to the ties binding members of human families. Imagery drawn from the spheres of conception, labor, and childbearing function to awaken sympathy, to convey a sense of incapacitating anguish (but also unexpected power), to illumine the ineffable origins of past, present, or anticipated realities, to castigate ungrateful sinners, and to signal Yahweh's blessings. Images of familial strife, pain, and alienation structure the reader's understanding of what has gone wrong in the divine/human relationship, but also suggest ways by which those relationships can survive and be healed.

In a society where adult males were normative, women were inevitably regarded as the "other" to some degree. Negative and/or threatening associations with women's distinctly female body functions (e.g., menstruation) appear in certain texts, as do references to the potential threat uncontrolled female sexual activity posed for Israel's patrilineal society. In Isaiah, metaphors containing discontinuous terms from the argot of female adultery and prostitution occasionally appear in descriptions of, or accusations against, personified Jerusalem. The functions of such imagery within Isaiah's vision could differ from those in certain other biblical books. Adultery charges against Jerusalem also appear, for example, in Ezekiel, a scroll whose period of composition falls within the same time span when Isaiah was in progress. But while Lady Jerusalem drops from sight when Ezekiel moves beyond judgment to a new beginning for God's people, the personified Jerusalem of Isaiah's vision appears not just in oracles of judgment, but especially in words of forgiveness, comfort, and restoration. What, for sequential readers, makes possible her transformation from illicit fornicator (1:21) to Yahweh's wife and the mother of his children? What contributions do the other ladies (cities) in Isaiah make to Zion's unfolding story? In order to answer these questions, we turn to a sequential reading of the "Ladies' Lots" in Isaiah.

4

THE LADIES' LOTS:
ISAIAH 1-39

The "ladies" of this chapter title are not human women (and, from the Isaian perspective, most of them weren't ladies either). They are, rather, cities personified as females. Many of the social and cultural associations with women identified in Chapter 3 are evoked in Isaian texts containing personified city imagery; and these associations function to persuade readers to particular perceptions of these "ladies" and, hence, of the peoples they embody. Frequently, personifications draw from the familial sphere: urban centers appear as (virgin) daughters, wives, mothers, and widows. Elsewhere, prostitution or perhaps menstrual imagery becomes the lens through which a city's activity or character is perceived.

Sequential readers attending to the "ladies' lots" theme (i.e., the fates of Jerusalem and her rivals) in Isaiah discover the cities' roles in Yahweh's unfolding "plan." Like the rebellious child metaphors examined in Chapter 2, personified city imagery appears already in Isaiah 1 and recurs throughout the scroll, while the "ladies' lots" is resolved (to Jerusalem's distinct advantage) by vision's end. References to personified cities contribute, therefore, not only to their contexts, but also to our reader's construal of Isaiah as a coherent literary work.

A look at recent commentary reveals a tendency either to ignore female imagery in Isaian oracles, or immediately to decode it, thereby disclosing its "real meaning." Female personifications of cities were conventional in Israel, but that does not mean their impact was nil. In discussions of relevant texts, I shall take seriously the poet's choices, as well as those other

124

factors influencing the reading process. Though my focus is female tropes, I shall occasionally "fill in" the discussion with texts where no such imagery appears. Assyria plays an important role in the topic to hand, for example, but the Isaiah traditions do not address a personified Lady Nineveh. Unless we trace our theme of personified cities against the broader background of Isaiah's vision concerning Zion's future among all the capitals and countries of the world, we cannot grasp its full import.

YAHWEH'S PLAN FOR ISRAEL AND THE NATIONS

The distinctive Isaian theme of Yahweh's plan for Israel and the nations plays a vital role in oracles concerning foreign cities and nations—indeed, in Isaiah as a whole. E. Conrad stresses the military nature of Yahweh's plan—a purpose devised long ago by the Lord of history against pretenders to that role. Consider, for example, the following threat against Assyria:

> As I have designed, / so shall it be;
> and as I have planned, / so shall it come to pass:
> I will break the Assyrian in my land,
>   and on my mountains trample him under foot;
> his yoke shall be removed from them,
>   and his burden from their shoulders.
> This is the plan that is planned
>   concerning the whole earth;
> and this is the hand that is stretched out
>   over all the nations.
> For the Lord of hosts has planned,
>   and who will annul it?
> His hand is stretched out,
>   and who will turn it back? (Isa 14:24-27)

The rhetorical purpose of this text is clear: to persuade readers of Yahweh's impending triumph, the vain boasts of Israel's rivals and its own bedraggled doubts notwithstanding. Even Jerusalem will become God's victim. But while she is not exempt from the punishment inflicted by God's "instruments," her *ultimate* fate and status among the nations are secure.

In this Chapter and the next, we shall see how attending to the ladies' lots theme in the course of a sequential reading of Isaiah reveals God's plan in all its fullness. How do these ladies fit into the values and goals that are part of the male god,

Yahweh's, world-wide strategy? Toward what ends is female imagery employed? Anticipating our conclusions, we suggest that aspects of our ladies' lots theme appear at strategic points in three principle movements within Isaiah 1–39: explaining Zion's current debased state (while affirming her ultimate glorification) in Isaiah 1–12; defining the roles of cities and nations, Jerusalem among them, in Yahweh's military plan (Isaiah 13–27); and anticipating Zion's survival, even in the face of her mightiest foes (Isaiah 28–39).

CITIES AS FEMALES

When Israel's prophets and other poets depicted and/or addressed cities as females, they were not creating fresh imagery. To the contrary, such tropes were part of a larger, variegated literary convention attested not only in Israel, but also elsewhere in the ancient Near East.[1] Scholars point to various origins for this convention, including appeals to psychology: "The image of a city as female makes good psychological sense," T. Frymer-Kensky concedes, "for the city contains the populace within her walls, nurtures it, provides for it, and defends it" (1992a:172). As we shall see, however, psychological explanations can be highly subjective.

Female city imagery assumed a variety of forms in Israel's ancient Near Eastern world. In the extant literature, cities appear, or are addressed, in familial (and not so familial) roles. But the biblical authors did not borrow slavishly from existing city-as-female poetic conventions; to the contrary, they adopted—but also adapted—certain features from their neighbors.

In a recent essay, M. Biddle (1991) identifies two distinctive expressions of a "city mythologem" that influenced Israel's depictions of cities. Turning first to Mesopotamia, he notes that Akkadian and Sumerian cities were not conceived in feminine terms. Gender mitigated against such a development, since the Akkadian term for city (*alu*) was masculine; and the Sumerian term, *URU*, was neuter. Nevertheless, Mesopotamian cities were thought to share a patron/protege relationship with their respective male and female deities: "the most fruitful such patron relationships, in terms of the mythologem under consideration," Biddle observes, "are those between city and patron goddess, often depicted as mother of her city. While the Mesopotamian city never fully assumes the status of goddess, it is *identified* in closest terms with its patroness and her fortunes (175)."[2]

In the Levant, by contrast, West Semitic languages facilitated the personification of cities as females, for common nouns for city were feminine in gender. The close *identification* between patron goddesses and their protege cities in Mesopotamia was, in the Levant, streamlined or "simplified" by the *deification* of the city "herself" (175).

Biblical Hebrew, like other Northwest Semitic languages, had common feminine nouns for "city" (e.g., 'îr, qiryah).[3] But for the biblical authors, Biddle reasons, notions of goddesses and divine cities were theologically unacceptable. They therefore modified both the Mesopotamian and the West Semitic versions of the mythologem: like their Mesopotamian counterparts, Israel's indigenous cities were presumed to have a patron deity, the (male) god Yahweh. Like West Semitic cities, Israel's cities were *personified* as females. Addressing or describing Jerusalem as a woman, for example, became "a theological device . . . allowing for dramatic development, but also setting Jerusalem in proper relation to her God." F. W. Dobbs-Allsopp (1993:75-90) and W. C. Gwaltney (1983:208) agree that in personified cities, Israel found a theologically acceptable substitute for the goddesses of its ancient Near Eastern neighbors. In the book of Lamentations, Gwaltney notes, "Daughter Zion" functions much like the female deities of Sumerian and Akkadian laments, who wandered through their cities' ruins bemoaning the destruction of town and temple.[4]

Gender markers appear on sundry feminine grammatical forms—for example, adjectives, participles, finite verbs, and many (though by no means all) feminine nouns—in both poetry and prose. Their appearance does not automatically signal personification; and their significance should not be exaggerated in the absence of other, explicitly personifying elements. Where such elements (e.g., verbs that can be applied literally only to animate objects) appear, however, they merit consideration both of the associations they evoke, and of their functions within their immediate and larger contexts. After all, even a subtle or familiar use of figurative language can contribute to the reader's construal of, and response to, its topic.

CITIES AND FAMILIAL IMAGERY

The City as (Virgin) Daughter

The phrase *bat-PN* (where PN is the name of a city or nation) occurs frequently in biblical poetry,[5] and has traditionally been translated, "the daughter of PN." But, following W. F. Stinespring (1965), the phrase is better understood as an appositional genitive referring not to some daughter of a city, but to the city itself.[6] Accordingly, the NRSV renders Isa 1:8 as follows:

> And daughter Zion is left / like a booth in a vineyard,
> like a shelter in a cucumber field, / like a besieged city.

The translator of *Tanakh* goes further, expunging any familial nuance from the phrase and rendering *bat-siyyôn* in Isa 1:8 as "Fair Zion." This has the effect of transforming an appositional genitive into a noun with attributive adjective. But it is in the spirit of Stinespring, who advocated greater flexibility in translating *bat* (like the Arabic *bint*, he noted, it can also mean "girl" or "maiden") and who pronounced J. Moffatt's translation, "dear Jerusalem" (for *bat-yerusalaim*), "free, but gets the right feeling" (1965:134, 138).

The phrase *betulat-(bat-)-PN* also appears within biblical poetry, addressing a community facing, or having experienced, disaster.[7] Much has been written about the meaning of *betulah*; specifically, the debate turns upon whether the noun refers simply to a nubile adolescent girl, or more narrowly to a young woman who has not yet engaged in sexual intercourse (Wenham 1972; Bowman 1978; Locher 1986; de Moor 1987). N. H. Walls (1992:79) examines contexts where *btlt* and its Semitic cognates appear and concludes that it is best translated "'maiden' since the primary significance of the term is as an age, social, and gender designation," rather than as an indicator of sexual inexperience. In Deuteronomy 22, *btlh* may refer more specifically to a young woman who has not yet become sexually active. In Joel 1:8, by contrast, it apparently designates a young woman who has recently married, but not yet borne a child. These examples suggest that *btlh* had more than a single meaning. In legal contexts, it could refer precisely to a woman who had never engaged in sexual intercourse. In other contexts, however, the term functioned to foreground certain of its associated commonplaces: youth; beauty; sexual ripeness; vulnerability; (potential) fertility; and value, including especially the value of her reproductive capacity.

Why characterize capital cities[8] as daughters, rather than as sons? Again, some scholars appeal to psychology. E. Follis, for example, explores what widespread associations with children of both genders can suggest about the personification of cities as daughters (1987:177):

> sons commonly are thought to represent the adventuresome spirit of a society. . . . Daughters, on the other hand, have been associated with stability, with the building up of society, with nurturing the community at its very heart and center. The stereotypical male spirit lies in conquest, while the stereotypical female spirit lies in culture. . . . As [daughter], the city becomes the quintessence of civilization and culture, of a stable lifestyle, of permanent relationships.

Critics dispute to what degree the city-as-daughter metaphor remained vital. Follis insists that as part of the phrase "Daughter Zion," the metaphor carried considerable rhetorical weight (1987:175): "the ancient poets accorded to *bat-siyyôn* an important place as an expression with considerable emotional and conceptual impact." But J. Galambush (1992:36) observes that "the expression 'daughter X' . . . is frequently used without further personification, and by prophets (e.g., Amos) who use no other forms of personification of cities, and so was probably a 'dead' metaphor, part of the ancient Near Eastern metaphoric conception of cities as females." While Galambush is correct that the expression "daughter X" could be used by the prophets without further personification or elaboration, this does not mean that the daughter metaphor was "dead," but only that it was conventional (the terms are not synonymous). When it became the focus of the poet's attention, however, it could be developed in various striking ways. In Isa 37:22 (= 2 Kgs 19:21), "virgin daughter Zion" exhibits youthful defiance. In Lam 2:18, however, her "wall" is urged to immerse herself in mournful weeping, activity especially, though not exclusively, associated with women:

> Cry aloud to the Lord! / O wall of daughter Zion!
> Let tears stream down like a torrent / day and night!
> Give yourself no rest, / your eyes no respite!

The poignancy is intensified when, at a critical moment, the poet assumes Jerusalem's female persona so that she ostensibly articulates her own plight (B. Kaiser 1987; Lanahan 1974:41–49). In Jer 4:30-31, for example, the prophet threatens:

> In vain you beautify yourself.
> For I heard a cry as of a woman in labor,
> anguish as of one bringing forth her first child,
> the cry of daughter Zion gasping for breath,
> stretching out her hands,
> "Woe is me! I am fainting before killers!" (Jer 4:30-31)

He uses the same poetic technique in yet another description of Jerusalem's impending destruction:

> they ride on horses, / equipped like a warrior for battle,
> against you, O daughter Zion!
> "We have heard news of them, / our hands fall helpless;
> anguish has taken hold of us,
> pain as of a woman in labor." (Jer 6:23-24)

The metaphor's impact depends, then, upon its development, rather than its freshness. Recurring metaphors should not be characterized as hackneyed or "dead" simply because they commended themselves repeatedly to Israel's prophets and other poets.

Addressing a city as daughter could function to foreground a variety of associations, including affection, pity, youthful scorn, mourning, incapacitating fear, joyful celebration, sexual abuse, shame, and vulnerability. The latter association appears endemic to most of the others, given the physical, legal, and social vulnerability associated with both females and minors. Depending upon the identity of *bat-PN* and the tone of its poetic context, the phrase with its attendant associations could function to enliven a sense of glee at her impending fate, as in Jer 23:12.

Alongside gloating references to daughter or virgin daughter PN, however, are depictions of her inviting pity rather than glee. Such frequently is the tone of passages containing *bat-siyyôn* (Follis 1987:177). Frymer-Kensky comments:

> The very "woman" upon whom the prophets direct our ire is also ourselves. The image of the young woman as *victim* focuses our attention on the vulnerability and perishability of the nation in God's eyes and allows the prophet and reader to

express a sadness that goes beyond questions of justice. . . .
[T]his image of the ruined-maiden victim enables the reader to
empathize with the people, to forget the cause of the devastation and join in the sorrow. (1992a:169)

Note, for example this passage from Lamentations:

What can I say for you, to what compare you,
  O daughter Jerusalem?
To what can I liken you, that I may comfort you,
  O virgin daughter Zion?
For vast as the sea is your ruin;
  who can heal you? (Lam 2:13; cf. 1:6; 2:4-5, 8, 10, 18)

At the other extreme, daughter imagery appears in biblical
poetry suffused with joy:

Sing aloud, O daughter Zion; / shout, O Israel!
Rejoice and exult with all your heart,
  O daughter Jerusalem. (Zeph 3:14; cf. Zech 9:9)

Daughter imagery contributes, then, to a variety of contexts
and toward a diversity of rhetorical ends. Its social and cultural associations are manifold, but vulnerability is prominent among them.

The City as Wife and Mother

Both Israel and its neighbors in the Levant personified cities as
women and, some scholars conclude, as wives of their patron
gods and mothers of their inhabitants. J. Lewy (1944) argued
on the basis of West Semitic and Akkadian town names, as well
as Assyrian personal names in which town names appear as
feminine theophoric elements, that cities were regarded as
female deities whose husbands were their respective patron
gods.[9] More recently, both A. Fitzgerald (1972, 1975) and J.
Galambush (1992:20) have championed Lewy's thesis. T. Frymer-Kensky, by contrast, flatly rejects it, acknowledging that
cities are called "lady" or "princess" in certain West Semitic
inscriptions, but claiming that "there is . . . no evidence . . . that
this female city was imagined to be married to the god of the
city" (1992a:269).[10] For our purposes, it suffices that personified Jerusalem appears as Yahweh's wife and her inhabitants'
mother in certain Isaian texts. Foreign cities also are depicted as
mothers of their inhabitants in Isaiah, but they are nowhere
described as wives of Yahweh or of other, rival gods.

Scholars propose various origins for the prophets' adulteress/ prostitute city imagery.[11] Fitzgerald claims the adultery motif developed when the ancient Near Eastern married city metaphor became part of Israel's monotheistic setting: "In a polytheistic society worship of other gods, in addition to the patron god of a city "was completely acceptable" (1972:405).

E. J. Adler (Goodfriend), on the other hand, argues that marriage would be an unlikely choice of metaphor for Israel's polytheistic neighbors, given their extremely negative attitudes toward adultery. Marriage and adultery/harlotry tropes had their primary origin in the exclusive nature of the covenant Yahweh forged with Israel at Sinai (1989:147-48).[12] The poetic convention of regarding cities as women may have facilitated development of such tropes (1992b:509), but it was not their source.

Galambush notes that polytheism need not inevitably have been equated with polyandry:

> Like the potential for butchery implicit in the OT metaphor of Yahweh as shepherd (who might not only "tend," but also slaughter, the sheep), the potential for adultery implicit in the marriage metaphor would be left inactive. The city might, for example, be understood as married and loyal to its patron god, but the residents of the city understood as her children, who might worship other gods. (1992:26)

Debates over the origins of adulteress/prostitute city imagery will continue. Most important for our purposes, however, is the recognition that such imagery could be developed by Israel's prophets and other poets in more than one way: foreign cities were sometimes accused of fornication (e.g., trade, treachery), though nowhere conceived as Yahweh's wives or wives of other male gods. Israelite and Judean cities were charged with adultery and harlotry (i.e., misplaced reliance on other deities or on earthly powers). Harlotry accusations are lodged against Jerusalem, in fact, yet in a way that leaves open the possibility of her eventual redemption and restoration as Yahweh's faithful wife.

The Widowed City

References to widowed cities appear not only in Isaiah (47:8, 9) but also in Jeremiah (51:5) and Lamentations (1:1). The Egyptian Stele of Merneptah contains the claim (Wilson 1969:378):

> Israel is laid waste, his seed is not;
> Hurru is become a widow for Egypt!

C. Cohen (1973) has investigated ancient Near Eastern references to widows in order to determine the precise meaning of the widowed city metaphor. He begins with §33 of the Middle Assyrian Laws, according to which a women whose husband died became the responsibility of an adult son. If she had no adult son, she became the responsibility of her father-in-law, who could either give her in marriage to another of his sons, or marry her himself. But, says the text, "If her husband and her father-in-law are dead and she has no son, she is an *almattu*." Clearly, Cohen avers, the term *almattu* refers to "a once married woman who has no means of financial support and who is thus in need of special legal protection" (1973:76).[13]

Turning to the Hebrew evidence, Cohen notes (77) that in contexts where marital status is the topic, the term *'almanah* should be translated "widow" (Lev 21:14; 22:13; Num 30:10; Ezek 44:22). But in contexts where protecting the rights of the socially disadvantaged is at issue, "a once married woman who has no means of financial support and who is thus in need of special legal protection" is a more appropriate definition.

> Tamar, the daughter-in-law of Judah, is not called an *'almanah* until she is told by her father-in-law to dwell in her father's household: "Dwell, *'almanah*, in the household of your father." By returning to her father's household, she is thus deprived of her father-in-law's support. Since, in addition, she has no adult son to support her, she certainly falls under the definition of Akkadian *almattu*. (Cohen 1973:77)

Likewise in Egyptian literature, (*h3rt*) sometimes refers to a woman whose husband has perished. In other contexts, however, it apparently designates a particularly vulnerable woman: "that her change of marital status is not the primary concern in these cases is further demonstrated by a text in which a *male* scribe, contending that his master is not taking proper care of him, compares himself to a *h3rt*" (78).

With this definition of widow as needy, once married woman in mind, Cohen turns to "widowed" city texts:

> When applied to a city, this concept would undoubtedly designate a once independent city which has lost its independence

133

and is now completely dependent upon another state for protection and survival. In short, *the "widowed" city motif seems
to refer to a once independent city which has become a vassal
of another state.* (78-79)

The logical transition from "widowed woman" to "widowed city"
is not so smooth as Cohen suggests. In the former case, a woman
dependent upon a male head of household (husband, father-in-
law, adult son) loses her protector (placing her "in need of
special legal protection"), while in the latter, a city's status
changes from independence, to dependence upon a suzerain.
Nonetheless, both situations move the woman/city from positive
to precarious circumstances. Cohen's thesis is compelling; we
would only emphasize that in both the literal and figurative references to widows, associations of *vulnerability* are foregrounded
in prominent ways. (Recall the male scribe who likened himself
to a "widow.") This is particularly true, as we shall see, in Isa
47:8-9a, part of a poem against Lady Babylon, where dwelling
as an *'almanah* (a possibility she denies in vs. 8) appears as the
precise opposite of dwelling securely (*hayyôsebet labetah*; vs. 7).

Summary

Within the Hebrew Bible, Israel's and Judah's cities have a male
patron deity, Yahweh. In the prophetic literature, these same cities, and foreign ones as well, are personified as women, though
not as goddesses. Familial models and metaphors lend rhetorical
power to many female depictions of cities, the latter appearing
as vulnerable maidens, beautiful and fertile wives, bereaved
mothers, forsaken spouses, defenseless widows, etc.

A CITY LAMENT GENRE

In ancient Mesopotamia, city laments described and bewailed
the destruction of ancient cities and their shrines.[14] Noting
similarities between these laments and certain biblical texts,
including Lamentations and a number of Isaian oracles relevant
to our ladies' lot theme, scholars have debated the existence of
an ancient Israelite city lament genre. Since genre, and the
presence of stock imagery, themes, etc., can predispose readers
to certain construals, instead of to others, the question is pertinent to our present inquiry.

Most recently, F. W. Dobbs-Allsopp (1993) has opted for a comparative approach to the problem, correlating motifs, themes, and structural elements appearing in Mesopotamian laments with similar features in relevant biblical texts, and affirming a generic connection.[15] To be sure, Mesopotamian and Hebrew expressions of such features can differ in significant ways. But positing a *generic* relationship between them accounts for both similarities and differences. In Israelite city laments, for example, divine warrior imagery replaces the devastating storm imagery of their Mesopotamian counterparts. And, as noted above, personified Jerusalem correlates to Mesopotamia's weeping goddess.

In the following pages, we shall note certain city lament features in Isaian oracles concerning cities and nations. The presence of such (ominous) features may not inevitably signal a city's demise, but they can certainly serve to threaten or presage such an end.

ISAIAH 1–4: FROM *SUKKAH* TO *SUKKAH*[16]

Initially in Isaiah's vision, Zion appears the pitiful victim of her inhabitants' rebellions and sins against Yahweh. Though labelled a prostitute, her fall from "faithful city" to "harlot" occasions a lament; and the onus for her impurity falls squarely upon her contaminating inhabitants, especially the leadership class. Isaiah 1 acknowledges the fiery destruction Jerusalem must endure, but it encourages our pity, not our ire. Our reader knows, of course, that Jerusalem burned in 587 BCE. Yet the rhetoric of Isaiah 1 invites the most positive construal possible of so great a disaster: Zion's rehabilitation is its ultimate goal.

Isaiah 1:8

Following the superscription in verse 1, Isaiah 1 begins with a summons: heaven and earth are called to witness charges that Yahweh's children have become rebellious (vss. 2-3), persistently forsaking and despising God (vss. 4-5) despite repeated beatings leaving them bruised and bleeding (vs. 6). Verse 7 details the destruction Israel's land has suffered on account of its inhabitants' sinfulness: it is desolate, burned, devoured. Our reader's first glimpse of personified Jerusalem is dismal indeed.

Three similes describes her sorry state:

> And daughter Zion is left / like a booth in a vineyard,
> like a shelter in a cucumber field, / like a besieged city.[17]

In this context, the phrase *bat-siyyôn* inclines the reader to pity and sorrow. Like Israel's land, Daughter Zion suffers not for some personal misdeed, but on account of the sins of her human inhabitants (detailed in vss. 2-6). All three similes convey a sense of perilous vulnerability. In the first, Judah's capital is likened to a temporary booth (*sukkah*) constructed from branches to provide shelter for the watchmen who guard a ripening vineyard (see also Job 27:18). In the second, it is likened to a *melunah*, also a rickety structure for the night-guard in the fields (Holladay 1971:197). Its precariousness is apparent from Isa 24:20:

> The earth staggers like a drunkard,
> it sways like a hut [*kammilunah*];
> its transgression lies heavy upon it,
> and it falls, and will not rise again.

Similar imagery appears in the Sumerian "Lamentation over the Destruction of Ur." There, Ningal, wife of Nanna, laments the ruin of her temple:

> My house founded by the righteous,
> Like a garden hut, verily on its side has caved in[18] . . .
> My faithful house . . .
> . . . like a tent, like a pulled-up harvest shed,
> like a pulled-up harvest shed indeed
>   was exposed to wind and rain.[19]

The epithet and first two similes, then, present Zion as vulnerable and precarious, if not already destroyed. The third simile, with its continuous term, "city" (*'îr*), drives home the *literal* truth of her sorry condition; it has exercised commentators, who variously translate *nesûrah* as "besieged" (so NRSV), "beleaguered" (so *Tanakh*) or "like a watch-tower" (so O. Kaiser 1972:6). G. B. Gray considered "a well-guarded city" to be the "safest rendering," though he was unable to make sense of the same only if it were a gloss. Yet the description of "Maiden Zion" as "guarded" may, in this context, be tragically ironic: Jerusalem, whose strength, beauty, and inviolability are elsewhere extolled by Israel's poets, is likened here to a field hut whose solitary inhabitants are her only defense. Verse 8 then leads fittingly to verse 9 with its first-person (pl.) admission that the city's survivors are few indeed:

> If the Lord of hosts
> had not left us a few survivors,
> we would have been like Sodom,
> and become like Gomorrah.

Commentators wishing to identify the original setting in life of once-discrete oracles within Isaiah 1 discern in these verses precisely the conditions pertaining in the aftermath of "Hezekiah's rebellion" (Isaiah 36–37; cf. Willis 1985:151-69). But the presence of temporary garden shelter imagery challenges interpretations of verse 8 as a description of a sole surviving city. As the examples cited above show, such imagery was traditionally associated with a temple's *destruction*, rather than a city's *survival*. "The image depicts Jerusalem's destruction. The once fortified city has now been made into something akin to a frail garden hut, useless and deteriorating after the harvest" (Dobbs-Allsopp 1993:146).

Because of its obscure third simile, the meaning of verse 8 remains difficult to ascertain. Unlike both of the ancient Near Eastern city laments cited above, Isa 1:8 does not explicitly state that the garden shelters have been *toppled*. Yet if Jerusalem's utter destruction is not envisioned here, one can at least argue that the use of imagery *associated* with city laments foregrounds the severity of Maiden Zion's plight. In any event, identifying a precise historical situation on the basis of stock imagery is a shaky undertaking.

Isaiah 1:21-26 (28)

Following Yahweh's rebuke of Israel's endless but insincere sacrifices and prayers (vss. 10-17) and the offer of a clear choice between obedience and life on the one hand, and rebellion and death on the other (vss. 18-20), the reader meets a second personification of Zion in a prophetic lament:[20]

> Alas, she has become a harlot—
> The faithful city. (Isa 1:21a; *Tanakh*)

The (once-) faithful city whose habitual fornications this lament bewails is not identified immediately by name. But a related epithet, *'îr ha'emet* ("faithful city"), appears in Zech 8:3; and both may have been traditional titles for Jerusalem. At any rate, verse 27 explicitly reveals Zion's identity.

How does our reader construe the claim that "the (once-) faithful city has become a harlot?" In his commentary, R. B. Y. Scott distinguished between the prostitution metaphor in 1:21, and other prophetic characterizations of Israel and/or its cities as unfaithful women: "The figure here is not, as in Hosea, that of an unfaithful wife," he wrote, "but of evil character in general; it is probably chosen by association of ideas, corresponding to the murderers, renegades, and thieves against whom the oracle is directed" (1956:176). The possibility that *zônah* refers to an unfaithful wife, and not just to a practicing prostitute, cannot be dismissed so easily, however. As we have seen, a married woman's illicit sexual activity could be characterized metaphorically as prostitution. True, murderers are paired with (male) adulterers in Job 24:14-15. Nevertheless, our reader, informed by extratextual knowledge of Israel's religious traditions, will likely presuppose that behind the prostitution charge lies a personified city who has failed to honor her obligation of fidelity to Yahweh.

Subsequent verses do not elaborate upon the harlotry imagery introduced in 1:21; they move in a different direction. Once, Jerusalem was full of justice; and righteousness habitually "spent the night in her"—a suggestive phrase given the preceding charge of harlotry, though its impact is blunted by its subject. But now, murderers pass their nights in her. The assertion scarcely flatters. But the reference to murderers populating the city (vs. 2b) deflects the reader's attention from Zion "herself," focusing it instead upon an element *in* Zion that is the cause of the (once-) faithful city's current debased state. Two following metaphors likewise describe something valuable—precious metal (silver), first-class drink (wine)—that has become contaminated or diluted. Verse 23 identifies Jerusalem's contaminants, her greedy and unscrupulous leaders. Rather than charge Jerusalem using extended promiscuity metaphors, then, the poet chooses several different tropes focusing not upon the "nature" or behavior of Jerusalem herself, but rather upon those elements *debasing her*.

The reappearance of the metallurgy metaphor in verse 25 further underscores our point:

> I will turn my hand against you;
> > I will smelt away your dross as with lye
> > and remove all your alloy. (1:25)

Metallurgy required prolonged periods of extreme heat inside the smelting furnaces; and we should not downplay the fierce intensity of the process to which she will be subjected. Its goal, nonetheless, is separating the silver from its contaminating elements, rather than the silver's (city's) destruction *per se*. Just as the silver and wine metaphors of verse 22 were decoded by immediately following references to dishonest and greedy leadership (vs. 23), so also the smelting metaphor of verse 25 is decoded in verse 26: Jerusalem's rebellious and sinful authorities will be replaced by a just leadership. Her dross and alloy removed, Zion will be restored to her former state: "Afterward you shall be called the city of righteousness, the faithful city."

Zion's lot, and that of the penitents within her, is assured already in 1:27. The fate awaiting those refusing to repent is declared in the very next verse: they will be destroyed. The concluding verses of chapter 1 are best construed as describing their end: though the smelting furnaces awaiting Zion have as their ultimate purpose her purification, the fire awaiting "the strong" in verses 29-31 is a complete holocaust. For the reader whose extratextual repertoire includes other texts employing flora and sexual imagery to describe illicit religious practices and their practitioners, the closing verses of chapter 1 further underscore that Zion has become a "harlot" *precisely on account of her rebellious and sinful inhabitants.*

In the Hebrew Bible, prostitution charges are lodged against *foreign* cities for a variety of reasons. Within Isa 23:15-18, we shall see, Tyre appears as an aging prostitute, apparently a slur against her indiscriminate trade practices. Nahum attacks Nineveh for "prostitution," that is, for using her guiles to deal treacherously with other nations. But biblical charges of adultery/prostitution against *indigenous* cities generally are motived by misplaced reliance: Israel depends upon other deities, or forms alliances with other nations, rather than looking to Yahweh for support and protection. Compared to such traditions Isa 1:21, with its emphasis upon Jerusalem's contaminants, is unusual. It is possible, of course, that prostitution (and adultery) metaphors were routinely applied to a wider swath of policies and practices than the biblical literature suggests. But for the critic whose objective lens permits interpreting Isaiah 1 within the larger work, this use of prostitution imagery is distinctive: the prompt, pointed move from harlotry accusation to indictment of Jerusalem's leaders foregrounds the prostitute as *victim* toward strategic ends. Will charges that Jerusalem is/acts like a harlot recur in subsequent chapters?

Summary

Zion first appears the pitiful, vulnerable victim of her inhabitants' rebellions and sins against Yahweh. Though later called a prostitute, the onus for her impurity rests squarely upon the contaminates within her, and especially her leadership classes. No precise temporal setting is specified. Readers may, on the basis of 1:1, be inclined to locate the situation during the reign of one of four Judean kings. It is not inevitable that they will do so, however; this is, after all, a vision.

Verses 21-26 contain several features characteristic of ancient Israelite city laments: use of contrast (vs. 21) and reversal (vss. 22-23); *qinah* meter (vs. 21); the presence of the divine warrior (vs. 24); the "faithful city" epithet (vss. 21, 26); lamentation (vs. 21); and restoration (vs. 26). These features lead Dobbs-Allsopp to a conclusion that might, on first flush, appear to contradict our own: "Yahweh, the divine warrior and agent of destruction, tells (through the prophet) the 'Faithful City' of her impending destruction. . . . The message, however oblique, is clear: Yahweh will treat Israel as an enemy" (1993:151).

We agree that the oracle, with its city lament features, proclaims Jerusalem's destruction (depicted metaphorically as a fierce smelting process). Our reader knows that Jerusalem has burned, and that Yahweh claims responsiblity for its demise. Our intent, however, has been to show how, largely through its choice of metaphors, the poem both focuses blame for Jerusalem's impurity upon certain *elements within her*, rather than upon Lady Zion "herself," and puts a positive "spin" on Zion's fiery destruction. The Lord's plan includes "treat[ing] Israel as an enemy," and Zion's destruction is certainly part of that treatment. But Yahweh acts ultimately *on behalf of Zion and those in her who repent.*

Isaiah 3:8

The glorious description of Zion's future exaltation following a second superscription in Isa 2:1 can be construed as elaboration upon the promise of 1:27. True, 2:2-4 do not personify the Zion whence instruction (*tôrah*) will go forth (2:3b). They articulate, nonetheless, Isaiah's "word" (2:1) concerning Zion's future elevation and international relations.

Verse 5 invites the "house of Jacob" to walk in Yahweh's light. But this invitation is followed by a catalog of accusations, including charges of hubris and idolatry, and warnings concerning their consequences (2:11-22). Isaiah 3:8, noted briefly in our analysis of Isaiah's "rhetoric of rebellion," marks the next personification of Jerusalem in Isaiah's vision. Here, Jerusalem is not going up (2:2); to the contrary, stripped of all competent military and governmental leadership, she's going down:

> For Jerusalem has stumbled / and Judah has fallen,
> because their speech and their deeds are against the Lord,
> defying [*lamrôt*] his glorious presence.

Isaiah 3:25-26

Lady Zion makes her next, brief appearance in the midst of the shaming of her haughty "daughters" (3:16–4:1). Features here appear also in Israelite and Mesopotamian city laments: *qinah* meter and female personification, including city gates personified as mourning figures (Dobbs-Allsopp 1993:147).

In discussing Thebes' destruction (recalled in Nah 3:8-10), J. Galambush notes the absence of the actual women of the city:

> In v 10 Nahum tells the fate of the men and children of the city but ignores the fate of the Theban women. The literal women of Thebes (unlike the literal men and children) have no place in the anticipated destruction. Because Thebes itself is depicted as the ravished bride of "her strong men" and the mother of "her" murdered children, the actual Theban women become superfluous. (1992:41)

In our text, by contrast, both Lady Zion and her despoiled and ravaged daughters appear. Indeed, descriptions of her daughters' dismal circumstances surround the two verses in which second feminine singular grammatical forms signal Lady Zion's presence. Yet the text links Zion's mourning with the

141

deaths of her (male) warriors. She laments on their account; and she is "cleaned out, plundered" (*niqqatah*; NRSV: ravaged) because of their demise.

Isaiah 4:4

Lady Zion and her female inhabitants are paired again in Isa 4:4, where Yahweh's redemption of both Jerusalem and her populace is being described. The passage ("on that day") speaks of despoiled daughters, mourning Zion, and the seven desperate women who must seize a single man in the aftermath of devastating warfare. We discussed this text above (Chapter 3) in connection with its menstrual imagery and need only note here that the author has used menstrual and other imagery of bodily excretions (with their attending associations) to shape the audience's understanding of the defilement that Yahweh will purge from the people. The result of that purging is described in verses 5-6 in language that does not personify Jerusalem and yet, evokes memory of the reader's earliest glimpse of "her":

> Then the Lord will create over the whole site of Mount Zion and over its places of assembly a cloud by day and smoke and the shining of a flaming fire by night. Indeed over all the glory there will be a canopy. It will serve as a pavilion, a shade by day from the heat, and a refuge and a shelter from the storm and rain.

The prophet promises divine care and protection reminiscent of what Israel experienced during its exodus and wilderness wanderings.[21] Note that *sukkah*, "pavillion" (vs. 6) is the same word appearing in the first simile of Isa 1:8. There, the noun meant "a temporary shelter" with associations of isolation, fragility, and precariousness. But in this context, positive associations with such structures prevail: shade from burning heat (see Jonah 4:5) and protection from storm and rain (see Ps 27:5).

Summary

In the opening chapters of Isaiah's vision, our reader encounters Lady Zion in several different guises. First introduced as "Maiden" or "Daughter," she appears a pitiful figure whose vulnerability and isolation result from her inhabitants' sins (1:8). As verses 21-26 acknowledge, there was a time when she was called "faithful city"—language that, by our reader's time, will be construed against the extratext of other prophetic traditions depicting Jerusalem as Yahweh's wife. Charges of prostitution, or habitual, illicit fornication—also part of that extratext—are damning; and Jerusalem's destruction assured. Nonetheless, her culpability is largely ameliorated in this context by the immediate shift to metaphors emphasizing contaminants of otherwise valued substances (silver, first-rate wine or beer) on the one hand, and by use of the metallurgy metaphor to evoke an intense but purifying process on the other.

Though dire predictions follow, including the defacement of Zion's daughters and her own bereavement (3:25-26), Isaiah 1–4 ends on a positive note. Again, fire functions as Yahweh's purifying agent (4:4). But now, additional associations with fire are foregrounded as Zion, illumined by God's glory and protected by cloud and flame, rises above harm's way. The vulnerable maiden who was abandoned like a "hut" (*sukkah*) in a field will be purified, protected by God's pavillion (*sukkah*), and populated by a holy people. For our reader, the repetition of *sukkah*, but in strikingly different contexts, underscores the magnitude of the envisioned transformation. This same pattern will recur elsewhere in Isaiah's vision, as expectations for Jerusalem's future coexist with threats of judgment.

"CRY ALOUD, O DAUGHTER GALLIM!
SING FOR JOY, O ROYAL ZION":
BEYOND THE ASSYRIAN THREAT

Personified city imagery does not reappear in Isaiah until 10:27b-33. For our sequential reader, however, intervening materials have stuck both familiar and more innovative chords: Israel and Judah, Yahweh's disappointing vineyard, are decried for their sins (5:1-7). The upper classes stand accused of land-grabbing (5:8-10), drunkenness (5:11-13), and rejecting the Lord's instruction (5:18-25). On account of these and other iniquities, Yahweh signals a distant nation whose army will roar over the people, "like the roaring of the sea" (5:30). The mostly prose passages in 6:1–8:23 [ET 9:1] recount Isaiah's prophetic call (Isaiah 6), his encounter with faithless Ahaz in the midst of the Syro-Ephramitic crisis (including the Immanuel prophecy; Isaiah 7), the conception and naming of Maher-shalal-hash-baz

(8:1-4), and another threat regarding "the king of Assyria and all his glory" (8:7). The tone is negative indeed: many of Jerusalem's inhabitants shall "stumble" (8:15; recall Isa 3:8). But with the poetry of 9:1 [2], the "thick darkness" of 8:22 gives way to "great light" and the royal birth announcement in 9:1-6 [2-7]. The remainder of Isaiah 9, with its specific references to Jacob, Israel, Ephraim, Samaria, and Manasseh, clearly intends to justify Yahweh's destruction of the Northern Kingdom. With 10:1-4, however, the reader remembers charges levied against the leaders of Jerusalem already in Isaiah 1. Such are not solely the past misdeeds of a justly-punished (Northern Israelite) nation, but sins plaguing Judah as well; perhaps, from the reader's perspective, they persist to his own day. In any event, Yahweh's wrath has not abated (10:4b). Assyria's role in Yahweh's punitive plan is reiterated:

> Ah, Assyria, the rod of my anger—
>> the club in their hands is my fury! (10:5)

Isaiah 10:27b-33

Made privy to the king of Assyria's thoughts, our reader knows from 10:10-11 that the threat he poses extends beyond the Northern Kingdom and into Judah itself. News of steadily advancing enemy troops spreads quickly, throwing Jerusalem's daughter towns into panic:[22]

> Cry aloud, O daughter Gallim!
>> Listen, O Laishah! / Answer her, O Anathoth!
> Madmenah is in flight,
>> the inhabitants of Gebim flee for safety.
> This very day he will halt at Nob,
>> he will shake his fist / at the mount of daughter Zion,
>> the hill of Jerusalem. (10:30-32)

Here, fleeting female personifications exploit associations with women and warfare—fear, weakness, vulnerability to rape, enslavement, or murder—to depict the despair of settlements in Assyria's path. The text is highly rhetorical. Yet our sequential reader construes the Assyrian threat not only in light of these verses, but also against the background of earlier ones, including the claim that "when the Lord has finished all his work on Mount Zion and on Jerusalem, he [MT: I] will punish the arrogant boasting of the king of Assyria and his haughty pride" (10:12). Yahweh's use of Assyria as an instrument of divine wrath will end (10:24-25). These sequentially prior verses reassure Zion's inhabitants (and our reader) that she will not share the fate of her Northern counterpart. Assyria's king may shake his arm at "the mount of Daughter Zion, the hill of Jerusalem," but the reader knows that he will not deal a fatal blow. The extended fist of Assyria's king is no match for the whip-wielding hand of Yahweh (vs. 26).

Isaiah 12:5-6

Zion is next personified in 12:6. Verses 5-6 are the culmination of hymns of thanksgiving joyfully sung in response to glorious deeds by the "root of Jesse" (Isaiah 11), whose rule will bring Israel edenic conditions (11:6-9) and an end to oppressive enemy nations (11:12-16). The passage begins, "You [masc. sing.] shall say in that day"; "With joy you [masc. pl.] will draw water" (12:3). In verse 6, however, the thanksgiving concludes with a shift to feminine singular forms:

> Shout aloud and sing for joy, yôsebet siyyôn,
> for great in your midst is the Holy One of Israel.

Specialists construe phrases like yôsebet siyyôn in various ways, perhaps because they bore more than a single possible meaning. The most common translation views yôsebet-PN as simply the semantic equivalent of yôsebê-PN, "the inhabitants of PN" (O. Kaiser 1972:167). The feminine singular participle (yôsebet) is taken as a collective, and its gender accorded no semantic significance (compare gôlah as a collective designation for the Babylonian exiles).[23] This approach does not consider the possibility that the prophets personified inhabitants of cities or countries as women in order to evoke and exploit certain associations with females. One could argue, however, that Jer 51:35 depicts Zion's populace as a physically-abused woman wishing upon Chaldea's inhabitants the same suffering she has endured:

> "May my torn flesh be avenged on Babylon,"
>   Zion-dwelling maiden shall say.
> "May my blood be avenged on Chaldea's dwellers,"
>   Jerusalem shall say.[24]

The critic knows that Isaiah 22 will address Jerusalem's populace as a woman climbing up to the rooftops to celebrate her
survival. According to this construal, then (and depending upon
the literary context), a city or country's inhabitants could be
depicted as a female bereaved, vulnerable, beloved, or joyous.

Yet another, quite suggestive approach understands *yôsebet-PN* as an epithet for the personified city or nation "herself,"
rather than as a collective for her inhabitants. But scholars have
long noted that the (masc. sing.) participle *yôseb* can mean
"enthroned"; and W. L. Holladay argues that *yôsebet* bears this
same meaning in a number of texts in Jeremiah, including Jer
10:17 ("Gather up from the land your bundle, [you who are]
enthroned under siege!").

"Enthroned" makes good sense in a number of passages
containing our phrase (including, as we shall see, Isa 47:8). So,
for example, Jer 22:23, which the NRSV renders:

> O inhabitant of Lebanon, / nested among the cedars,
> how you will groan when pangs come upon you,
>   pain as of a woman in labor.

This verse is translated by Holladay in a way that makes the
"inhabitant's" identity clearer, and her physical relationship *vis
à vis* Lebanon less confusing (1986:600):

> You who are enthroned in Lebanon, / nested in the cedars,
> how you have groaned when pangs come upon you,
>   writhing like a woman in labor!

This translation makes clear that "Jerusalem is accused of
self-deification, surrounded as she is in both palace and temple
by cedar from Lebanon (see v 7). But Lebanon's cedars suggest
height: if Yahweh is enthroned on (the height of) Zion (Ps
9:12), then Jerusalem takes pride in being enthroned on (the
height of) Lebanon" (Holladay 1986:603).

Cross and Freedman have suggested that *yôseb* also developed a more technical meaning: "technical usage seems to have
produced a development in the meaning of the root *ysb* in
special idioms from 'sitting' on a throne to being a 'throne-
sitter,' i.e., a king, and finally to the virtually denominative use
of the verb and its derivatives with the meaning, 'rule'"
(1955:249). The feminine singular counterpart of *yôseb*, "throne
sitter, king" would be "queen"; such seems to be the thinking

behind the NRSV translation of *yôsebet siyyôn* in Isa 12:6 as "O royal Zion" (RSV had "O inhabitant of Zion").

Finally, T. Frymer-Kensky offers a different understanding of *yôsebet-PN* that moves beyond simple personification. In her view, Jerusalem (for example) was not just personified as a female; in the Israelite mind, "she" existed as a woman living within the city (1992a:172-73):

> Zion is very much the physical city of houses and walls, but Zion is also a *person* who dwells within this physical city. . . . Yoshevet Zion is the essence of the city seen as a female, the immanent presence that lives within the walls. The great all-encompassing love that Isaiah feels for Jerusalem, and his belief that Jerusalem will always be the center of God's activity and attention, combine with this image of Zion-the-dweller to produce a powerful vision of the inner spirit of the city.

Whether or not Frymer-Kensky has identified an aspect of the Israelite mindset regarding personified Jerusalem is difficult to determine. Her distinction between the city itself, and an "inner spirit of the city" named "Yoshevet Zion," however, seems contrived. Isaiah 12:6 is better understood either as the celebrative singing of Zion's population, personified as a joyful woman, or (more likely) as enthroned Zion herself. Earlier the object of the Assyrian king's threat, she is urged to give thanks for her salvation, and to celebrate the Holy One in her midst.

Summary

Already in Isa 5:26-30, Yahweh threatens to bring a mighty foreign army against Israel. That threat is repeated, and the foe identified, in 7:17: Assyria's king is the agent of Yahweh's wrath, the "instrument" of the hour in God's unfolding plan. Assyria's destruction of Northern Israel is described, and Yahweh's role in that judgment defended (9:8-21). So long as miscarriages of justice persist, Yahweh's anger continues; and Judah is not immune to its devastating effects. But Assyria's king misconstrues the reason for his military success. His arrogant thoughts of adding Jerusalem to his conquests (10:11) elicits from Yahweh both a threat of destruction and a promise to Zion's inhabitants that they will not share the Northern Kingdom's fate. Though Assyria's army is on the march (10:27-32), Zion is assured that she can look beyond the Assyrian threat to songs and shouts of joy in thanksgiving to God.

With the conclusion of chapter 12, we have arrived at the end of our first major movement in Isaiah 1–39. Concern for Zion's "final destiny," to borrow from the title of C. Seitz's recent monograph, has appeared at significant junctures throughout these chapters—in Isaiah 1, 4, 10, and concluding with the songs of thanksgiving in Isaiah 12. Our reader has no doubt that Jerusalem stands under God's word of judgment. But that word is not God's last word to Zion.

Who or what does personified Zion (and, *mutatis mutandis*, other cities as well) represent in these texts? Is she the city itself, its inhabitants, or a female presence living within the city walls? No single answer to this question suffices. Rather, the referent evoked in female form must be identified text by text.

"TUMULT ON THE MOUNTAINS": ORACLES AGAINST THE NATIONS IN ISAIAH 13–27

Our reader arrives at Isaian oracles against foreign cities and nations with songs of praise to Yahweh ringing in his ears. Those songs celebrated Yahweh's sovereignty over a world where even the great Assyrian empire acts at God's behest; and Yahweh gathers the remnant from among the nations, promising Judah and Ephraim a prominent place in a reordered world, and ensuring Zion's eventual exaltation.

A series of superscriptions introduces the entities addressed in chapters 13–27, the second major movement within Isaiah 1–39.[25] It begins with oracles against Israel's paradigmatic foes—Babylon followed by Assyria—but also addresses neighboring enemies and potential allies, including Egypt.

Isaiah 13–14:30

Isaiah's first oracle against Babylon contains a number of features associated with city laments: *qinah* meter (13:4, 5, 8a and b); enemy invasion (13:17); descriptions of the city as a haunt for wild animals (13:20-22); references to Sodom and Gomorrah (13:19), to exile (13:14), to the glorious city (13:19), and its restoration (13:6; see Dobbs-Allsopp 1993). But while chapters 13–14 refer to the horrors that are women's lot in the midst of warfare, they include no female personifications of

Babylon. (The imperative, "Wail!" in 13:6, for example, is masculine plural, not feminine singular.) To the contrary, the king of Babylon, rather than his capital city, is singled out for severe rebuke (14:4-20) in this essentially militaristic oracle. A subsequent oracle against Assyria likewise contains no female imagery. It is noteworthy, nonetheless, for its affirmation that Yahweh has an inexorable plan for the earth:

> This is the plan that is planned
> concerning the whole earth;
> and this is the hand that is stretched out
> over all the nations. (14:26)

The oracle against Babylon undoubtedly post-dates the eighth-century Isaiah of Jerusalem. From our reader's perspective, however, its presence underscores the *prima facie* claim that the prophet Isaiah's vision extended to events lying beyond his lifetime. Because Isaiah of Jerusalem could accurately predict Babylon's defeat by the Medes (13:17), our 400 BCE reader is emboldened to believe that other, as yet unrealized, aspects of Yahweh's world-wide plan will also be fulfilled.

Isaiah 14:31

Personified city imagery next appears in the following oracle against Philistia. Because Isaiah 14:31 is our first personified *foreign* city, a few remarks are in order.

When Israel's prophets personified foreign cities, their purpose was not to extol them. To the contrary, foreign capitals were personified toward precisely the opposite ends. The great "ladies" or "princesses" of Israel's ancient Near Eastern world were reduced, in the prophets' poetry, to desperate straits and/or dubious moral states. J. Galambush (1992:38) succinctly identifies the motives underlying personifications of the foreign capitals of Israel's enemies:

> the personification of foreign capitals served as a rhetorical tool by which the prophets could malign and belittle enemy strongholds. The virtues traditionally attributed to the personified cities—wisdom, strength, and care of their "children"— were denied by the prophets, who instead focused upon the vices that might be implied by the cities' personification. In place of the positive commonplaces associated with womanhood, the prophets exploited negative commonplaces such as

deceit, weakness, sexual infidelity, and finally, vulnerability to rape, to belittle and threaten these neighboring powers.

Such oracles were uttered, Galambush claims, "to affirm Israel at the expense of its enemies" (1992:38). The derisive function of oracles against Israel's principal foes (e.g., Assyria and Babylon) must be kept in mind, even when genre (e.g., lament) suggests sorrow:[26] it is one thing to lament the destruction of one's own city, but quite another to "lament" the anticipated demise of an enemy metropolis.

But what of oracles uttered against Israel's neighboring states—potential allies in coalitions against Assyria or Babylon? Were they construed as bad news for Israel, as well as for Philistia, Moab, or the like? Since the destruction of one party presaged a similar fate for its allies (see G. R. Hamborg 1981), such oracles were likely—on first utterance—to cause despair in Israel and/or Judah (Hillers 1965:86-89). In their canonical arrangement, however, Isaian oracles against Israel's neighbors coexist with assurances that Zion will not share her neighbors' fates. Isaiah 14:31, for example, urges Philistia's gate,[27] and the city herself, to wail, cry, and melt in fear of an approaching army. But the notice of Philistia's impending demise is immediately followed by an announcement that Zion will provide refuge for Yahweh's needy people. It is unlikely, therefore, that our reader shares the terror and grief soon to replace the Philistines' joy (vs. 29).

Isaiah 16:1-4

The ostensible "lament" over Moab in Isaiah 15 (but see above and the sentiment expressed in vs. 9b!) employs primarily masculine, rather than feminine, grammatical forms. Even in verse 4, where a feminine verb describes the outcry of Heshbon and Elealeh, an immediately following masculine plural pronoun refers to "their" voices. Moreover, male mourners are described in verses 2b-3, and a male or mixed-gender group is presupposed by the masculine forms in verses 5-9.

Isaiah 16:1-4 contains references to both "the mount of daughter Zion" and "the daughters of Moab":

> Send lambs to the ruler of the land,
> from Sela, by way of the desert

> to the mount of daughter Zion.
> Like fluttering birds [ke'ôp nôded],
>   like scattered nestlings,
> so are the daughters of Moab
>   at the fords of the Arnon.

The phrase "daughters of Moab" is ambiguous, since it can plausibly refer either to female Moabite refugees, or to personified Moabite cities. If the latter referent is preferred, then the personified cities seek on their inhabitants' behalf the shelter and safety they can no longer provide. Two similes shape the reader's perception of "the daughters of Moab."[28] According to the first, they are like fluttering birds; the root *ndd* means not only "to flutter," but also "to flee," and, as a participle, "fugitive." (It recurs with the latter meaning in vs. 3b.) The image of fluttering birds evokes associations of panic, flight (in the obvious sense, but also in the sense of escape from danger), helplessness, and vulnerability. Hence, the simile, "like fluttering birds" is particularly well-suited to refugees who have escaped the bloodbath, but seek sanctuary in Jerusalem. A related image, "scattered nestlings," likewise evokes associations of panic and vulnerability. Both similes are striking, given the sequentially prior boast of Assyria's king:

> My hand has found, like a nest,
>   the wealth of the peoples;
> and as one gathers eggs that have been forsaken,
>   so I have gathered all the earth;
> and there was none that moved a wing [noded kanap],
>   or opened its mouth, or chirped. (10:14)[29]

In their present arrangement, the images of 15:8–16:4 interlink to describe Moab's distress: vivid depictions of its plight—wailing (15:8) and blood (15:9)—motivate Moab's distressed daughters (16:1); the threat posed by lions (15:9) is followed by the gift of a lamb (16:1); and the entreaty in 16:3-4 appears, not as petition by Moab's rulers, but as piteous pleas for asylum by the panicky "daughters" of Moab. Moreover the juxtaposition of "the mount of daughter Zion" and "the daughters of Moab" intensifies the contrast between their circumstances: Zion's fate is not that of her neighboring states. For sequential readers, the reference to Jerusalem's shade (16:3), which can make the noonday sun like night, recalls Jerusalem's protective pavillion in 4:6, "a shade by day from the heat, and a refuge and a shelter from the storm and rain."

Isaiah 17–21

Personified city imagery next appears in Isaiah 22. Several intervening texts merit our reader's attention, however, for they will play an important role in assessing the fates awaiting the world's capitals and nations, including Lady Zion. Isaiah 17 begins with a judgment oracle against Damascus, but also against Israel. Thundering nations imperil Yahweh's people (vs. 12), yet the text affirms that these very nations will themselves be destroyed (vs. 14).

In their final forms, Isaiah 17 and 18 also affirm Zion's eventual exaltation over the nations. Isaiah 19 insists several times that Yahweh has a "plan" for Egypt (vss. 12, 17), involving punishments but also the *conversion* of both Egypt and Assyria: "On that day Israel will be the third with Egypt and Assyria, a blessing, in the midst of the earth, whom the Lord of hosts has blessed, saying, 'Blessed be Egypt my people, and Assyria the work of my hands, and Israel my heritage'" (19:24-25). This text goes considerably beyond other biblical affirmations about these nations' future roles. For our purposes, we note again that promises of a positive outcome for Israel appear among oracles against foreign nations. When the author(s) of Isaiah 19:18-25 envisioned Yahweh's conversion of Egypt and Assyria ("striking and healing"; recall Isa 1:5-6), did he astonish our ancient reader as he astonishes his twentieth-century audience? Yet the reconciliation anticipated in verses 16-25 was presaged already in 2:1-4 with its promise of universal peace.

Isaiah 20, a narrative, condemns reliance upon Egypt and Ethiopia. Oracles against Babylon, Edom, and Arabia (Isaiah 21) follow. These do not personify the nations and cities addressed, though feminine grammatical forms appear, for example, in 21:2, 9. Again, Yahweh's knowledge (and control) of events is affirmed throughout (21:6-10, 16-17).

Isaiah 22

The assertion that Israel's God directs the nations' fates is repeated in Isaiah 22: "But you did not look to him who did it, or have regard for him who planned it long ago." Here, however, Jerusalem and her inhabitants are the objects of Yahweh's rebuke.

The chapter begins with the superscription "the oracle concerning the valley of vision," borrowing from verse 5 and conforming the beginning of this oracle to preceding and subsequent ones. Verses 1-3 address the city's revelling inhabitants as personified Jerusalem, using second feminine singular grammatical forms. The presence of personification leads to some grammatical awkwardness: "What do you [f.s.] mean that you have gone up, all of you [f.s.] to the housetops?" Clearly, however, Zion's populace appears in the guise of a woman rejoicing over her own survival, despite the devastation and death inflicted upon her environs and their inhabitants.

With verse 4, a first person singular speaker bewails "the destruction of the daughter of my people."[30] As noted, obscurities attend this phrase. It may be an appositional genitive, to be rendered "the daughter, my people." But "the daughter of my people" can also refer to an indigenous city, perhaps Jerusalem "herself." If the latter, then verse 4 anticipates Jerusalem's future destruction, even as its inhabitants celebrate a narrow escape from harm's way. Subsequent verses, with their references to battering down walls (vs. 5), and to Elam and Kir (vs. 6), lend concrete detail to that destruction. Even more ominous is the phrase, "he has taken away the covering (*masak*) of Judah," since it threatens the removal of Jerusalem's protection (4:5-6). Yahweh's people are not exempted from judgment. Hence the folly of Zion's failure to pity and mourn the victims of an earlier military incursion from which she escaped, but other of God's people did not.

Isaiah 23

Isaiah 23 begins with the superscription, "the oracle concerning Tyre," but the subjects of this chapter, which contains elements common to city laments, include Sidon and the elusive Tarshish as well.[31] Verses 1-14 ostensibly lament the destruction of Phoenician seaports and with them, a thriving commercial empire (note that the *hêlîlû 'anîyôt tarsîs*, "Wail, O ships of Tarshish" of vs. 1 is repeated in vs. 14). Verses 15-18 look beyond Tyre's destruction to a restoration of sorts; the text is prose, rather than poetry, but it is linked to preceding verses by the opening phrase, "and on that day."

While Isaiah 23 raises multiple, complex historical and textual conundrums,[32] its gist is clear enough: thriving Phoenician seaports will be destroyed for their pride; and—the poet is at pains to assert along the way (vss. 8-9, 11-12, 18)—their destruction is attributable to none other than Israel's God, Yahweh of hosts.

Isaiah 2:5-22, the great poem against "all that is proud and lofty," listed the ships of Tarshish among those against whom Yahweh "has a day." That day arrives with Isaiah 23. Returning from their voyages, the ships (and so, synecdochically, their crews) bewail the destruction of their ancient seaports—the Phoenician cities of Tyre (an island off the eastern Mediterranean coast) and Sidon (located about twenty-five miles north of Tyre). Scholars debate the precise location of Tarshish (Baker 1992:331-33). But its ships were, apparently, proverbial for their size and grandeur. Ezekiel 27:25 claims that such ships carried Tyre's wares, and that Tarshish traded its silver, iron, tin, and lead for Tyre's goods (27:12).

In Isaiah 22, Zion was castigated for celebrating her survival when the dismal plight of fellow Israelites warranted acts of lament and mourning. In 23:4, by contrast, a city (or perhaps the sea; see below) expresses profound bereavement. Verse 4 addresses Sidon, herself called "merchant of the nations":

> Be ashamed, O Sidon, for the sea has spoken,
>> the fortress of the sea, saying:[33]
> "I have neither labored nor given birth,
>> I have neither reared young men nor raised maidens."[34]

Here the Hebrew imperative "be ashamed" refers to "both the subjective and objective loss of *kabod*, honour, that which brings a person dignity, respect and well being" (Kaiser 1974:165). The text clearly threatens Sidon with this shame, but who speaks in verse 4b? Is the lamenter the sea, or the fortress of the sea; and if the latter, is the fortress Sidon, or some other city, e.g., Tyre?

Given the preponderate convention of personifying cities as females, it is most likely that a city lifts the lament in verse 4b (Dobbs-Allsopp 1993:119). Kaiser believes that she is Sidon, whose shame derives explicitly from her childlessness: "the poet reminds Sidon of her own lamentations at her childlessness, that is, at the loss of her sons and daughters in the conquest."[35] S. Erlandsson (1970:98) understands things differently, however, claiming that "the stronghold of the sea" is "presumably Tyre." In other words, Sidon is shamed by Tyre's pitiful plight. Whatever her identity, the speaker laments her childlessness, assuming the persona of a barren woman (and, therefore, a victim of divine punishment, lack of fulfillment, and low social status), in order to mourn her deceased sons and daughters (whose deaths leave her grief-stricken and facing an uncertain future).

A second, albeit brief, example of female imagery appears just three verses later. The NRSV offers a conventional translation: the coast's inhabitants are urged to lament their fallen city; and the metaphor of Tyre's feet carrying her away describes Phoenician colonization, or its far-flung trade routes:

> Is this your exultant city
> > whose origin is from days of old,
> whose feet carried her / to settle far away?[36]

What associations are evoked by this brief personification? The question functions to exacerbate the Phoenicians' grief, emphasizing the stark contrast between Tyre's former glory, power, and influence, and its impending devastation. So construed, the claim that her feet once carried her afar is positive, at least from the perspective of those enjoined to wail. But negative associations dog the steps of peripatetic women as well. Dangers threatened females who ventured too far from home (Deut 22:25-27), and foreign women could be dangerous. Isaiah's reader may experience disdain for this "walking woman" who embodies Phoenician enterprise;[37] indeed, as reading progresses, these negative associations may be strengthened by the reader's encounter with Tyre, the strolling prostitute, in verses 15-18.

Verses 8-9, which question the source of Tyre's undoing and affirm Yahweh's control of the world's proud cities and nations, also contain a brief female personification. The opening question is usually rendered "Who has planned this against Tyre, the bestower of crowns (*hamma'otîrah*)?" An alternative translation, however, renders Tyre as "the crown wearer" (BDB; Kaiser 1974:160). Indeed, crowns, and particularly mural crowns, were part of the poetic stock of personified city imagery (Biddle 1991:179; Dobbs-Allsopp 1993:88-89). Isaiah 23:8 has no interest, of course, in praising Tyre as a deified city. To the contrary, we have noted the tendency to do precisely the opposite, namely, to exploit certain negative associations with females in order to belittle enemy strongholds. Here, however, Tyre's former glory is extolled precisely to emphasize how far she has fallen, and to attribute that fall to no other than Israel's God, Yahweh of hosts. If verse 8 describes Tyre as crown-wearer, rather than as bestower of crowns, then the reader glimpses her glory, the better to appreciate Yahweh's ultimate sovereignty over a wealthy, powerful, and haughty queen.

Verse 10 contains the briefest of female personifications, the epithet, "O daughter Tarshish." Verse 11 reiterates Yahweh's control over Canaan's fortresses. The following verse portrays Sidon (note the piling up of epithets) as a vulnerable, young, female refugee:

"You will exult no longer,
    O oppressed virgin daughter Sidon;
rise, cross over to Cyprus—
    even there you will have no rest." (vs. 12)

Through his wide-angle lens, the critic may detect in this address to fugitive Sidon an historical reference to Lule, its king, forced into exile by Sennacherib in 701 as his land was devastated by the Assyrian army (Erlandsson 1970:101). Our reader need not know of Lule's flight to Cyprus to make sense of verse 12. But if he knows of the island's reputation as "a suitable refuge for the oppressed rulers of Sidon" (Clements 1980b:194), that knowledge will enrich his understanding of the verse and heighten the effect of its oppressed female refugee imagery. (Modern readers sometimes pass over such imagery, forgetting that female refugees, forced to the margins of society [as prostitutes, beggars, etc.], were ubiquitous figures during periods of military aggression in Israel's ancient Near Eastern world.) Ironically, flight is futile. Sidon will find no rest, even in asylum.

The mostly prose conclusion of Isaiah 23 predicts that Tyre "will be forgotten" for seventy years; the phrase "like the days of one king" ostensibly refers to a single human lifespan (so Clements 1980b:195). Verses 15-16 claim that at the end of that period, the city's situation will become *like* that described in the song of an aging harlot. This is a female fornicator's song (note the feminine construct form of *sîrah*). In the "trollop's tune," a "forgotten" prostitute is urged to take up a harp and stroll the streets so that she will be "remembered." "She is evidently being encouraged," Galambush wryly observes, "to come out of retirement and strum [she says "drum"] up a little business" (1992:39). The song consists of two tricola, each line having two stresses. Watson (1984:184) translates as follows, noting its end rhyme (five words end in î, two in îr) and wordplays:[38]

> Lift your lyre, / circle the city, / worn-out whore.
> Sweetly strum, / sing many a song, /and so be remembered.

Yahweh will visit Tyre, and she will resume her "intercourse" with the nations. But how her circumstances have changed! The crown wearer of verse 8, "whose merchants were princes, whose traders were the honored of the earth," has slid all the way down the social scale. And her future clientele will be no better, presumably, than such women can hope to attract. The prostitution metaphor casts a sorry shadow on all parties involved in Tyre's continual and indiscriminate trade. Clements speaks of the "marked tone of irony and contempt for Tyre, the opulence of which is evidently resented" (1980b:195). There is irony aplenty in these verses, and contempt as well. But while likening Tyre's commercial enterprises to prostitution was certainly no compliment, the image of the forgotten whore is as pathetic as it is contemptuous. Galambush notes the structural function of the "trollop's tune" in verses 15-18 (1992:39-40):

> Isaiah moves from predicting that the commercial capital will be "forgotten," to a comparison between Tyre's situation and that of a "forgotten" but newly enterprising whore, and finally to a prediction that after seventy years Tyre (likewise) will return, not to her commerce—but to world-wide prostitution. Isaiah uses the song about the whore as a kind of hinge connecting his depiction of Tyre as city with his depiction of Tyre as whore. Playing on the already available comparison between city and woman, Isaiah exposes Tyre's much vaunted commercial success as a type of commerce particularly associated with women: prostitution.

The final blow falls, then, with the assertion that Tyre's earnings (*'etnah*, "harlot's hire") will be dedicated to Yahweh, providing food and fine clothing for "those who live in the presence of the Lord." The conclusion's unfortunate consequence is to turn Yahweh and Israel into Tyre's pimps. By this ignominious end, Phoenicia's seaports—once powerful queens—are reduced to childless refugees who can find no security, and to prostitutes whose gainful employment brings them shame, but no personal gain. The NRSV notation to verse 18, "even these sordid treasures will finally be dedicated to God," attempts, but fails to redeem its glee at the prospect of religio-national supremacy for Yahweh and Israel, and disgrace for Israel's once-prosperous neighbors.

Isaiah 24–27

The so-called "Isaian Apocalypse" contains no female personifications of cities. We include it, nonetheless, because its images of world-wide judgment function as the climax of oracles against foreign nations and cities, and Jerusalem, in Isaiah 13–23.

We examined Isaiah 27 in our Chapter 2, and we shall turn to Isaiah 26 in Chapter 6. In this context, therefore, we simply observe that these chapters include descriptions of the devastating effects of God's judgment upon the entire earth. In one already-quoted verse, imagery appearing in certain biblical and extra-biblical city laments describes the earth's devastation. The garden hut imagery in Isa 24:20 resembles its Mesopotamian counterparts even more than do the similes of Isa 1:8, since this hut is explicitly described as falling to the ground: "and it falls, and will not rise again."

In addition to such descriptions of world-wide ruin, however, the reader encounters songs of praise to Yahweh:

> O Lord, you are my God
> I will exalt you, I will praise your name;
> for you have done wonderful things,
> plans formed of old, faithful and sure. (25:1)

Yahweh's destructive acts abound, stretching even to Jerusalem; yet expressions of trust and confidence in Yahweh's plan affirm the eventual restoration of God's people:

> Come, my people, enter your chambers,
>   and shut your doors behind you;
> hide yourselves for a little while
>   until the wrath is past.
> For the Lord comes out from his place
>   to punish the inhabitants of the earth for their iniquity;
> the earth will disclose the blood shed on it,
>   and will no longer cover its slain.

Isaiah 24–27 ends on an auspicious note, with the people of Israel gathered together, worshipping Yahweh "on the holy mountain at Jerusalem" (27:13).

Summary

Isaiah 13–23(27) speaks primarily of the fates awaiting Israel's foes—both world powers and nearer neighbors. Significantly, the oracle concerning Babylon appears first; that the prophet Isaiah could predict the eventual destruction of Israel's paradigmatic foe by the Medes underscores the authenticity of his words. But more than just Babylon is at issue; Israel's God has determined:

> I will punish the world for its evil,
> and the wicked for their iniquity;
> I will put an end to the pride of the arrogant,
> and lay low the insolence of tyrants. (13:11)

This verse effectively summarizes much of what Isaiah 13–27 says about Yahweh's plan for the nations (e.g., 14:24, 26-27; 19:12, 17; 22:11; 23:8), a plan ultimately leading to Zion's exaltation (14:1-2; 16:4b-5; 18:7; 23:18). True, the threat of Jerusalem's destruction—an event announced already in Isaiah 1—appears amidst these oracles against her rivals. Our reader knows Jerusalem fell to the Babylonians. But he also knows Yahweh's promise that Zion, and those in her who repent, have a future beyond the smelting furnace.

In these chapters, female personifications evoke and exploit associated commonplaces with women toward strategic ends, depicting the foreign cities and nations under Yahweh's control as a terrified female refugee, a bereaved mother, a deposed queen, an aging harlot. Such painful, scornful associations contrast sharply with positive associations of nurture, protection, and faithfulness that, frequently in Isaiah's vision, are fully exploited on Lady Zion's behalf.

"SHE DESPISES YOU, SHE SCORNS YOU— MAIDEN DAUGHTER ZION": ISAIAH 29:1–8

Personified Zion next appears in an oracle that, in its canonical form, moves from judgment against Jerusalem to a promise that her enemies, erroneously believing they can possess her, will find their victory as illusory as a dream in the night. Verse 1 begins with a cry, "Woe," followed by the twice-repeated epithet, "Ariel." The term has generated considerable debate, but Jerusalem is clearly its referent. Many commentators consider it a reference to the temple's altar of burnt-offering (Clements

1980b:235; see Ezek 43:15).[39] Yahweh, the first person speaker of verses 1-4, threatens that Jerusalem "shall be to me like an ariel" (vs. 2) In other words, burning imagery—though of a different sort than found, for example, in 1:25 or 1:30-31—again serves as the discontinuous term by which God's judgment is described. Verse 3 depicts Yahweh's future siege against Jerusalem—devastating proof that her God has become her foe:

> And like David, I will encamp against you;
>> I will besiege you with towers
>> and raise siegeworks against you.

The conjunction of Jerusalem and siege imagery evokes memory of Isaiah 22. In that chapter, personified Jerusalem was threatened with a destructive siege (vss. 5-11) because, at a time of national distress, "she" went up to the housetops to celebrate personal survival. But here, in the aftermath of God's siege, Lady Zion manages only a barely audible whisper "deep from the earth" (vs. 4):

> Then deep [(we)sapalt] from the earth [me'eres] you shall speak,
>> from low in the dust [(we)me'apar tissah] your voice
>>> shall come;
>> your voice shall come from the ground [me'eres] like the voice
>>> of a ghost,
>> and your speech shall whisper out of the dust [(we)me'apar].

O. Kaiser suggests that 29:4 juxtaposes two images: "the first, that of a person who has fallen to the ground and begs his [sic] conqueror for mercy, and the second that of a dead person who speaks out of the earth like a ghost with a voice reduced to a whisper" (1974:267-68). While acknowledging the personification, however, he overlooks that the entity addressed is female.

Two other Isaian imprecations against cities show interesting lexical correspondences with 29:1-4. A Moabite city is first:

> The high fortifications of his [MT "your" (m.s.)] walls
>> will be brought down [hesah],
> laid low [hispîl], cast [higgî'a] to the ground [la'ares],
>> even to the dust ['ad-'apar]. (Isa 25:12)

The second oracle threatens an unnamed "lofty city":

> For he has brought low [hesah]
>> the inhabitants of the height;
>> the lofty city he lays low [yaspîlennah].

He lays it low to the ground [*yaspîlah 'ad-'eres*],
     casts it to the dust [*yaggî'ennah 'ad-'apar*]. (Isa 26:5)[40]

In 29:3, the poet provides a literal description of Yahweh's siege against Jerusalem; and personification is not foregrounded. Verse 4 presupposes that the siege resulted in Jerusalem's destruction. But by means of personification, the reader is invited to perceive her demise not (only) as urban decay, but also as mourning, profound despair (as in "Down, sit on the dust, maiden daughter Babylon," 47:1), and death (*'apar*, "dust," appears in descriptions of death in Job 7:21; 17:16; 20:11; and 21:26). The depiction of Jerusalem's demise at the hand of her God-turned-foe is profound indeed; and her faint, ghost-like whisper bespeaks (to borrow from Clements) "abject weakness" (1980b:236). But that whisper also functions as a pivot upon which the poem turns from destruction to deliverance, for those who can talk, however softly, are yet alive. The shades cannot speak (Ps 88:10b), but Lady Zion whispers from the dust (*'apar*), prompting a promise that her foes (MT has "strangers") shall be "like fine dust" [*'abaq*, a synonym of *'apar*], and the multitude of tyrants like flying chaff when Yahweh of hosts "visits" her (vss. 5-6). Though in verse 2 Yahweh threatened, "I will distress ([*we*]*hasîqôtî*) Ariel," by the end of verse 7, the tables have turned; and her foe has become her defender once more. With Yahweh's theophany (vs. 6) comes a promise:

And the multitude of all the nations that fight against Ariel,
     all that fight against her and her stronghold,
     and who distress [(*we*)*hammesîqîm*] her,
shall be like a dream, a vision of the night. (vs. 7)

Though Yahweh's siege against Zion succeeds, she will not remain a perpetual desolation. Again, beyond Zion's devastation lies a central, glorious role in Yahweh's plan.

ISAIAH 37:22

Subsequent chapters address foreign and domestic cities (and nations), but female personification does not occur in them to any significant degree. Assyria's king is the target of 31:4-9. Isaiah 34 predicts the end of God's enemies, Edom principle among them. But these foes are not evoked in female form.

Only in 37:22 does a personified city reappear. Daughter Zion's appearance is brief, but memorable.

Isaiah 36–37 are strategic for the sequential reader, because they describe in stunning fashion the end of Assyrian aggression—a threat occupying a prominent place thus far in Isaiah's vision (and see further below, Chapter 6). To summarize the situation only briefly: Sennacherib's deadly march against the fortified cities of Judah during Hezekiah's fourteenth year of rule brings him to Jerusalem. Isaiah reassures Hezekiah, and when presented by the king with a second threatening communiqué from the Assyrians, the prophet conveys God's response:

> "Thus says the Lord, the God of Israel: Because you have prayed to me concerning King Sennacherib of Assyria, this is the word that the Lord has spoken concerning him:
>> She despises you, she scorns you—
>>> maiden [NRSV: virgin] daughter Zion;
>> she tosses her head—behind your back,
>>> daughter Jerusalem." (37:22)

Here, maiden daughter Zion exhibits youthful courage and defiance. Defiant daughters were not especially esteemed by ancient Israel's parents. If 37:22 described Zion's attitude toward Yahweh, she would certainly be strongly censured.[41] But Daughter Jerusalem here defies an arrogant foe brandishing derisive gestures of his own:

> This very day he will halt at Nob,
>> he will shake his fist
> at the mount of daughter Zion
> the hill of Jerusalem. (Isa 10:32)

The Assyrian king's pretensions (10:8-11) and threatening advances have been decidedly rejected, and his destruction declared, by Yahweh. He may boast:

> "I have gone up the heights of the mountains,
>> to the far recesses of Lebanon;
> I felled its tallest cedars,
>> its choicest cypresses;
> I came to its remotest height,
>> its densest forest." (37:24)

But the reader has long known that only Yahweh does such things:

> Look the Sovereign, the Lord of hosts,

will lop the boughs with terrifying power;
the tallest trees will be cut down,
    and the lofty will be brought low.
He will hack down the thickets of the forest with an ax,
    and Lebanon with its majestic trees will fall. (10:33-34)

Now, Assyria's army faces destruction. Yahweh and Zion will get the last scoff when 185,000 Assyrian soldiers lie dead in the field, and Sennacherib returns home for an unanticipated appointment with two assassination-minded sons (37:36-38). The Assyrian threat has ended. Has the danger of Jerusalem's destruction passed as well? Immediately, the reader is reminded that it has not. Only Yahweh's instrument has changed:

Then Isaiah said to Hezekiah, "Hear the word of the Lord of hosts: Days are coming when all that is in your house, and that which your ancestors have stored up until this day, shall be carried to Babylon; nothing shall be left, says the Lord. Some of your own sons who are born to you shall be taken away; they shall be eunuchs in the palace of the king of Babylon." (39:5-7)

And readers recall that the oracle against Babylon in 13:1-22, proclaiming Babylon's eventual destruction, nonetheless affirmed that Yahweh chose Babylon "to destroy the whole earth" (vs. 5).

On a bare hill raise a signal,
    cry aloud to them;
wave the hand for them to enter
    the gates of the nobles.
I myself have commanded my consecrated ones,
    have summoned my warriors,
    my proudly exulting ones,
to execute my anger. (13:2-3)

CONCLUSION

What does Isaiah 1–39 reveal about the ladies' lots in Yahweh's unfolding plan? First and foremost it speaks of Zion. We encounter her initially in a three-fold description conveying precariousness and inducing pity, her plight the consequence of Israel's rebellions against Yahweh. Subsequent verses lament that she has become a harlot. But the onus for her unfaithfulness lies with her contaminating elements. Though she must undergo a fiery "purification," her future, and that of her inhabitants who repent, will be glorious indeed (1:21-28). The point is repeatedly made in following chapters: Yahweh has a plan. That plan concerns not only the people of Israel, but also all the nations of the world. It calls for just punishment of God's people, and also of proud and arrogant rulers, cities, and nations. On occasion, the scroll anticipates that restoration (and Yahwistic religion) awaits certain of Israel's foes, including Egypt and Assyria, conforming to the world-wide peace proclaimed in 2:1-4. Repeatedly, however, *Isaiah's vision affirms Zion's eventual exaltation among the nations, even while acknowledging that she also must experience destruction at Yahweh's hand.* Her fate lies with her God, not with an arrogant and undiscerning Assyrian "instrument" of divine aggression.

Like rebellious child imagery, the "ladies lots" theme is far from ubiquitous in Isaiah 1–39. Although personified Jerusalem appears along the way, the city is not always personified to any significant degree. The same is true of foreign cities and nations. Oracles concerning Assyria are numerous, for example, but their focus is Assyria's king, rather than Nineveh, his capital. This scarcely surprises, since the king and his troops, rather than that distant city, cast a shadow upon Israel, Judah, and their neighbors. Babylon also is not personified as a female in these chapters, though she will appear in a lengthy poem in Isaiah 47. Where personification does appear, however, it contributes— whether overtly or more subtly—to the reader's perception of the subject suddenly endowed with life. Foreign cities and nations, for example, are cast as women in order to evoke and exploit certain negative associations, thereby belittling both them and the people they embody.

When our reader turns toward chapters 40–66, he does so with certain ideas about Lady Zion and other cities (and nations) already in place. To be sure, such expectations may be revised in light of subsequent chapters. To this point, however, our reader knows why Assyria conquered Northern Israel, but was unable to quash Judah. He knows that Babylon is Yahweh's instrument for Jerusalem's destruction, but that Israel's God controls Babylon's lot as well. He knows the folly of Judean reliance on any power save Yahweh, and he knows Lady Zion's ultimate fate: beyond the Assyrian threat, beyond even the Babylonian debacle, lie honor, status, prosperity, and shouts and songs of joy.

5

THE LADIES' LOTS: ISAIAH 40–66

n recent years, several scholarly articles on female imagery in Isaiah 40–66 have appeared. This scarcely surprises, since these chapters contain more female imagery than any other comparable block in the Hebrew Bible.

Most scholars studying Isaiah's female imagery act as if, to quote M. Gruber, "the idea of Zion appears first in *the introductory chapter 40*" (emphasis mine; 1985:561). One can examine personified city imagery only in Isaiah 40–55 and against a sixth-century, Babylonian background, or attempt to correlate female tropes in 56–66 with scenarios from the social world of the post-exilic period, irrespective of Isaiah 1–39. As we saw in Chapter 4, however, our sequential reader brings to Isaiah 40–66 fully-formed ideas and expectations concerning Jerusalem and her rivals. Will these expectations be realized, or will they require reassessment as Isaiah's vision progresses?

ISAIAH 40–55:
"THE PEOPLE WHO SURVIVED THE SWORD FOUND GRACE IN THE WILDERNESS"[1]

Our reader, fully accustomed to sudden shifts in literary style, subject, and tone, does not wonder that the prose narrative of Isaiah 39 gives way to poetry in chapter 40. The two chapters are closely linked, for Isaiah 39 is vital to a coherent construal of chapters 40–55: Isaiah's last-quoted words to Hezekiah (39:5-7) set the stage for the geographical and chronological leaps made explicit by 43:14. According to Isa 39:8, Hezekiah responds to Isaiah's prophecy that Babylon will plunder Judah and take his sons captive as follows: "There will be peace and security in my days." But 40:1-2 presupposes that subsequent to the "peace and security" of Hezekiah's lifetime, Jerusalem has "served her term," paid her penalty, and "received double for all her sins." The peaceful days of Hezekiah ended; and in the years since his death, "my people/Jerusalem" have endured judgment described already in Isaiah 1 and reiterated at points along the way in Isaiah's unfolding vision.

Some scholars affirming Isaiah's redactional unity nonetheless insist that the prophet's vision—which was to continue "Until cities lie waste without inhabitant, and houses without people, and the land is utterly desolate; until the the Lord sends everyone far away, and vast is the emptiness in the midst of the land" (6:11-12)—concludes with Isaiah 39. Such a reading is not so inevitable as some would argue. Yet even those scholars holding this view insist that Isaiah 40–66 are intimately related to preceding chapters. C. Seitz, for example, identifies links between the "new things" proclaimed in Isaiah 40–48 and the "former things" of 1–39:

> The voice of 40:6b-7 acknowledges that the plan of old has come to pass, not in 701 but in 587. . . . The Assyrian has been replaced by the Babylonian instrument of judgment (so 23:13), and the voice speaks of the destruction experienced in 587—a return to the chaos depicted in chaps. 24–27. The world has become the wilderness (40:3) spoken of long ago (13:5), about which the Babylonian had boasted (14:17); for this he will be punished (14:3-21)—like the arrogant Assyrian before him (14:24-27)—at the hands of Persians (13:17-22), the "birds of prey" (18:6) who do God's bidding. . . . The "new things" are about to take place, including above all the calling of Cyrus, "the bird of prey from the east" . . . The prologue of 40:1-11 signals that the old age is passing away and a new day is dawning. . . . It is time for the herald of good tidings to replace the voices of past guilt and former judgment. (1990:243)

Isaiah 40:1-11:
"Speak Tenderly to Jerusalem"

The concern for Jerusalem's fate that surfaced time and again in Isaiah 1–39 persists—indeed, blossoms—in following chapters. The opening words of Isaiah 40 bespeak tenderness and devotion toward Zion ("Comfort, O comfort my people"), even while affirming that she has received her punishment ("*double for all her sins*") at Yahweh's hand. Clearly, the text intends to affirm that Yahweh's care for Zion has not abated.

Isaiah 40:1-11 vexes scholars. Does it represent a return to the divine council, last visited during Isaiah's commissioning as a prophet (Isaiah 6)? Is a new commissioning or re-commissioning taking place? Who does the reader understand to speak in verse 6—a member of the divine council,[2] personified Zion,[3] or a prophet—Isaiah, or some other mouthpiece for Yahweh?[4] Such questions may well have vexed our reader as well, since no explicit clues resolve them.[5] Clearly, however, this text constitutes good news for Israel and Jerusalem. In his commentary, J. L. McKenzie observes: "the disintegration of the people and kingdom of Israel was a shattering disaster, and the prophet throughout his poems is awed by the unexpected miracle of survival. Yahweh's judgment could not have been more complete and decisive than it was, yet Israel has survived it" (1983:17). The survival of "my people/Jerusalem" certainly is celebrated. But our reader is not surprised to discover that Jerusalem has survived Yahweh's judgment. To the contrary, her survival beyond destruction was announced time and time again in Isaiah 1–39.

Following the exchange in verses 6-8 with its crowning affirmation, "the word of our God will stand forever," feminine singular grammatical forms again signal personified Jerusalem:

> Get you up to a high mountain,
> O Zion, herald of good tidings;
> lift up your voice with strength,
> O Jerusalem, herald of good tidings,
> lift it up, do not fear;
> say to the cities of Judah,
> "Here is your God!" (vs. 9)

The translations "O Zion, herald of good tidings" (*mebasseret siyyôn*) and "O Jerusalem, herald of good tidings" (*mebasseret yerûsalaim*) are rejected by some critics, who would render these phrases "O herald of good tidings *to* PN." It is true that a masculine herald of good tidings will appear in 52:7 (see also 41:27). Because our reader moves sequentially through Isaiah, however, he will not interpret 40:9 on the basis of a later text.[6] Personified Zion is a well-established figure by this point; and there is nothing implausible about her ascending a mountain to proclaim to her (daughter) cities the news of Yahweh's approach.[7] To the contrary, the image of a strong and vocal Zion is congruous with our last glimpse of her (37:22), and serves well the rhetorical end of affirming her ongoing survival. When she is told, "get you up to a high mountain," the reader remembers an earlier oracle, "In days to come the mountain of the Lord's house shall be established as the highest of the mountains" (2:1). When she is told, "lift up your voice with strength," he recollects her weak whisper from the dust (29:4) following Yahweh's ravaging siege.

A question remains: who or what does personified Zion represent? In 40:1, "Jerusalem" could plausibly be construed either as a synonym for "my people" (an example of synecdoche) or as the city "herself," frequently the object of direct address in Isaiah's vision. But Zion cannot be a female personification of the *golah* (the exiles) in verse 9, for her announcement is precisely that Yahweh is returning from victory with the exiles as spoils of war. We conclude, therefore, that she represents the city. Though Jerusalem lies in ruins, the poet can still speak of her, as the book of Lamentations demonstrates. And by describing her as a herald seeking higher elevation whence to shout her glad tidings, the poem not only depicts the dissemination of good news, but also presages her imminent exaltation.

Isaiah 45:14: "They Shall Come Over in Chains and Bow Down to You"

Having summoned personified Jerusalem to a high mountain, there to proclaim Yahweh's victorious return, the text turns to divine self-asseverations of incomparable power and knowledge (e.g., 40:18-20; 41:7), and of control over past, present, and future events (e.g., 40:21; 41:2-6; 42:9; 45:1-7), including Israel's imminent release (43:14) and salvation (e.g., 41:8-16; 44:1-5). Idolatry and its practitioners are disparaged (e.g., 40: 18-20; 41:7). Repeatedly, Yahweh invites Israel to perceive its history through God's eyes, and to trust that its deliverance lies with its all-knowing, omnipotent deity alone.

Amidst these claims, promises, and disparagements, female city imagery and references to Jerusalem are rare.[8] True, reassuring words concerning Zion's future occasionally appear (41:

27; 44:26, 28), buttressing not only Isaiah 40, but also earlier texts promising Zion's restoration. With 45:14, however, our reader encounters a promise to Zion that is of a piece with Yahweh's ultimate plan regarding her role among the nations:

> The wealth of Egypt and the merchandise of Ethiopia,
>   and the Sabeans, tall of stature,
> shall come over to you and be yours,
>   they shall follow you;
>   they shall come over in chains and bow down to you.
> They will make supplication to you, saying,
>   "God is with you alone, and there is no other;
>   there is no god besides him." (45:14)

This verse does not explicitly describe Zion's enthronement. Yet the description of prostrate, wealthy merchants makes her exalted status clear, even as their words glorify her God. Our reader recalls the royal Zion of 12:6, but also the gifts brought to Mount Zion from "a people tall and smooth, a nation mighty and conquering" (18:7). He remembers, as well, the glory formerly enjoyed by Tyre, the crown wearer, whose merchants were princes, honored across the earth (23:8). Tyre's glory will be transferred to Zion, even as Yahweh reduces her to shameful circumstances. The promise of Isa 2:1-3 concerning Zion's fate, including her exaltation among the nations, appears again, while her supplicants' words, "God is with you alone, and there is no other; there is no god besides him," presages a forthcoming challenge by a woman who falsely fosters divine pretentions.

Isaiah 47: "Sit on the Ground without a Throne, Daughter Chaldea!"

Isaiah 47, the great "lament" over Babylon, marks a significant stage in Yahweh's plan for Israel and the nations. Lady Babylon's dethronement signals the demise of Israel's paradigmatic foe, or course. But as E. Conrad claims, it also represents "the Lord's final victory over all the nations" (1991:81). Future references to foreigners will stress their roles in, rather than opposition to, Zion's exaltation.

Personification is a pervasive poetic feature of Isaiah 47. Throughout its verses, the poem exploits various associations with females in order to describe, justify, and exploit Lady Babylon's fall from power. This text also bears features of city laments in biblical and extra-biblical literature: *qinah* meter (especially in vss. 1-9); the contrast between past status and present plight; identification of the divine agent responsible for her circumstances, etc. (Dobbs-Allsopp 1993:109-13). But while the grief expressed in Mesopotamian city laments and the biblical book of Lamentations is all too real, Isaiah 47 mocks Babylon and relishes her demise at Yahweh's hand.

Readers arrive at this text on the heels of a sharp contrast between immobile Babylonian idols borne off to exile on the backs of beasts, and Yahweh carrying Israel from birth to old age (46:1-4). This derisive scene certainly bodes ill for the Empire! And it is followed by the assertion that Israel's God, who has no equal (vss. 5-7) and is Lord of history, planned from ancient times to bring "a bird of prey" upon Babylon:

> I am God, and there is no one like me,
> declaring the end from the beginning
>> and from ancient times things not yet done,
> saying, "My purpose shall stand,
>> and I will fulfill my intention."
> calling a bird of prey from the east,
>> the man for my purpose from a far country.
> I have spoken, and I will bring it to pass;
>> I have planned, and I will do it. (46:9-11)

Commentators note that Isaiah 47 constitutes the sole oracle against a foreign nation in the Deutero-Isaian corpus. It is by no means the only such oracle in Isaiah, however. How does it relate to its predecessors? C. A. Franke claims that the chapter "functions as a pivot on which the principal ideas and themes of Second Isaiah turn" (1991:410). But his claim may be too modest, since he does not consider its broader significance for Isaiah as a whole. Our reader recalls that in an earlier oracle, Yahweh determined first to use Babylon's military prowess toward certain ends, but then to destroy the city:

> See, I am stirring up the Medes against them . . .
> Their bows will slaughter the young men;
>> they will have no mercy on the fruit of the womb;
>> their eyes will not pity children.
> And Babylon, the glory of kingdoms,
>> the splendor and pride of the Chaldeans,
> will be like Sodom and Gomorrah
>> when God overthrew them. (Isa 13:17-19)

Now, Babylon's fall becomes Yahweh's victory, confirming Isaiah's earlier oracle and providing yet another proof of the efficacy of God's plan for Israel and the nations. Isaiah 13-14 focused upon warfare and its atrocities, but Isaiah 47 exploits female personification in order to depict Lady Babylon as foolish, vulnerable, and weak.

In verse 1, Lady Babylon is ordered to lament her own destruction, much as Lady Zion lamented her ruin in the book of Lamentations:

> Come down and sit in the dust,
> virgin daughter Babylon!
> Sit on the ground without a throne,
> daughter Chaldea!
> For you shall no more be called tender and delicate. (47:1)

Although the city's royal status is presupposed in this verse, we never behold her enthroned. Rather, Yahweh orders her to ritual acts of mourning. Yet the imagery "is not simply indebted to the language of mourning in general, but is indebted to the language of mourning specifically as it relates to death" (J. G. Taylor 1988:165). Here is a reversal the reader can relish: in 3:26, Lady Zion sat on the ground, her gates lamenting and mourning. In Isaiah 29, Yahweh's siege left her ravaged, whispering out of the dust. But now, immediately upon Yahweh's promise to "put salvation in Zion" (46:13), the capital city of the human agents who have inflicted Yahweh's punishment against Jerusalem is herself ordered to the ground, there to sit "without a throne," mourning her demise. Associations of mourning, death, and destruction are astir, then, in Yahweh's imperatives.

Babylon is called virgin, J. Muilenburg believed, "because she is as yet unravished, unconquered" (1956:544). That interpretation is possible, of course, but the epithets especially evoke conventional associations of youth and vulnerability to victimization. The following statement denying Babylon her traditional titles, "tender" (*rakkah*) and "delicate" ('*anuggah*), reminds readers who are thoroughly conversant with Israel's religious traditions of another text, a horrific description of siege conditions threatening Israel should it fail to observe Yahweh's commandments. Deut 28:56-57 describes a mother who secretly cannibalizes her children, though she was "the most tender (*harakkah*) and delicate ([*we*]*ha'anuggah*) among you, so tender

171

and delicate that she does not venture to set the sole of her foot on the ground." The reader knows that Babylonia's army successfully laid siege to Jerusalem, creating the conditions Deuteronomy envisioned (Lam 2:20; 4:10). But now, the tables are turned as tender, delicate Babylon goes down to the ground.

Verses 2-3 further describe her humiliation. Like a menial slave woman, she will be forced to grind grain (Exod 11:5; Job 31:1). Muilenburg notes the "remarkable onomatopoeia" of verse 2a (1956:544), where each of four words containing a *h* emulate the sound of the mill stones. But coarse labor is only the beginning of her shame:

> Remove your veil, / strip off your robe, uncover your legs,
>   pass through the rivers.[9]
> Your nakedness shall be uncovered,
>   and your shame shall be seen.[10]
> I will take vengeance, / and I will spare no one. (vss. 2b-3)

Scholars construe these lines variously. O. Kaiser (1969:190) believes they continue the slave girl imagery of verse 2a:

> she . . . is no longer "the tender, the delicate one" . . . she is now a slave, brusquely ordered about and forced to do the most menial tasks. Her humiliation extends even to her dress: veil and train, the apparel denoting high rank, are torn off her; she works with her clothes tucked up, like a servant girl.

His comments fail, however, to take seriously the threat of public exposure and concomitant shaming in verse 3. J. McKenzie also perceives slave girl imagery here, but is more sensitive to the sexual vulnerability of female servants: "In Egyptian paintings women slaves at work are sometimes represented as very scantily clad. The image also suggests the harsh fact that women prisoners were at the pleasure of their captors" (1983:91).

J. Muilenburg, by contrast, suggests that servant girl imagery is abandoned after verse 2a and replaced with an allusion to captives forced into an alien land. If that is indeed the case, he claims, "we have excellent archaeological illustration for our passage from the bronze doors of Balawat, which picture the women of Dabigi taken captive by Shalmanezer III raising their clothes." Regarding verse 3a, he says only that "Babylon is stripped like an adulteress" (546).

Comments by McKenzie and Muilenburg regarding the sexual vulnerability of female slaves and captives are apropos. But

Muilenburg's remark on Babylon being stripped "like a adulteress" is crucial as well. She is not accused of adultery in this poem—Babylon is not Yahweh's wife (though Israel's male god has her firmly under his control [vs.4]). And while the poem will later speak of her becoming a widow, it does not deign to utter the name of her spouse.[11] Rather, the poet invites his audience (and the reader) to "*see*" the shaming of Babylon through the metaphorical lens of a woman who is stripped in a public place, a naked object of fascination, contempt, and disgust.[12]

Verses 5-6 again address Babylon and deny her a traditional epithet. For the first time in the poem, a charge is levied:

> "Sit in silence, and go into darkness, / daughter Chaldea!"
> For you shall no more be called / the mistress of kingdoms.
> I was angry with my people, / I profaned my heritage;
> I gave them into your hand, / you showed them no mercy
> on the aged you made your yoke exceedingly heavy.

Here, Yahweh claims Babylon's defeat of Jerusalem as a personal victory over "my people." God placed Israel in Babylon's hand, but her cruelty exceeded acceptable limits, extending even to the elderly.

Babylon lacked pity, but she abounds in pride. Her assertion, "I shall be mistress forever," is ill-founded: the remainder of verse 7 suggests that she should have known as much. She is threatened with (conventionally) a woman's greatest loss:

> Now therefore hear this, you lover of pleasures,
>   securely enthroned woman,
> who say in your heart,/ "I am, and there is no one besides me;
> I shall not sit as a widow / or know the loss of children"—
> both these things shall come upon you / in a moment, in one day:
> the loss of children and widowhood
>   shall come upon you in full measure,
> in spite of your many sorceries
>   and the great power of your enchantments. (vss. 8-9)

Lady Babylon believed herself inviolable. But the claim, "I am, and there is no one besides me" properly belongs to Yahweh alone (e.g., 43:11). The loss of husband and children will turn her proud boast into grim reality. No apotropaic rituals or charms can protect her from Yahweh's threats to remove provider, protector, and her hope for the future. Though she, secure in her wickedness (*bera'atek*), believes that "No one sees me," evil (ra'ah) will come upon her. The twice-repeated "you do not know" (lo' tede'î; vs. 11) underscores the inefficacy of the "wisdom and knowledge" she believes her sorcery and charms provide. Here, the author plays upon yet another commonplace with women, for they were especially, though not exclusively, associated with sorcery and witchcraft in Israel's ancient Near Eastern world (S. Rollin 1983). The ironic imperative that she continue to rely on her charms and star gazers mocks Babylon's knowledge of, and reliance upon, astronomy. Commentators disagree concerning the identity of those with whom she has "trafficked" (vs. 15); are they her sorcerers, or her partners in trade? If the latter, then Babylon is tainted by the same behavior threatening to reduce Tyre to the status of an aging prostitute. In any event, she will receive no protection from those who wander about lost (ta'û). They, like Israel's persistent rebels, will be consumed by fire.

In summary, Isaiah 47 exploits the conventional personification of cities as females to describe Babylon's demise in terms of tragedies and afflictions endured by women. Enslaved, exposed, defenseless, and bereaved, she is Yahweh's victim; and he shows her no mercy. Through the powerful rhetorical tool of personification, the "mistress of kingdoms" becomes a cruel, proud, but ultimately humiliated and defeated woman.

SONGS OF COMFORT TO ZION
Isaiah 49:14-26

Yet another hymn of praise (49:13) follows the second so-called "servant song" (49:1-6) with its attending words of assurance (vs. 8-12). This hymn promises Yahweh's compassion on "his suffering ones." But personified Zion counters that Yahweh has abandoned her. For the first time in Isaiah's vision, our reader actually hears Jerusalem speak:

> But Zion said, "The Lord has forsaken me,
>   my Lord has forgotten me." (49:14)

Her words elicit Yahweh's immediate response: a rhetorical question evokes thoughts of the strong physical and emotive bond linking mother and infant, but Yahweh claims a devotion to Zion that is greater still:

> Can a woman forget her nursing child,
> > or show no compassion for the child of her womb?
> Even these may forget, / yet I will not forget you. (vs. 15)

Yahweh's rhetorical question is well-suited to what follows, since Zion's reunion with her children is the primary vehicle by which Yahweh expresses love for her. Personification is not so pervasive here as in Isaiah 47. Yahweh's claim, "See, I have inscribed you on the palms of my hands; your walls are continually before me," reminds the reader of Zion's "city-ness," as do references to her builders (MT: your sons) and destroyers (vs. 17), her waste and desolate places, and devastated land (vs. 19). Nonetheless, the poem reiterates familial images of homecoming and reunion. By Yahweh's oath (vs. 18b), Jerusalem will adorn herself with her children as a bride dons wedding jewelry. The appearance of her astonishingly large brood will leave Zion confounded:

> Then you will say in your heart, / "Who has borne me these?
> I was bereaved and barren, / exiled and put away—
> > so who has reared these?
> I was left all alone— / where then have these come from?"

Her self-descriptions—bereaved, barren, exiled, put away—bespeak women's lot in warfare and remind the reader of other ladies' lots in Isaiah: Sidon too faces bereavement and barrenness, her children victims of military defeat; and she also is forced into exile. Lady Babylon will know the loss of children, the vulnerability of having no male protector. But Zion's despair is coming to an end. "Soon," the text promises (vs. 22), kings and queens will carry her children home, bow before her, and lick the dust from her feet. The image of prostrate royalty suggests Zion's reenthronement.

From the perspective of this poem, then, Yahweh is Jerusalem's "Savior, Redeemer, the Mighty One of Jacob" (vs. 26). Nary a word about Yahweh as Zion's destroyer intrudes. Because God's devotion is greater than a mother's for her infant, her children will return to her, restoring the Yahweh-Zion-Israel relationship to familial harmony. Addressing personified Jerusalem as a mother, the poem invites its readers to perceive Yahweh's tender compassion through the metaphor of the exiles' imminent homecoming—the reunion of barren, bereaved Jerusalem and her precious sons and daughters. But it goes on to address Zion's status among the nations as well (vss. 23-26), for that too is an integral part of Yahweh's plan for Israel and the world.

Isaiah 50:1

The next female personification of a city follows immediately upon Yahweh's pledge to save Jerusalem's children, but to destroy her oppressors. Isaiah 50:1 also was discussed in our Chapter 2. In this context, we need only reiterate that Yahweh's and Jerusalem's children are held responsible for the family's estrangement. Though the husband concedes that Zion was "sent away," her dismissal resulted from the children's rebellion, and not from misdeeds on her part. Since Zion is blameless and no formal statement of divorce exists, Yahweh can reclaim his wife. Once again, Jerusalem is exculpated at Israel's expense.

Isaiah 51:1–52:12

Virtually all commentators acknowledge the rhetorical intensity of verses following the third servant song. Imperatives (51:1, 2, 4, 6, and 7) summon those addressed to recognition of Yahweh's power, promising comfort, consolation, and paradisiacal conditions for Zion's desert-like, ruined environs (vs. 3). Concomitantly, God's people—"you who have my teaching (*torah*) in your hearts" need not fear reproach, since divine deliverance is assured. Verses 9-11 recall Yahweh's battle with the primeval chaos monster, combining mythical language with imagery from the exodus. God's people need fear no "oppressor." Human beings are mere mortals, after all; and none can compete with the Lord of hosts.

In their canonical form, then, these verses interweave images of Yahweh as creator and sovereign of the cosmos with references to God's past, present, and future acts on Israel's behalf. Consider, for example, 51:16, where Zion and the people of Israel are equated:

> I have put my words in your mouth,
>> and hidden you in the shadow of my hand,
> stretching out the heavens
>> and laying the foundations of the earth,
>> and saying to Zion, "You are my people."

The following verse addresses Jerusalem: just as Yahweh's "arm" (an example of synecdoche) was summoned to strength in verse 9, so Zion is urged to arise in the aftermath of a poisonous punishment:

> Rouse yourself, rouse yourself!
>   Stand up, O Jerusalem,
> you who have drunk to the dregs
>   the bowl of staggering. (51:17)

Jerusalem has drained Yahweh's cup of wrath; and none of her children can guide her safely home, for all have perished (vs. 20). But Yahweh promises to remove the cup from her hand and to efface her humiliation, inflicting it instead upon her oppressors. Again, imperatives urge Jerusalem:

> Awake, awake, / put on your strength, O Zion!
> Put on your beautiful garments,
>   O Jerusalem, the city of the holiness.
> for the uncircumcised and the unclean
>   shall enter you no more.
> Shake yourself from the dust, rise up,
>   Sit [on your throne], Jerusalem;[13]
> loose the bonds from your neck,
>   O captive daughter Zion! (52:1-2)

Though the severity of her punishment is vividly acknowledged and her plight, like that of her children, pitiful indeed, Jerusalem is summoned to a future that is the opposite of Babylon's. Beautiful garments will replace her dust-covered slave attire. As the city of the sacred she is assured, in a perhaps sexually-suggestive way, that "the uncircumcised and the unclean shall enter you no more." Even as Babylon is ordered from her throne to the dust, Jerusalem rises from the dust to sit enthroned.

Isaiah 54

The address to Zion in Isaiah 54 is, J. F. A. Sawyer has observed, as striking as the suffering servant passage that immediately precedes it, though "the one [has been] studied almost to the point of idolatry by Christian exegetes, the other almost totally ignored" (1989:93). Zion, not named but whose identity can scarcely be doubted, is personified as a woman throughout; and that fact has everything to do with how the poem unfolds. So it is interesting to read the commentaries and realize how many ignore her, looking through or past the metaphor to discern the poem's cognitive content and theological core. In order fully to appreciate this poem, however, the reader must take seriously its images of a childless, estranged woman and of Yahweh, a male god who wishes to be reconciled with his wife. Simply decoding the imagery as interpretation progresses robs it of much of its power, pathos, and joy.

On the other hand, the fact that the woman is *Zion* should not be lost either. Sawyer rightly emphasizes the oracle's female metaphor, but he errs when he says that our chapter "is not a story about Jerusalem, any more than the servant songs are about Israel or Jesus or the prophet. It is about a woman, and to neglect this is to miss the dynamic of the passage" (1989:94). Zion is *both* a city and the central female character in Isaiah's vision. Indeed, word plays remind the reader of her "city-ness" at various points. Consider the phrase "children of the desolate one" (*benê-sômemah*) in verse 1. Sawyer writes:

> *Swmmh* 'abandoned' . . . in v. 1 is used in some contexts of ruined city-walls and gates (e.g., 49:8, 19; 61.4; Lam. 1.4), but here surely its usage in the story of Tamar, raped, humiliated and abandoned by her brother (2 Sam. 13.20), is more relevant—although few commentaries note this. (1989:95)

I agree that the Tamar reference is apropos. But *swmmh* is the perfect word for this particular poetic context precisely because it elicits thoughts of ruined cities *and* desolate women. Forcing a choice between the two impoverishes the text, since both sets of associations are appropriately astir. Sawyer's analysis extends only through verse 10, but if we look further in the chapter, we discover additional vocabulary appropriate to both women and cities. To give but one example, "antimony" (*puk*; vs. 11) refers to a powder used by women to darken their eyelids (2 Kg 9:30; Jer 4:30) but also appears in the list of construction materials gathered by David for Solomon's temple in Jerusalem (1 Chr 29:2). R. N. Whybray (1975:188) prefers this second understanding of *puk* to the first. But again, both are meaningful.

Following J. Muilenburg, we divide the poem into six strophes: verses 1-3, 4-5, 6-8, 9-10, 11-15,[14] and 16-17 (633). The first strophe begins with "two series of imperatives, each followed by a solemn asseveration" (vss. 1-2); these in turn are followed by a triad of interpretive clauses (vs. 3; Muilenburg

633). The woman addressed, called *'aqarah*, "barren one," is urged to rejoice:

> Sing, O barren one who did not bear;
>> burst into song and shout, / you who have not been in labor
> For the children of the desolate woman will be more
>> than the children of her that is married, says the Lord.
> Enlarge the site of your tent,
>> and let the curtains of your habitations be stretched out;
> do not hold back; lengthen your cords
>> and strengthen your stakes.
> For you will spread out to the right and to the left,
>> and your descendants will possess the nations
>> and will settle the desolate towns. (54:1-3)

The substantive adjective *'aqarah* here makes its only appearance within the Latter Prophets. Elsewhere, however, it describes Sarah (Gen 11:30), Rebekah (Gen 25:21), and Rachel (Gen 29:31). Hence, along with thoughts of Jerusalem, these verses evoke thoughts of Israel's sterile, but then miraculously fertile, matriarchs. References to tents, flaps, cords, and stakes likewise stir thoughts of Israel's ancestors. Yet "tent" (*'ahal*) has distinctive associations with Jerusalem as well (as the prophet Ezekiel knows and exploits in Ezekiel 23).

Like Lady Sidon (Isa 23:4), Zion is bereaved and barren. Like Israel's matriarchs, however, she will not remain childless. Indeed, she will experience a veritable population explosion as her childen swarm out into the land, filling it and reoccupying ghost towns. The verb translated "you will spread out" (*tiprosî*) occurs also in God's promise to Jacob (Gen 28:14): "and your offspring shall be like the dust of the earth, and you shall spread abroad to the west and to the east and to the north and to the south." Lady Zion will experience fulfillment of that ancient vow.

Strophe two further details the imminent reversal:

> Do not fear, for you will not be ashamed;
>> do not be discouraged, for you will not suffer disgrace;
> for you will forget the shame of your youth,
>> and the disgrace of your widowhood you will remember no more.

The poem does not pause to clarify what constitutes "the shame of your youth," or "the disgrace of your widowhood," but rather rushes to reassure her that her period of abandonment has ended. Muilenburg finds in the former phrase a reference to "the whole pre-exilic period of infidelity" (635). The latter he identifies with the years of Babylonian exile. Such comments, though reasonable, run right over the metaphors inviting us to perceive the city of Zion's plight through the lens of a shamed girl, a solitary woman. The reader might plausibly, based on information gleaned thus far, construe "the shame of your youth" as a reference to sexual promiscuity (recalling 1:21). But this particular poem certainly does not invite such an interpretation. Rather it evokes thoughts of barrenness and abandonment:

> In order to appreciate the plethora of verbs (v. 4a) and nouns (v. 4b) expressing the shame, ignominy and humiliation, we must remember that, with Israel and the nations round about her, suffering and shame went together as the outside and the inside of the same phenomenon. Thus, in the case of the childless woman's suffering, it is not anything she does, such as behaving immorally, that involves her in shame, but childlessness as such. It is exactly the same with a vanquished nation—its defeat costs it its honour in the eyes of the rest of the nations. (Westermann 1969:273)

Similarly, the disgrace of widowhood foregrounds the vulnerability of being without a protector or provider. As noted at the beginning of Chapter 3, "widow" too is a word associated with both women and vassal cities in Israel's ancient Near Eastern world.

Strophe three acknowledges a breach in Yahweh's relationship with Zion, but downplays its gravity:

> For the Lord has called you
>> like a wife forsaken and grieved in spirit,
> like the wife of a man's youth when she is cast off. . . .
> For a brief moment I abandoned you,
>> but with great compassion I will gather you.
> In overflowing wrath for a moment
>> I hid my face from you,
> but with everlasting love I will have compassion on you,
>> says your Redeemer, Yahweh.

Here God acknowledges Jerusalem's grief, confesses culpability, but insists that they can be reconciled nonetheless. He abandoned his wife "for a brief moment," but he is returning her to himself "with great compassion." The contrast between past and imminent future is underscored not only semantically in the opposition between "small" and "great," but also in the opposition between the singular "brief moment" (*rega' qaton*) and the plural "great compassion" (*rahamîm gedolîm*; Berlin 1985:137). The reference to overflowing wrath in verse 8 is both intensified by alliteration (*besesep qesep*) and qualified by the repetition of *rega'*, " a moment." Sawyer attempts to paraphrase these lines:

> The last four verses of the poem are apologetic in tone: "it was just for a moment—I lost my temper . . . I won't do it again . . . I promise . . . I love you." She is physically weaker than he is and socially dependent on him. He has the power to give her happiness and dignity and freedom; she knows he also has the power to punish, humiliate and abuse her. So he has to convince her that he really loves her and that she can trust him. To do this he sets aside all hardness and pomposity, the frightening manifestations of his power and his status as "God of all the earth," and comes to her, on bended knee as it were, to plead with her to let bygones be bygones and start again. (1989:95-96)

Whether our reader would have construed Yahweh's words precisely as Sawyer understands them cannot be known, of course. But it is clear that this description of what Jerusalem has endured, and of what Yahweh desires beyond her punishment, cannot be discerned apart from the poem's marriage metaphor; the two are one.

Strophe four buttresses Yahweh's promise with the evocation of an ancient and enduring oath (vs. 9). The impact of the reference does not turn upon whether the initial line reads "the days," or "the waters," of Noah. For the author and reader of this text, Yahweh's commitment to Noah (neither J nor P refers to an oath) was an immutable reality. And it is followed by a reference to the most stalwart of God's creations, mountains and hills (Muilenburg 637). Yet Yahweh's steadfast love for, and covenant of peace with, Jerusalem are even more reliable than these. For Muilenburg, verses 9-10 constitute the "highest climax" of the poem (637). Many scholars would identify them as its conclusion as well. But the reader, encountering a triad of feminine singular adjectives in verse 11 with no obvious, other referent, will surely construe them as continuing the address to Lady Zion. And indeed, the afflicted (cf. 51:21), storm-tossed, and "not comforted" entity addressed is Jerusalem, whose "city-ness" obtrudes in ways consonant with stock city imagery and themes already introduced in Isaiah. In 49:14-18, for example, Yahweh claimed to have incised Jerusalem's walls on the divine hands, promising that she would wear her children like bridal ornaments. In 54:11-13, her gates, battlements, and walls are like jewelry studded with precious stones (see Biddle 1991:182-83). Amidst such splendor, her sons sit as Yahweh's students; and Lady Zion is reassured that she shall never again experience the terrors that have plagued her past (vss. 11-14).

Following verses elaborate upon this assurance that Zion need fear no foe, since Yahweh controls all military might (vss. 15-17). Of particular note for our purposes is verse 17b ("This is the inheritance of the servants of the Lord and their vindication from me, says the Lord"), for it links the preceding, *positive* description of personified Zion and her children on the one hand, with God's servants on the other. To this point in Isaiah, the term "servants" has embraced all Israel, rather than a particular component within the larger community. As we saw in our Chapter 2, however, it will come to designate those who acknowledge and repent of Israel's history of rebelliousness, committing themselves to a life of obedience to Yahweh's teaching, as opposed to those who persist in rebelling against God. Interpreted on the basis of preceding material, Isa 54:17b constitues a reassuring promise to Israel as a whole. In retrospect, however, our reader will come to regard it as a polemical claim by the "servants" to Lady Zion's bountiful heritage.

Summary

The next personified city imagery appears in Isa 57:3-13, part of what most modern scholars, myself included, regard as the post-exilic Trito-Isaian corpus (Isaiah 56–66). I pause, therefore, to summarize the ladies' lots theme in Isaiah 40–55, beginning with the recognition that our reader already brings to these chapters expectations for Zion and her foreign counterparts formed earlier in the book: Yahweh has a plan; it involves all nations, but especially Israel. Its goal is world-wide recognition of Yahweh's unparalleled sovereignty. Proud cities and nations have fallen and will continue to fall. Israel is reduced to a remnant; and Daughter Jerusalem has survived the Assyrian threat, but must undergo punishment at Babylon's hand. Yet that mighty empire, too, is subject to Yahweh's rule and will be brought to ruin. Beyond Zion's destruction, by contrast, lies a future of world-wide acclaim for her, and for those in her who repent of their history of rebellion against Yahweh.

Such expectations are not, by in large, confounded in Isaiah 40–55 where Yahweh's sovereignty and control of the cosmos are prominent themes. Babylon, Israel's paradigmatic foe, teeters on the brink of destruction. Lady Jerusalem awaits a reversal of her present plight: a wealth of children; peace; prosperity; and reconciliation with her husband. The furnace of affliction has been endured. It is time to be at home again.

One expectation formed on the basis of Isaiah 1–39 has demanded our reader's reassessment. In Isaiah 1–39, Israel's rebels, and particularly its corrupt and intemperate leadership, were frequently decried. A distinction was drawn between penitents on the one hand, and perdurable sinners on the other. Isaiah 40–55 contains frank acknowledgments of Israel's rebellious and sinful past, but it nonetheless offers rebels a "clean start": that fresh beginning does not depend upon the repentence of Zion's contaminating elements. It only requires the acceptance of what God is offering for God's own sake:

> I, I am He who blots out your transgressions for my own sake,
> and I will not remember your sins. (43:25)

This astonishing message is fully apparent only to sequential readers of Isaiah's vision to this point. It stands at odds with the flat assertion that unrepentant rebels and sinners will be utterly destroyed (1:28). Yahweh has determined to blot out Israel's rebellions! The people need only accept the offer and step out in faith. They, all of them, be they addressed as Lady Zion, or as Jacob, or by any other epithet the poet employs, can participate in a marvelous future as part of God's family. For the reader arriving at Isaiah 55, the imminent unfolding of Yahweh's plan awaits but one thing: Israel's response.

"ANNOUNCE TO MY PEOPLE THEIR REBELLION, TO THE HOUSE OF JACOB THEIR SINS": ISAIAH 56–66

Because Chapter 2 carefully traced developments in Isaiah 56–66, I shall not do so again in this context. Presupposing that discussion, we shall focus instead upon passages containing personified city imagery, referring only to those additional features significant for the reader's construal of Jerusalem's lot. Recall, for example, the asseveration concerning Yahweh's servants that concluded the great love poem in Isaiah 54:

> This is the heritage of the servants of the Lord
> and their vindication from me, says the Lord. (vs. 17b)

In that context, "servants" apparently designated all Israel. Only two chapters later, however, Isaiah 56:6-8 will identify as Yahweh's servants those members of the community (including righteous foreigners and eunuchs) who keep the Sabbath and hold fast to the covenant. Yahweh promises to bring them "to my holy mountain, and make them joyful in my house of prayer" (vs. 7). Israel's corrupt leaders, by contrast, stand condemned of sin—again. Have the expressions of grace found in Isaiah 40–55 come to an end for them?

Isaiah 57:6-13

We termed Isaiah 40–55 "grace notes" because in those chapters Yahweh's judgment upon a rebellious people did not spell their doom, transgressions notwithstanding. Instead, divine promises of forgiveness and restoration, along with various other rhetorical strategies, attempted to reawaken Israel's belief in Yahweh as sovereign of the cosmos and planner of destinies. In Isaiah 56, however, the joyous hymn of praise concluded in 55:13 gives way to a two-fold imperative ("maintain justice [*mispat*] and do what is right" [*sedaqah*]) motivated by a divine promise ("for soon my salvation [*yesû'atî*] will come, and my deliverance [*sidqatî*] be revealed"; 56:1). Hence, divine words of assurance are linked to divine demands. As our reader moves further into Isaiah 56–66, he will realize that these chapters address a setting later than the Babylonian exile; and that the issue to hand is not motivating the diaspora to return home, but learning how to negotiate life there.

As noted in Chapter 2, 56:3-8 insist upon a worshipping community inclusive of all the faithful, even foreigners and eunuchs. Others will join those Israelites whom Yahweh has already returned home (vs. 8):

> Thus says the Lord God, / who gathers the outcasts of Israel,
> I will gather others to them / besides those already gathered.

But then, we observed, the text's tone shifts abruptly as wild animals are summoned to devour Israel's sinful leaders (56:9-12). Accusations against Israel's leadership were all too common in Isaiah 1–39, non-existent in 40–55. Now, they return in a striking vituperation that reminds the reader of precisely those conditions described at the outset of Isaiah's vision (56:9-12): Israel's religious and civil leaders are blind and without knowledge; they are mute animals, sharing a dog's love of slumber and food. What energy they can muster is expended securing wine and strong drink; the latter term, *nisbe'ah*, recalls the choice liquor (*sobe'*) that, cut with water, metaphorically represented the debased state of Zion, the once-faithful city who became a harlot (1:22). The lament over the suffering righteous whose deaths no one heeds (57:1-2; compare Ps 12:1 [ET 2] and Mic 7:2) is followed by charges and words of judgment that, like Isaiah's inaugural oracle, take the form of a trial speech. Poisonous epithets reminiscent of 1:4 slur the leaders' progenitors ("you children of a sorceress, you offspring of an adulterer and a whore") and so their own natures as well. They are "children of transgression" (*yildê pesa'*)—again an echo of Isaiah 1—and offspring of deceit who engage in heinous cultic acts. Verses 3-5 use masculine plural grammatical forms: [15]

> But you, draw near, / you sons of a sorceress,
> seed of an adulterer and of her who plays the harlot . . .
> Are you not children of transgression, / offspring of deceit,
> who burn with lust among the terebinths, / under every green tree,
> who slaughter children in wadis, / among the clefts of the rocks?

In verses 6-13, however, the leaders are addressed using almost uniformly feminine singular forms. This shift, presaged perhaps by two of the three epithets in verse 3, invites the reader to perceive their sins through the lens of an illicitly-fornicating female also engaging in necromancy and child sacrifice:

> On a mountain high and lofty / you have set your bed.
> There you went up / to offer sacrifice.
> And behind the door and the doorpost/ you set up your symbol.
> For a hundred times[16] you stripped
> and you mounted and spread out your bed . . .
> . . . the love of their bedding,
> the phallus which you envisioned. (vss. 7-8)[17]

A framework of phrases from the Psalms (vss. 2, 13b) contrasts the suffering righteous with the wicked leaders addressed in verses 3-13a, as Westermann notes (1969:320). But Westermann goes on to argue that verses 7-10, 11, and 12-13 consist of three anonymous, pre-exilic prophetic utterances, which found their way into the corpus as "the break-up into two different groups which began after the return, the one regarding itself as that of the devout and righteous as over against the transgressors, caused earlier prophetic oracles of judgment to be taken up and interpreted with reference to the new situation" (1969:320). While we agree that Isaiah 56–66 provides considerable evidence of division within the post-exilic community, verses 3-13 are better construed as a unified literary composition borrowing from the well-established convention of personifying a city as a woman—and more precisely as a fornicating, sorcery-dabbling, child-sacrificing woman—and introducing an innovation into that convention.

S. Ackerman also regards 57:3-13 as a literary unity, and a finely-crafted one at that. She notes, for example, a structural pattern, such that references to the fertility cult, child sacrifice, and the cult of the dead recur, in that order, twice in verses 5a-9b. "Clearly," she states, "this structure indicates that in the prophet's mind an organic unity exists among sexual fertility rituals, child sacrifice and cults of the dead" (1990:42). Throughout the poem, the inextricable link (i.e., fertility) joining these practices is reenforced through the use of polyvalent vocabulary and wordplays. In verse 5, 'elim can plausibly be construed to mean either "terebinths" or "gods"; and both meanings are apropos to the context. The noun miskab, "bed," recurs three times in verses 7 and 8 (twice). It refers, of course, to the site of the wanton woman's repeated fornications. But, Ackerman notes, miskab can also refer to one's grave or resting place; it appeared with just that meaning in Isa 57:2, a lament over the unheeded deaths of the righteous. Hence, it bears associations with not one, but two of the poem's three major themes. Again, the word for "symbol" (zikkaron; vs. 8) signifies some sort of fertility cultic object. Because it puns the Hebrew word zakar, "male," it also suggests a phallic image (see also Ezek 16:17). But zikkaron can refer to a memorial stela as well. And the reference to yad, usually translated "hand," but possibly referring in this context to the phallus, elsewhere denotes a monument for the dead; see, for example 2 Sam 18:18. Hence, these and other word plays bind the woman's activities into an inextricable morass of iniquity.

Not a few commentators are at pains to argue that charges lodged against the wanton woman of 57:6-10 reflect *actual* cultic activities of the post-exilic period. J. L. McKenzie, for example, observes:

> That fertility rites of some kind are described seems to admit no doubt. There are also allusions to necromancy. . . . There are no explicit references to these superstitions in other post-exilic literature; but there is no difficulty in supposing that the theological and cultic condition of the early post-exilic community was primitive. . . . Such rites could well have been practiced by those who lived in the land after the Babylonian wars; there seems to have been no center in the country which would have preserved genuine Yahwism. (1967:158)

P. Hanson, by contrast, correctly reminds his readers that "the description of their activity in verses 5-10 is to be taken no more literally than is the designation 'sons of a witch, offspring of the adulterer and the whore'":

> The metaphorical use of language found here is illustrated clearly by verse 6. Various attempts have been made to identify the pagan cultic practic being attacked here. But note the roots being used: *hlq* ("apportion"—"be slippery"); *nhl* ("inherit"—"wadi"); *grl* ("allotment"—"stony place"). Although the exact translation of this colon must remain uncertain, one thing is clear: this is no objective description of a cultic practice, but rather a highly sardonical paronomasia used to ridicule the cult of those being attacked. (1975:198)

Though Hanson does not say so, the metaphorical depictions of the leaders' acts are associated with women, and so particularly appropriate to the poem's female personification. Moreover, such metaphors were already part of Israel's literary and religious traditions. Ezekiel, for example, knows of women's propensity toward sorcery, witchcraft, and other practices lying beyond the orthodox Yahwism whence they were largely excluded (Ezek 13:17-23). He describes Jerusalem and Samaria's "intercourse" with foreign gods and nations as sexual intercourse, accusing them of child sacrifice (Ezek 16:20; 23:39). He describes in pornographic detail Jerusalem's assent to her lofty platform, where she offers herself to every passerby (Ezek 16:23-25). And like the wanton of Isa 57:9, Oholah and Oholibah send envoys afar, in their case explicitly to seek out new paramours (Ezek 23:40-42). Ezekiel's personified city passages excoriate his people as a whole. In Isaiah 57, by contrast, one group of Israelites castigates another.

Who does the fornicator in Isaiah 57 represent? Do textual clues allow a more precise identification? As noted, the word for "bed," *miskab*, can also mean "grave." But *miskab* sounds quite like another noun, *miskan*, meaning "tabernacle" or "shrine." As Ackerman observes, "the description of offering sacrifice at the 'bed' in verse 7 confirms that the bed/shrine pun is intended, as does the reference to a 'door and doorpost' in the beginning of verse 8: Shrines have doors and doorposts; beds do not" (39).

Now *miskan* refers to God's abode in Zion in Ezek 37:27 and Ps 132:5, 7. Moreover, the phrase describing the wanton's ascent to her bed "upon a high and lofty mountain" (*har-gaboah wenissah'*; vs. 7) recalls similar phrases used to describe Jerusalem (e.g., *wenissa' miggeba'ôt* in Isa 2:2; see also Isa 40:8; Ezek 17:22, 40:2; Mic 4:1). We conclude, therefore, that Jerusalem as temple-site is particularly at issue here. The wanton woman is not unrelated to the "(once-) faithful city" of Isa 1:21-26. But an important innovation has occured. *While the Zion of Isaiah 1 became a harlot on account of her defiling inhabitants, here her defiling inhabitants appear in the guise of a personified, harlotrous Zion.* In other words, "she" is *precisely* those persistently rebellious, insolent leaders excoriated in 56:9–57:5. In later texts, encouraging words addressed to "Zion"/"those in Jacob who turn from transgression" (59:20) will employ the language of love. There are *two* Zions, then, in Isaiah 56–66: the harlot who—in a single, graphic appearance—embodies Israel's evil leadership; and the beloved wife and mother who represents Yahweh's faithful servants (recall 54:17b).

Other features also remind readers of Isa 1:21-28: both texts focus upon Jerusalem's corrupt and defiling leadership. Both utilize the poetic technique of female personification, and both contain charges of illicit fornication. In fact, 57:6-13 can be construed as a vivid illustration of the accusation presumed, but not further developed through sexual metaphors, in Isa 1:21-23.

How will our reader understand the relationship between these texts? Two answers are possible. On the one hand, he may regard the situation described in Isa 57:3-13 as far removed temporally from that reflected in Isaiah 1. The city whose fate he has followed—who narrowly escaped the eighth-century Assyrian threat, but was destroyed by Babylon in the sixth century, whose inhabitants endured the "furnace of affliction," but were offered forgiveness, comfort, and reconciliation at exile's end—here represents debasing and pernicious post-exilic leaders. He may conclude, in short, that the harlot is back, though she embodies her sinful inhabitants, not the penitents or the city "herself." That being the case, something more must be done to eliminate her (=them) before the glorious exaltation of Zion and her penitents can take place. The remainder of the scroll, then, details the substance of that "something more."

Yet another possibility exists, however. The reader of Isa 57:3-13 may conclude that, though he has thus far construed Isaiah's vision along the lines just described, he must now rethink his understanding of it, and especially of the scroll's opening chapter. We have noted that 1:1-31 situates the prophet Isaiah chronologically, but not necessarily the conditions he envisions. It might, as historical critics so often have concluded, depict a Judean landscape ravaged by Assyrian forces in the aftermath of "Hezekiah's rebellion," so that Jerusalem alone survives among Judah's cities. But it might also be construed to describe conditions during the exilic or early post-exilic periods, when the land lies devastated, its towns destroyed, Jerusalem in ruins, and the population sparse.

Our sequential reader of Isaiah—reflecting upon Isa 56:1–57:13 and its many similarities to Isaiah 1—may become convinced that the vision's inaugural chapter, which he first construed as a description of pre-exilic circumstances, actually describes conditions pertaining (also) during the post-exilic period. R. Rendtorff suggests this possibility when he claims that the entire book in its final form addresses post-exilic Israel (1985; 1991b). If the reader, encouraged by the recurrence of harlotrous Zion imagery and accusations against Israel's cultic leadership, concludes that Isaiah's vision's begins with a description of early post-exilic conditions, then he will recognize that the great purge promised in 1:21-31 refers not to the past with its Babylonian catastrophe (though that event might be construed as a portent of things to come), but rather to a future conflagration when the rebellious leaders whom harlotrous Jerusalem represents (1:21-23; 57:6-13), and who are responsible for the land's present plight (Isa 1:7-8), finally are utterly consumed (1:28-31). The remainder of the scroll can then be understood to detail this ultimate purge (Yahweh, the Divine Warrior, will effect it without recourse to a foreign "instrument") and its consequences for Lady Zion and her penitents on the one hand, and perdurable sinners on the other.

Personification of Isa 57:6-13 puts a female face and form to Jerusalem's insolent, self-indulgent, and blasphemous leadership. "She" is not, as some would have it, a flashback to an earlier state of defilement that, for some elusive reason, is permitted some play here. Neither has she found her way into the text because a redactor discerned at this point an opportunity to slip in some snippets of pre-exilic prophecy (now reinterpreted by virtue of their redactional framework). Rather, she appears in order that the audience or reader might perceive the cultic activities of their current leadership through the lens of a fornicating, child sacrificing, female devotée of the cult of the dead. An image evoked by earlier prophets to describe the sins of cities and nations—defiled and defiling, shameless, promiscuous, idolatrous, cruel, and unnatural—here functions to evoke extreme revulsion and disgust toward a (*male*) subgroup within the larger community.

Isaiah 60

Isaiah 58–59 figured prominently in Chapter 2: an announcement of Israel's rebellious history resulted in a confession by some, though not all, Israelites of their transgressions (59:12-13). Presently, these penitents "stumble at noon as in the twilight" (59:10). But they live, nonetheless, in the expectation that "your light shall rise in the darkness and your gloom be like the noonday" (49:10b). That prospect verges on fulfillment as a voice summons Yahweh's servants with the news of a great, impending theophany (chap. 60). Double feminine imperatives address the personified Jerusalem embodying *obedient* Israel:

> Arise, shine; for your light has come,
> and the glory of the Lord has risen upon you.

For darkness shall cover the earth,
    and thick darkness the peoples;
but the Lord will arise upon you,
    and his glory will appear over you.
Nations shall come to your light,
    and kings to the brightness of your dawn. (vss. 1-3)

Here, in J. Muilenburg's words, is "a strophe flooded with light" (1956:699). Addressed as Lady Zion, "those in Jacob who turn from transgression," groping "like those who have no eyes" (59:10), will soon be suffused with the divine effulgence. The discontinuous language of sunrise describes Yahweh's glory rising, casting its brilliance upon the city. Hence, the dazzling light of the rising sun,[18] more than the fire of Sinai, is foregrounded in this metaphorical description of Yahweh's theophany. "The image of Zion as not only the recipient of God's light but as herself shining with the reflected light of Yahweh's glory is," R. N. Whybray observes, "an original contribution by this author" (1975:230). While Zion basks in the bright light of Yahweh's glory, the remainder of the earth lies shrouded in darkness. The initial *kî-hinneh* (vs. 2a) sharpens the contrast between the light of verse 1, and the gloom of verse 2.[19] "But *upon you*," the poem continues (note that *'alayik* is emphatic), "Yahweh will dawn, and his glory upon you will be seen." Verse 3 ("Nations shall come to your light, and kings to the brightness of your dawn") functions as a pivot between the light theme of verses 1-2, and the ensuing theme of the nations streaming to Jerusalem. Once again, both sides of our "ladies' lots" theme are emphasized—God's relationship with Zion, and Jerusalem's status among the nations.

Verses 4-9 extravagantly detail the international procession returning Zion's children and bringing her great wealth. Like its predecessor, this second section begins with two feminine singular imperatives. Lady Zion is urged to look around, witnessing the approaching convoys. In language reminiscent of Isa 49:12, 22-23, her children return—sons walking, daughters carried upon the hip. Verse 5 appears to describe her great joy at their impending arrival:

Then you will see, you will beam;
    your heart will tremble and swell. (vs. 5)[20]

But the second half-verse, with its initial *kî*, would link her joy

191

to the approaching treasures she espies. From Midian, Ephah, and Sheba, places of "venerable association" (Muilenburg 1956:701), come caravans of gold and silver-laden camels. The flocks of Kedar and Nebaioth willingly offer themselves as acceptable sacrifices upon Yahweh's altar (vs. 7). Turning from east to west, Lady Zion witnesses the swift-flying sails of the ships of Tarshish leading a fleet loaded with her children and with additional coffers of precious metals. These ships were once, the reader recalls, an important part of the thriving Phoenician trade enriching Sidon and Tyre the crown wearer, "whose merchants were princes, whose traders were the honored of the earth" (Isa 23:8). Here, however, they are not "in her majesty's service," but in Yahweh's! As Muilenburg notes, forms of the verb *ba'* appear frequently throughout the poem (vss. 1, 4, 5, 6, 9, 11, 13, 17 [twice]), signaling what is so richly affirmed in verses 4-9: "the world is coming to Zion's hill" (1956:697).

"Beholding" this remarkable influx of persons and riches, readers may recall the nations' eager streaming to Jerusalem envisioned in Isa 2:1-4. But while that text attributed their pilgrimage to a yearning for Yahweh's instruction, the present poem emphasizes the vast importation of their material wealth to Zion. Note, for example, that forms of the verb *pa'ar*, "to beautify, glorify," appear six times in the text, half in verses 7-9. In Isa 3:18 and 20, nouns from the same root referred to finery adorning Jerusalem's haughty, promenading women; and the tone was reproving. Here, however, *pa'ar* bears no trace of the disdain permeating that earlier text. In this case, of course, the ultimate recipient of the world's wealth is not only Zion, but also Yahweh (vss. 6b, 7b, 9b).

Who does personified Zion represent in this poem? Noting the presence in verse 4 of phrases original to Isaiah 49 (e.g., "Lift up . . . come to you"; see Isa 49:18a), R. N. Whybray nonetheless insists that her identity differs in these two texts:

> In their original context these phrases refer to the repopulation of "bereaved," that is, uninhabited, Jerusalem who is pictured as watching with amazement the arrival of her "children," the exiles and other dispersed Israelites. Here Zion is the community of Jews already returned from exile and living in and around Jerusalem, and the promise is of the comple-

tion of this return: the restoration of all the people of God to their land. (1975:231-32)

I also have claimed that personified Zion embodies her inhabitants, though I argue more precisely that for the sequential reader, those inhabitants include "those in Jacob who turn from transgression" (‖ "Zion"; 59:20), but not their wicked leaders. With the beginning of the poem's third part (vss. 10-16), however, thoughts of Jerusalem as *city* are foregrounded by Yahweh's promise that her destroyers shall become her rebuilders— certainly a reversal worth relishing: note the references to walls (vs. 10a), gates (vs. 11), "the place of my sanctuary" (vs. 13), building materials (vs. 17), and the additional reference to walls and gates in verse 18. Verse 10b, by contrast, evokes thoughts of Zion as an abandoned wife, using terms paired also in Isa 54:8 ("In overflowing wrath [*qesep*] for a moment I hid my face from you, but with everlasting love I will have compassion on you [*rihamtîk*], says the Lord, your Redeemer") to contrast Yahweh's past and present disposition toward her:

> for in my wrath [*beqispî*] I struck you down,
> > but in my favor I have had mercy on you [*rihamtîk*]. (vs. 10b)

"Who" Zion represents can shift within a single poem, therefore; and thoughts of two or more referents—a city, its populace, a young woman—can be astir simultaneously as the poem foregrounds first one and then another.

Perpetually-open gates not only ensure the constant influx of the world's wealth (vs. 11), but also testify to Zion's unimpeachable security. The phrase "with their kings led in procession" is problematic; many commentators would emend *nehûgîm* to an active participle, *nôhagîm*, "with their kings leading them." The MT can be construed, Muilenburg notes, to mean "their kings led into captivity" (1956:703). The point, in any event, is that Israel need not fear nations and their rulers, since their divinely appointed business is to serve Zion and her God in perpetuity. Verse 12 then cuts to the chase:

> For the nation and kingdom that will not serve you will perish;
> > those nations shall be utterly laid waste. (vs. 12)

The NRSV stichometry suggests that this verse is poetry, but commentators generally regard it as prose and a gloss (see, e.g., Westermann 1969:360; Muilenburg 1956:703). But R. N. Whybray correctly concedes that its sentiment "is not as far removed from verses 10-11 in tone as many have held."[21] Indeed, both critic and "reader" know that throughout Isaiah, intervening prose passages often contain the most succinct and explicit articulations of points that are crucial both to Isaiah's rhetoric of rebellion, and to the ladies' lots theme. Why should we, as critics, insist that such pointed prose assertions be devalued or disregarded (235)?

For sequential readers, verse 12 is of a piece with other of the scroll's claims concerning Yahweh's plan: universal acknowledgment of God's unparalleled power and sovereignty as creator and sustainer of the cosmos; the eventual exaltation of Zion among the nations; the ingathering of the peoples to Zion, there to be instructed in Yahweh's Torah, to serve her inhabitants, to beautify and enrich her environs, and to glorify her God; the survival of auspicious foes who will themselves become Yahwists (e.g., Egypt and Assyria in Isaiah 19), but also the perpetual, enforced, and demeaning servitude of formerly proud and prosperous enemies (e.g., Tyre in Isaiah 23) and the destruction of Babylon (Isaiah 47). Given the pervasive claim that Zion's eventual glorification is integral to Yahweh's plan for Israel and the world, what fate other than that asserted in 60:12 could befall the recalcitrant nation or king refusing to honor her?

Moreover, as this poem itself demonstrates, serving Jerusalem and serving God cannot be separated: witness how flocks and herds from the west become fodder for Yahweh's altar, while the precious woods of Lebanon beautify the sanctuary. Earlier we noted how, in a threat against Jerusalem, Jer 22:23 addressed her disparagingly as "you who are enthroned in Lebanon, nested in the cedars." In Isaiah 60, by contrast, Lady Zion is promised a return to her (and Yahweh's) place of prominence and majesty:

> The glory of Lebanon shall come to you,
> > the cypress, the plane, and the pine,
> to beautify the place of my sanctuary;
> > and I will glorify where my feet rest. (vs. 13)

Yes, the nation that refuses to play its part in God's plan is guilty of rebellion; and, of course, the fate awaiting persistent rebels was announced long before this point in the scroll.

Images of her enemies' children prostrate at Zion's feet

constitute yet another reversal worth savoring:

> The descendants of those who oppressed you
>> shall come bending low to you,
> and all who despised you
>> shall bow down at your feet;
> they shall call you the City of the Lord,
>> the Zion of the Holy One of Israel. (vs. 14)

Her former foes' epithets point to Zion's inextricable link with Yahweh. Verse 15, by contrast, shifts to Yahweh's speech and terms drawn from the conjugal sphere: formerly, Zion was "forsaken" (recall Isa 49:14; 54:6) and "hated" (senûʼah; the technical term for a repudiated wife).[22] Here, however, her former, forlorn status is sharply contrasted with her glorious future:

> Whereas you have been forsaken and hated,
>> with no one passing through,
> I will make you majestic forever,
>> a joy from age to age. (vs. 15)

Verse 16, then, takes up the earlier image (e.g., 49:23) of kings and queens tending Israel's returning infants, so transforming it that Jerusalem herself becomes a babe suckling at royal breasts! The notion strikes moderns as strange. R. N. Whybray best construes its meaning when he states that the author has used the nursing metaphor "to express the idea that Zion will drain the foreign nations of their wealth" (1975:236). Such an assertion is certainly consonant with the poem's general proposition. In any event, only here in Isaiah is Jerusalem depicted as a baby.

The remainder of Isaiah 60 contrasts past Jerusalem (even in its Solomonic "glory days") with the immeasurably more magnificent Zion of the (imminent) future. Her overseer will be "Peace"; her taskmaster "Righteousness." Even her walls and gates—normally vital to urban security, and once urged to mourning and a flood of tears—will symbolically be named "Salvation" and "Praise" respectively (T. Anderson 1986:76), their former defensive functions unnecessary because:

> Violence shall no more be heard in your land,
>> devastation or destruction within your borders. (vs. 18a)[23]

With verse 19 the poem returns to the theme of light whence it began, declaring the sun and moon extraneous since "your God will be your glory" (v. 19b). Lady Zion's mourning is ended; her people, grown numerous and powerful, "shall possess the land forever" (vs. 21a).

Isaiah 60 is not about an act of divine *deliverance*; it is, rather, a "sky's the limit" description of Jerusalem's state of glorification consequent upon that deliverance. It therefore moves Lady Zion's story beyond God's great salvific act on her behalf, to what will constitute "everyday life" for a redeemed people serving the Lord of all the earth in God's beautified city. The poet's delight at thoughts of Israel enjoying a magnificent excess of the world's riches elicits comments from commentators. J. Muilenburg cautions against a material/spiritual dichotomy: "It is a mistake . . . to divorce the literal and material from the symbolic and spiritual. The external and internal manifestations of Yahweh's presence and his eschatological and redemptive deeds belong together" (1956:698). R. N. Whybray, by contrast, remarks,

> it is difficult to understand why some commentators insist on spiritualizing these promises. The author is saying that the promises of world dominion which go back ultimately to the time of David, but which had much more recently been confidently reiterated by Deutero-Isaiah, remained valid and would soon be amply fulfilled. (1975:231)

Both points of view have bases in the text. Muilenburg repeatedly notes how each of the poem's strophes ends in "theocentric asseverations" (705). Yet Whybray's claim that "the note of nationalism—albeit of 'religious nationalism'—is unmistakable" rings true as well. Here, a community embraces an edenic vision despite exceedingly harsh physical conditions, affirming its sovereign God's good pleasure that Zion and her faithful inhabitants enjoy both a priviledged position among the nations, and the best of the earth's wealth.

Several commentators ascribe the final verses of Isaiah 61 to Zion (the Targum prefaces: "Jerusalem has said"). According to J. McKenzie, Isa 61:1-7 consists of the prophet's words, verses 8-9 belong to Yahweh, and Zion concludes in verses 10-11 (1967:181): "the figure of the bride, suggested in verse 10, is amplified in the following poem" (182). While wedding imagery abounds in Isaiah 62, we would note, the bridal *simile* in verse 10 follows immediately on a bridegroom simile. Since first person singular grammatical forms do not betray the speaker's gender, McKenzie's identification remains tenuous. J. Muilenburg's comments are more nuanced: the same prophet of glad tidings in verses 1-3 here speaks as Zion's representative—"her words are his words" (1956:714). But the eschatological hymn of praise proclaiming Yahweh's inevitable, salvific acts is best attributed to the first person singular speaker (in 61:1-7) who will intercede on Zion's behalf in Isaiah 62.

Isaiah 62

Isaiah 62:1-12 constitutes the penultimate personified Zion passage in Isaiah. Sharing with the two preceding chapters certain key terms and themes, the poem details Jerusalem's restoration and glorification. And, as R. N. Whybray notes, its dependence upon Isaiah 40–55 is even greater than that of Isaiah 60–61 (1975:246).

Commentators dispute the speakers' identity in Isaiah 62. For Whybray, Yahweh proclaims a partial oracle of salvation in verse 1; verses 2-5 are prophetic comment. Yahweh speaks in the first person, addressing Jerusalem in the third; the prophet addresses Zion in the second person feminine, speaking of Yahweh in the third person (1975:246). J. McKenzie, by contrast, attributes the entire poem to the prophet, with the exception of Yahweh's oath in verses 8-9. Muilenburg also identifies the speaker of verses 1-5 as the prophet, whose concern for Jerusalem, whence flows "the thought of the whole poem," is expressed in finely-balanced lines reminiscent of Isa 60:1-2:

> For Zion's sake I will not keep silent,
>   and for Jerusalem's sake I will not rest,
> until her vindication shines out like the dawn,
>   and her salvation like a burning torch. (62:2)

Turning to verses 6-7, however, Muilenburg asserts that the first quatrain consists of Yahweh's words, the second of the prophet's response.[24]

I attribute the anonymous first person singular voice in Isaiah 61 and 62 to a speaker (Isaiah? the Servant, one of his disciples?) whose purposes are: to speak words of comfort and reassurance to those in Zion who have repented of their sins and are obedient to Yahweh's instruction, awaiting God's as-yet-unfulfilled promises ("to comfort all who mourn; to provide for those who mourn in Zion"); and to remind Yahweh constantly of those very promises (vss. 6-7).

Our focus appropriately falls upon the poem's use of female personification. The poetry brims with care for Jerusalem (and the penitents she embodies), and many of its features are pertinent to our analysis, including references to renaming (or the repudiation of names), crown imagery, and wedding imagery. Are these features in some sense interrelated?

Renaming appears first in verse 2a, again in verse 4, (where two negative epithets are replaced by two positive ones), and yet again in verse 12, where two additional pairs of names occur, one for the people of Israel, and the other for Zion. In verse 2a, we encounter—as in 60:3—concern that nations and kings witness Zion's exaltation. Jerusalem will receive a "new name" [sem hadas] that the mouth of the Lord will give." The phrase forms something of a crux since it appears nowhere else in the Hebrew Bible. In any event, verse 2 does not reveal this new name: "God keeps it to himself" (Westermann 1969:375).

When and why did renaming occur in Israel's world? Cities could be renamed by their conquerors (e.g., Num 32:41-42), T. D. Anderson notes, to commemorate a significant event (e.g., Gen 35:6-7), or when they were rebuilt (e.g., Num 32:37-38; 1986:75). Because Jerusalem is personified in Isaiah 62, however, Anderson must also consider circumstances where *persons* were renamed: "Generally, renaming is associated with a change in the status or condition of the person receiving the new name" (75). People coming under new authority might be given a different name as a sign of subjugation (e.g., Dan 1:7); suzerains, for example, sometimes bestowed new throne-names upon vassal kings (e.g., 2 Kgs 23:34; 24:17). In a somewhat different vein, the establishment of a covenant relationship between God and an individual could lead to renaming, e.g., Abram to Abraham (Gen 17:5), Sarai to Sarah (Gen 17:15), and Jacob to Israel (Gen 32:28; 35:10). In the latter case, Anderson notes, the old name (Jacob) continued in use alongside the new, but "this does not change the fact that an authentic renaming has taken place" (76). Marriage also entailed renaming, as Isa 4:1 attests. In that case, however, the wife did not drop her original name, but simply added her husband's as an "additional appellation" (76). Finally, names could be changed for purposes of "naturalization" (Esth 2:7?).

These examples contrast with renaming formulae lacking any intent actually to replace an older epithet. Their purpose, he writes, "is rather a dramatic form of predication—to describe forcefully the character and condition of the person renamed. It is the meaning of the new name which is important, not its labelling function" (76). In such instances, Anderson asserts, use of the old name could persist. In a number of passages, for example, Jerusalem is given a new, symbolic name: Jer 3:17 ("Jerusalem shall be called the throne of the Lord"); Jer 33:16 ("And this is the name by which [Jerusalem] will be called: 'The Lord is our righteousness'"); Ezek 48:35b ("And the name of the city from that time on shall be, The Lord is There"); and a text we have already examined, Isa 60:14b ("They shall call you the City of the Lord, the Zion of the Holy One of Israel"). These epithets convey a sense of "ownership or belonging" (see also Isa 44:5). Isaiah 1:21 and 26 are related, since they characterize the city as "(once-) faithful" (76). Nowhere, however, does the text explicitly state that symbolic names will render the name "Jerusalem" obsolete.

What have these comments to do with renamings in Isaiah 62? The appearance of *'azûbah*, "Forsaken" (cf. 1 Kgs 22:42), scarcely surprises, since descriptions of Zion as a forsaken wife (49:14; 54:6; 60:15), and Yahweh's responses (54:7), have already appeared in the scroll. A second term, the feminine noun *semamah* ("destruction, waste"), often describes ruined, depopulated land and cities, and so is apropos to verse 4a with its reference to "your land." Nonetheless, many commentators, following 1QIsa[a] and other textual traditions, repoint the consonants to read *somemah*, "Desolate" (see also Isa 54:1). Perhaps *smmh* was again intended to evoke both a desolate woman and desolate land.

While "Forsaken" and "Desolate" describe the deleterious conditions of an abandoned wife, Hephzibah ("My Delight is in Her"; vs. 4b) expresses the joy of conjugal love. Whybray refers to an ancient Near Eastern parallel to verse 4a: "this image, a variation on the theme of the city Jerusalem as Yahweh's spouse, has its origins in a Semitic concept of the procreator god who fertilizes the land. A similar phrase occurs in one of the Amarna letters (fourteenth century BC)" (1975:248). The expression may well have stirred such thoughts in the minds of readers familiar with said Semitic concept. A more proximate description of the fructifying effects of Yahweh's comforting presence for Jerusalem's land was to hand, however:

> For the Lord will comfort Zion;
>> he will comfort all her waste places,
> and will make her wilderness like Eden,
>> her desert like the garden of the Lord;
> joy and gladness will be found in her,
>> thanksgiving and the voice of song. (Isa 51:3)

Finally, the twin epithets for Israel in verse 12, "The Holy People" and "The Redeemed of the Lord" express Yahweh's ownership of Israel. Zion's two names, "Sought Out" (derûsah) and "a City not Abandoned" are, of course, the precise antithesis of the epithets she has borne (vs. 4).

Our second major motif in Isaiah 61, crown imagery, appears already in verse 3:

> You shall be a crown of beauty ['ateret tip'eret]
>> in the hand of the Lord,
> and a royal diadem [seniwp melûkah]
>> in the hand of your God.

Because verse 4 abruptly returns readers to the subject of naming, (or, more properly, "unnaming"), some commentators suggest repositioning verse 2b after verse 3. Others do not relate the two ideas. Whybray, for example, struggles to discern the significance of, and associations with, crown imagery in verse 3, quite apart from Jerusalem's renaming. Muilenburg grants Isa 28:1 as a possible source for the crown imagery in 62:3:

> Ah the proud garland of the drunkards of Ephraim,
>> and the fading flower of its glorious beauty,
> which is on the head of those bloated with rich food,
>> of those overcome with wine.

But more likely, in his view, the imagery "derived from the ancient custom of representing the tutelary deity of a city as crowned with the city walls" (1956:718). Muilenburg describes the crown as a "visual representation of Israel's glory" (718); like C. Westermann (1969:375), he construes the metaphor of Jerusalem as crown or ornament as indicative of how very precious Zion is to Yahweh. "And this comparison in v. 3 shows,"

Westermann adds, "how from Trito-Isaiah's time onwards . . ., terms taken from aesthetics made their way into the language of theology" (375).

Unlimited by the space constraints of commentary writing, M. E. Biddle addresses the mural crown motif within its larger ancient Near Eastern context, surveying Mesopotamian, West Semitic, and Hellenistic sources, as well as selected texts from the Hebrew Bible. Like Muilenburg and Whybray, he quotes a Babylonian inscription, "Borsippa is your (Marduk's) tiara," further explaining that "the city and its temple, the earthly representative of the cosmic circle, physically represented by the city walls, can be likened to a great crown adorning the head of the city and its deity" (1991:178). In fact, Biddle notes, mural crowns, often distinguished by their crenelated form, appear frequently on the heads of royalty and divinities in the iconography of Mesopotamia (178-79). In West Semitic and Hellenistic regions, mural crowns circled the heads of deified cities. So inextricably related were the city and its principal deity, Biddle writes, that "the mural crown, a powerful symbol of the divinity of the WS and Hellenistic city, . . . makes it clear that the deification of the city represents a fusion of city and goddess and not an abstraction of the principle of protection" (181).

Turning to the Hebrew Bible, where cities were not deified, Biddle nonethelesss identifies passages containing the mural crown motif with "expected modifications":

> The *personified* city Jerusalem, like the Mesopotamian city in that she has a distinct patron deity and like the WS city in that she is, nevertheless, depicted personally. . . . appears not only where she is explicitly named, but also in a number of texts which address, discuss, or give voice to an apparently unspecified female figure and in another group of texts, whose significance has been previously unrecognized, which liken her to the mural-crown. (182)

In Biddle's view, the mural crown motif informs Yahweh's assertion in Isa 49:14-18: "YHWH reassures Mother Zion that she has not been forgotten, that indeed YHWH has inscribed the outline of her walls on his hands so that he may always consider them, and that, furthermore, YHWH is reassembling her sons whom she will wear as wedding jewelry" (182-83). The motif reappears in the description of Zion's reconstructed walls

(54:11-13) and is "finally resolved" in Isa 62:1-5, where Zion's walls, "once inscribed in plan-form upon YHWH's hands to be constructed of the jewels of her children, are now a crown in Yahweh's hands" (1991:183). Ancient Near Eastern parallels to the mural crown motif are apparent in this passage, Biddle observes, yet so are its distinctive Israelite features: "Zion is the celebrated city, crown in the hand of the deity, but the crown is not worn by the deity, nor is the deity her spouse. . . . She is, after all, a personification, a poetic figure" (1991:184).

T. D. Anderson, by contrast, understands Isaiah 62 primarily in terms of coronation and marriage imagery with their concomitant renamings and joyous associations.[25] The appearance of *pe'er* in Isa 61:10, coupled with the explicit references to marriage in verse 5, support the view, in Anderson's opinion, that the crown in verse 3 evokes associations not only with coronations but also with weddings.[26]

> The most instructive parallel reference is the use of *'ateret* in connection with a royal wedding in Cant 3,11: "and behold King Solomon, with the crown with which his mother crowned him on the day of his wedding" . . . Cant 3,11 shows that one part of the wedding ceremony (at least in a royal wedding, though probably also in others) was the placing of a crown on the bridegroom's head. If on his wedding day a bridegroom receives two beautiful things—a beautiful crown and a beautiful bride—it would be tempting for a poet to use one as a metaphor of the other. (78)

If, in fact, our poem [metonymously] substitutes crown for bride, then the problem posed by verses 2-3 is resolved:

> Zion is the bride at a royal wedding. The "new name" of v. 2 may be the renaming of the bride associated with marriage. Since it is a royal wedding the renaming is simultaneously associated with being installed as queen. . . . In v. 3 the image changes a little and Zion is seen as the crown which the Lord, as officiator of the marriage, is to place on the bridegroom's head. The reference to *senîp melûkha* shows that it is a royal wedding. It is likely that of all the 'crown' vocabulary, *'ateret* and *sanîp* were chosen since they are the only terms which can give the double connotation of both royal and ornamental (wedding) crown. The fact that the new names of v. 4b make reference to being married, and to the delight of a bridegroom in a bride, supports this interpretation. (Anderson 1986:78-79)

Yahweh, the officiator, holds the crown. But who is the bridegroom? According to verse 5, two possibilities exist, "your sons" (*banayik*) and "your God" (*'elohayik*). Anderson initially opts for the former: "In 62,5 the image of sons returning to their mother and the image of Zion as bride are combined in the idea of the sons, representing the returning people, being the bridegroom of Zion" (79). Aware of the fluidity of characters in Isaian familial imagery, however, he later suggests that God also can be construed as Zion's bridegroom:

> The fact that the procession consists of the Saviour, God, accompanied by the people, explains why the bridegroom in v. 5 can be seen in terms of both God and the sons. The return of the sons to Zion, which is seen as a marriage, is also the return of God to Zion. God's rejoicing over Zion is manifested concretely in the rejoicing of the returning exiles. God can be seen both as the bridegroom, who shows his love and joy to Zion, and as the officiator of the marriage, who causes the restoration to take place. (80)

Anderson's interpretation is forced at points. Nevertheless, he has shown how our three principle poetic motifs—renaming, coronation, and marriage imagery—interweave to create a scene of joy, reconciliation, and possiblities for new life. The divine oath of verses 8-9 may sound a far cry from the extravagant claims for every life in Jerusalem recounted in Isaiah 60. Yet references to *dagan* ("grain") and *tîros* ("new wine") in 62.8 evoke thoughts of Yahweh's gifts to his wife in Hos 2:11. Taping into an ancient tradition, then, the poem describes remarriage, re-enthronement, a new beginning for an ancient love story. God and Zion are not just to be reconciled, their family re-membered. Yahweh will rejoice over his bride.

CONCLUSION

Earlier, we noted that Isaiah 62 constitutes the pentultimate personified Zion passage in Isaiah. Like Chapters 60–61, with which it is closely linked, it proclaims a future existence for Jerusalem that could make the proverbial Queen of Sheba pale with envy. Though these chapters acknowledge Zion's present ruined state (61:4) and those in her who mourn, a first person voice (60:1-4; 62:1-6) speaks words of comfort—promising Zion's penitents an everlasting covenant (see 59:21), salvation, and the wealth of the nations. "For Zion's sake," he refuses to be silenced; sentinels remind both Jerusalem and, especially, her Lord of his oath to her.

Despite promising prospects and proleptic announcements, the situation in Isaiah 56–66 in many respects resembles that with which Isaiah's vision began. Discussing Isaiah 56–57, we noted features reminiscent of Isaiah 1—stinging vituperations against Jerusalem's leadership, harlotry imagery, a trial speech, poisonous epithets, charges of heinous cultic acts. These reminiscences remind readers that Israel's history of rebellion against Yahweh, its principle offense since "childhood," persists to the present day; and that for all Israel experiences, Yahweh's plan for Lady Zion, and for all the "ladies" of the world, cannot be fulfilled until such time as the Divine Warrior, independent of any national "instrument," destroys enemy foes, rids Israel of its sinful and idolatrous leaders (embodied in harlotrous Jerusalem), and ushers in a new, edenic age for Yahweh's "servants." The ladies' lots, though proclaimed with great joy in Isaiah's vision, have yet to be realized.

A final personified Jerusalem passage appears in Isaiah 66. Before we can understand its impact fully, however, we must analyze a natal proverb spoken by an important Judean king at a crucial moment in Israel's history.

6

NO STRENGTH
TO DELIVER:
BRINGING TO BIRTH

In Israel's ancient Near Eastern world, the principle purpose of marriage was to produce children, especially sons. Hence, a wife's most important function was bearing a male heir to her husband's line. As noted in Chapter 3, however, that function was fulfilled at the risk of natal complications that could claim the lives of both mother and infant.

This Chapter focuses on a proverb about childbirth complications purportedly uttered by the esteemed king, Hezekiah, at a critical moment in Judah's history (Isa 37:3b = 2 Kgs 19:3b).[1] Our goals are fourfold: first, we shall discern what we can about the proverb's possible meanings within Israel's ancient Near Eastern world; second, we shall determine its function within the narrative world of Isaiah 36–37; third, we shall assess the proverb's significance for the reader's assessment of Hezekiah in Isaiah; finally, we shall identify two additional Isaian texts in which trust in God's strength and readiness to deliver appear.

A CITY IMPERILED

Moving from Isa 35:10 to 36:1, our reader experiences yet another sudden shift in tone. A poetic description of the joyous march of Yahweh's redeemed upon a sacred highway gives way to a prose account of Sennacherib's ferocious march against the fortified cities of Judah: "In the fourteenth year of King Hezekiah, King Sennacherib of Assyria marched against all the fortified towns of Judah and seized them."

According to Isa 36:2, Sennacherib sent his Rabshakeh (commander-in-chief) to Jerusalem with a large force to quell the city. In the hearing of Jerusalem's inhabitants, the Rabshakeh shouted demoralizing messages at Hezekiah's representatives. His words ridiculed Hezekiah's ostensible *trust* in Egyptian assistance, and ultimately in Yahweh, and stressed God's *inability* to save the city.

Learning of the Rabshakeh's message, Hezekiah tore his clothes, donned sackcloth, and went to the temple. But he also sent a small group of influential government and religious leaders to Isaiah with a message. The communication began with a straightforward assessment of the disastrous circumstances: "Thus says Hezekiah," his envoys told the prophet, "'This day is a day of distress, of chastisement, and of contempt'" (37:3a). But this literal statement was followed by a traditional saying, or proverb:[2] "Babes are positioned for birth, but there is no strength to deliver" (vs. 3b; my transl.). "Perhaps," Hezekiah's message continued, "the Lord your God will take note of the words of the Rabshakeh, whom his master the king of Assyria has sent to blaspheme the living God, and will mete out judgment for the words that the Lord your God has heard—if you will offer up prayer for the surviving remnant" (vs. 4; *Tanakh*). Here, at the end of his message, Hezekiah finally has revealed its purpose. He wishes the prophet to offer intercessory prayer to Yahweh on behalf of Jerusalem and its populace, the "surviving remnant" among the Judean cities attacked.

According to Isa 37:5-7, Yahweh responded through the prophet immediately with comforting words of deliverance.

> Do not be afraid because of the words that you have heard, with which the servants of the king of Assyria have reviled me. I myself will put a spirit in him, so that he shall hear a rumor, and return to his own land; I will cause him to fall by the sword in his own land."

HEZEKIAH'S PROVERB

Many commentators have agreed that verse 3b is a proverb. This classification is suggested by the phrase's brevity (just seven words in Hebrew), and by its nicely-crafted binary structure.[3] The first colon, introduced by *kî*, describes an event drawn from everyday human experience:

(kî)	ba'û	banîm	'ad	masber
(because)	have come	babes	to the	birthing position
		[lit. sons]		[lit. breaking]

But a second colon supplies additional, alarming information:

wekoah	'ayin	leledah
but strength	there is not	to deliver[4]

Combined, these two halves become the briefest of narratives, producing the proverb's message.[5]

Crucial for recognizing Hezekiah's proverb *qua* proverb, however, is its out-of-context subject matter. We noted in Chapter 1 that in some other literary context, vs. 3b could be construed literally as the aggrieved king's dramatic and somewhat stylized report of childbirth complications in the royal harem. Given the situation identified in the preceding verses, however, the audience (both Isaiah and our reader) almost certainly will recognize that a literal interpretation of the statement is highly improbable and identify it as a metaphorical proverb.[6]

A MODEL FOR PROVERB ANALYSIS

When a proverb is uttered, P. Seitel explains (1969;[7] see also Fontaine 1982), three separate situations or domains are involved: the one present in the proverb itself when understood *literally*; the domain to which the proverb will be applied; and the one in which the proverb is actually spoken. The following diagram illustrates these three domains:[8]

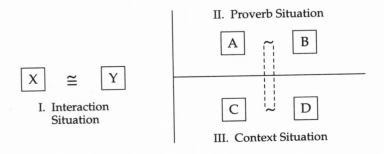

207

According to this model, a proverb speaker (X) asserts to the intended hearer (Y) in an *interaction situation* that the relationship that obtains between persons or entities (A and B) in the *proverb situation* is analogous to the relationship between persons or entities (C and D) in the *context situation* (1977:77). The broken lines connecting the proverb and context situations illustrate the analogous relationship asserted by the speaker to exist between these two domains.

Hezekiah's proverb situation, understood literally, sketches the following scenario: labor has progressed to the point that birth is near, but the mothers-to-be, utterly exhausted by painful and protracted travail, lack the strength needed to push out their babies. These women are not mentioned explicitly in Hezekiah's proverb, but they are implicitly present. (Possibly, the proverb describes the dilemma of a single woman pregnant with two or more babies.)[9]

The context situation for Hezekiah's proverb is the already-identified Assyrian threat against Jerusalem. Its interaction situation, however, is in some ways more difficult to detail. In our text, Hezekiah (X) utters the proverb, and the prophet Isaiah is its intended hearer (Y).[10] The symbol linking X and Y represents the relationship between speaker and hearer including gender, age, and social status (Seitel 1969:147-48). Although Isaiah's precise age in 701 is unknown, he was certainly the elder of the two males. As king of Judah, Hezekiah's status and concomitant authority were presumably second to none among his subjects, be they younger or older. But Isaiah testifies to the prophet's willingness to chastise Judah's monarchs, give them unpopular advice, and even condemn their actions (see, for example, his confrontation with King Ahaz in Isaiah 7). Over against the status and authority of the crown, therefore, readers must weigh the status and authority of the prophet averring to speak for God.

What correlation is Hezekiah making between entities in the proverb and context situations? Our answer to this question is important; for, as Seitel demonstrates, the same proverb, correlated in different ways, can suggest various meanings and perform diverse social functions. What might be the meaning and purpose of verse 3b, for example, if Hezekiah were understood to be identifying Yahweh and members of the divine council (see Isa 6:1-7) with helpless females? In light of the Rabshakeh's accusation that Judah's god is powerless to save Jerusalem, Hezekiah's proverb could be construed as a lamentable admission that Yahweh is indeed unable to rescue the city's inhabitants. Or imagine that Hezekiah employed the proverb in a joyous communication to Isaiah about Judah's victory over a Moabite city. In such a situation, Hezekiah might intend a correlation between Moabite deities and powerless women; and his strategy of proverb usage would be to mock and belittle foreign gods. In its present context, however, neither of these hypothetical correlations pertains. Hezekiah is concerned with Jerusalem's plight, not with some other nation's troubles. Moreover, the king does not believe Yahweh incapable of delivering Jerusalem, as his request that Isaiah pray to God demonstrates.

One could be content simply to say that the correlation is as follows: just as in the proverb situation there is no strength to give birth, so in the context situation there is no strength to repel Assyria.[11] This reading is accurate in the sense that Hezekiah's proverb in fact invites Isaiah (and the reader) to perceive the military crisis through the "lens" of childbirth imagery. We should not let matters rest there, however, for questions immediately arise: Why did the king (or, at least, the author of this narrative) select a proverb about parturition complications when numerous other options surely existed? What is characteristic about unbirthed babies that best captured Jerusalem's plight? And if lack of strength is strategic, then whose powerlessness did Hezekiah emphasize?

It is also possible, however, that instead of correlating crisis to crisis, Hezekiah's proverb correlates entities *within* the respective crisis situations. Imagine, for example, that only one entity in the proverb situation is to be identified with an entity in the context situation—a single correlation proverb (Seitel). In that case, two options would be possible. On the one hand, Hezekiah could be correlating himself and his subjects with *women* incapable of delivering their infants:[12] his proverb then could be understood to emphasize the inability of Jerusalem's inhabitants to rescue themselves from a desperate situation.[13] On the other hand, he could be identifying himself and his subjects with unborn *babes* (i.e., "we are trapped and in danger of death").[14]

If, however, Hezekiah's saying is a proverb in which *two* entities in the proverb situation can be identified with entities in the context situation (a dual correlation proverb, in Seitel's terms), then he might be understood to correlate Jerusalem's inhabitants with endangered babies and himself, along with his advisors, with the helpless women.[15]

We cannot resolve questions of correlation, and of strategy, until we delve more deeply into the proverb situation as understood *within Hezekiah's culture.* This saying is not, after all, a product of our own social and temporal context, and we dare not blithely assume that biblical Israelites would have perceived this proverb situation as we do, or that it would have triggered for them the same intellectual, imaginative, and emotive responses.[16]

ANCIENT NEAR EASTERN REFERENCES TO AN INABILITY TO BRING TO BIRTH

Archaeologists have recovered ancient Near Eastern texts that, like Hezekiah's proverb, refer to inability to bring to birth. A Hittite myth, for example, describes the ruinous results of the god Telepinus' angry abandonment of the land:

> So grain (and) spelt thrive no longer. So cattle, sheep and man no longer breed. And even those with young cannot bring them forth. (Goetze 1969a:126)[17]

Here is presented the same scenario encapsulated in Isa 37:3b, although Hezekiah's saying is a metaphorical proverb, whereas the Hittite myth purports literally to depict barrenness, famine and its consequent weakness, and childbirth difficulties in the wake of Telepinus' departure.

Even more interesting for our purposes is a Middle Assyrian medical text dating, perhaps, from the time of Tiglath-pileser I (*ca.* 1100 BCE; W. G. Lambert 1976:28-39). This text combines four medical prescriptions for treating colic in pregnant women (lines 1-31) with two incantations on behalf of females experiencing difficulty in childbirth (lines 33-50; 51-62). The second incantation rehearses the already-cited myth of Gi-Sin and probably was recited as a woman in labor was anointed with oil and sprinkled with amniotic fluid, in hopes of ensuring an imminent, normal delivery (line 62).

The first incantation reads as follows (Lambert 1976:32):

(33) The woman in childbirth has pangs at delivery,

(34) At delivery she has pangs, the babe is stuck fast,

(35) The babe is stuck fast. The bolt is secure—to bring
life to an end,

(36) The door is made fast—against the suckling kid . . .

(37) The mother is enveloped in the dust of death.

(38) Like a chariot she is enveloped in the dust of battle,

(39) Like a plough she is enveloped in the dust of the woods,

(40) Like a warrior in the fray, she is cast down in her blood.

(41) Her eyes are diminished, she cannot see; her lips are
covered,

(42) She cannot open (them)* the destiny of death and destinies*
her eyes are dim,[18]

(43) . . . ever fears; her ears cannot hear.

(44) Her breast is not . . ., her locks are scattered,

(45) She wears no veil and has no shame.

(46) Be present and . . ., merciful Marduk.

(47) "Now is the battle on, I am surrounded! Reach me!"

(48) Bring forth that sealed-up one, a creation of the gods,

(49) A creation of man. Let him come out to see the light.

(50) Enenuru, an incantation for a woman in childbirth.

In Lambert's view, lines 37-40 have no inherent connection
to labor and delivery and may well have been borrowed from
some prior literary context. Lines 41-43 also lack a specific link
with birth pangs and do not appear in other extant birth incantations. Lines 44-45, he believes, relate even less to their present context; they apparently describe a "shameless woman . . .
breasts bare (?), hair loose and no veil" (36). The corrupt line
46, an appeal to a deity for help, is a common element in such
incantations. Line 47 has a counterpart in another Akkadian
inscription; in this context, Lambert surmises, the line constitutes
the unborn babe's cry for help. Finally, a variation of lines
48-49 appears in the Akkadian inscription containing line 47.

Such a comparative analysis, Lambert concludes, illustrates
"the way in which incantations were being built up from literary
elements and motifs in the period 1500-500 B.C." (1976:37). He
undoubtedly is correct; yet more should be said about this text's
final form, whatever the prehistory of its parts. True, lines 37-40
could describe a mother whose situation was other than the inability to achieve parturition. Here, however, it certainly describes movingly the travailing woman's plight. Moreover, that

she should be likened to a fallen warrior ironically reverses the numerous extrabiblical and biblical texts in which warriors are described pejoratively either as becoming women (e.g., Jer 50:37; Nah. 3:13), or as acting like women, including women in travail (e.g., Jer 49:22; see Hillers 1964:66-68).

References to a woman's diminished senses, disheveled appearance, and lack of shame despite the absence of proper attire, are not inappropriate to a description of prolonged and difficult childbirth, although they could make sense within other literary contexts as well. Particularly poignant, however, is the baby's cry: "Now is the battle on, I am surrounded! Reach me!" Lambert finds the military imagery distasteful. The line, he remarks, "seems to be intended as the cry for help from the babe yet in the womb, whose immaturity ill agrees with the military metaphor" (1976:36).[19] But the infant's cry is not just military imagery. It is siege imagery ("I am surrounded! Reach me!"); and the image of an army or city hemmed in and unable to escape is both powerful and apt for a baby trapped in the birth canal of the nurturing body that suddenly threatens "to bring life to an end."[20] Finally, the climactic lines 48-49 stirringly challenge not only the deity but also the exhausted woman to "bring forth that sealed-up one."[21]

Summary

Our earlier examination of literal and figurative references to labor and delivery in Chapter 3 sheds light on Hezekiah's proverb. From Queen Puduhepa's metaphorical depiction of herself as a travailing woman, we discerned—at least in Hittite culture—the belief that deities attend particularly to petitions of women in labor. In both biblical and extrabiblical texts, labor imagery illumines human psychological and physiological responses to danger, while suppressing thoughts of actual labor's outcome, i.e., the emergence of some new entity. Childbirth imagery, on the other hand, invites readers to particular apperceptions of the genesis of other, less well-understood phenomena, and sometimes highlights the intimate link between progenitrix and offspring.

Our investigation of literal references to certain childbirth complications in Israel's ancient Near Eastern world also has illumined our understanding of Isa 37:3b. Should problems render a mother incapable of expelling her baby, both were in danger of dying. The Telepinus myth linked the inability to bring to birth with the weakness consequent upon famine and brought on by divine anger and abandonment. Hittite and Akkadian midwives sought, through rituals and prayers describing their patients' suffering, to move the deities to pity and intervention on behalf of mother and child. Clearly, the inability to achieve parturition was a religious, as well as a physical, crisis within the ancient Near Eastern world.

But what of figurative references to the inability to bring to birth? Do biblical texts other than Hezekiah's proverb contain such imagery?[22] We shall address this question later in this Chapter. At this point, however, we return to those few Akkadian incantations in which siege imagery was invoked to describe the plight of an infant surrounded by—and trapped inside—its mother's body. Was Hezekiah (and/or the author of this text) familiar with such use of military imagery? And did the threat of a besieged Jerusalem suggest to him that inability-to-bring-to-birth imagery was particularly apt for describing the crisis facing the city's inhabitants? We cannot answer these questions with certainty. For the composers of certain Akkadian texts, however, siege imagery best conveyed a sense of the unborn babe's distress.

Having recovered, at least in part, the range of culturally-defined meanings associated with the inability to achieve parturition in Israel's world, we return to questions of correlation between entities in Hezekiah's proverb and context situations, and of the strategy motivating his proverb performance.

HEZEKIAH'S STRATEGY FOR
PROVERB PERFORMANCE

Earlier, we identified four possible correlations for Hezekiah's proverb that merited serious consideration. First, his saying could suggest that lacking strength to give birth is analogous to lacking strength to repel Assyria. Such an analogy is understood better in light of our analyses of both literal and figurative references to childbirth, for we have gained a better sense of *how a proverb about parturition complications might appear especially appropriate to the military crisis at hand.*

Alternatively, Hezekiah's proverb could be understood to

correlate entities *within* the respective crisis situations. In that case, the following options ensue. On the one hand, we could view Hezekiah's saying as a single correlation proverb in which he identified himself and his subjects either with the helpless women (i.e., "we are powerless to change our desperate situation"),[23] or with their unborn babes (i.e., "we are trapped and in danger of death").[24] On the other hand, it could be construed as a dual correlation proverb in which Hezekiah identified Jerusalem's inhabitants with trapped infants and himself, along with his advisors, with helpless women (i.e., "our babes are stuck fast and we are unable to deliver them").

If one views Isa 37:3b as a single correlation proverb, its import is not altered greatly regardless of the correlation option chosen. Because the lives of both mother and child were threatened by the inability to bring to birth, the proverb's point in either case would be that both Hezekiah and his subjects face imminent death and cannot save themselves. One might argue on the basis of a text like Gen 35:17 (in which the dying Rachel is consoled by her midwife with the words, "Have no fear, for it is another boy for you") that a correlation with the unborn infants would produce the greatest rhetorical effect, since the prospect of losing sons would be regarded as the greater tragedy. If one chooses to view the saying as a single correlation proverb, however, we must concede finally that either correlation is possible.

But what of the possibility that Hezekiah's saying is a dual correlation proverb: the king identifies Jerusalem's inhabitants with the endangered infants ("we are trapped and in danger of death"), and himself, along with his advisors, with the helpless women (i.e., "our babes are stuck fast and we are unable to deliver them")? Is this option the more compelling way for readers to understand Hezekiah's proverb *within its larger Isaian context*? Answering this question requires that we move beyond our investigation of the proverb's possible meanings in Israel's ancient Near Eastern world, and within the narrative world of Isaiah 36–37, to our third task of examining more particularly the proverb's interaction situation—ascertaining the proverb's significance for our reader's assessment of Hezekiah, based upon his sequential reading up to and including Isa 37:3b.

The Strategic Confession
of a Powerless Monarch

Read in isolation from their Isaian context, Isaiah 36–37(38) say much about Hezekiah that is positive.[25] But readers of 36:1–37:4 face questions: Why is Sennacherib destroying Judean cities, and what of his charges and threats? Why must Hezekiah send Isaiah a penitent message culminating in a request for intercessory prayer on behalf of Jerusalem and its inhabitants?

When these chapters are read within their broader Isaian context, however, readers are able to resolve such questions: Sennacherib's initial charge that Hezekiah is relying on Egyptian assistance is understood to mean that Judah's king has violated the prophet Isaiah's frequently voiced opposition to such policies, whereas his claim that Yahweh has ordered Sennacherib to attack Judah's cities must at least be considered in light of sequentially prior assertions that Assyria is the weapon of God's wrath against a sinful nation. Will the reprobate actions of Hezekiah and his advisors lead to Jerusalem's demise? The Rabshakeh's second speech sharpens the issue lying at the heart of these chapters: *Who do you trust? Will you rely on Yahweh, or place your fate in the hands of Assyria's "great king"?* Readers of Isaiah 1–35 already know what the answer *should* be. But how will Hezekiah respond?

> When King Hezekiah heard it, he tore his clothes, covered himself with sackcloth, and went into the house of the Lord. And he sent Eliakim, who was in charge of the palace, and Shebna the secretary, and the senior priests, covered with sackcloth, to the prophet Isaiah son of Amoz. They said to him, "Thus says Hezekiah, 'This day is a day of distress,[26] of chastisement,[27] and of contempt.[28] Babes are positioned for birth, but there is no strength to deliver.'"
>
> (Isa 37:1-3; my transl.)

Understood within its Isaian context, Hezekiah's saying functions as the confession of a now-powerless monarch who, violating the expressed policy of Yahweh's prophet, has chosen willfully to rely on his own strength and that of his allies. Note the proverb's emphasis upon lack of strength (*wekoah 'ayin leledah*). It is not, of course, the babies' lack of strength that is bemoaned. Unlike Hosea (Hos 13:13), Hezekiah does not expect infants to assist in their own deliveries. Neither does he believe that Yahweh lacks the strength to rescue. Rather, the mother's strength is required to push out a baby. And Hezekiah, along with his advisors, bears responsibility for delivering his city and its inhabitants—a task that at this desperate hour he is utterly unable to perform.[29]

But his proverb performance also marks a turning point for Hezekiah, albeit a strategic one intended to maximize the chances that Isaiah, and ultimately Yahweh, will respond favorably despite his past disobedience. At this most crucial moment, Hezekiah—unlike his predecessor, Ahaz—chooses *to repent and trust in Yahweh*. Here is our paradigmatic Hezekiah: he is exemplary not because he never acts contrary to God's wishes, but because at the calamitous moment he does what was called for already in Isa 1:27. He repents. Once the rupture in his relationship with Isaiah and with "Yahweh your God" is repaired through a humble confession of weakness and other acts of contrition (torn clothes, sackcloth, a trek to the temple, Isa 37:1), and he receives Isaiah's positive oracular response (37:5-7), Hezekiah can approach God directly in prayer, without Isaiah's further intercession (37:15-21).

Assuming that the correlations in Hezekiah's proverb are between endangered babes and Jerusalem's inhabitants on the one hand, and the powerless women and Jerusalem's leadership on the other, what can we conclude about Hezekiah's reason for including the saying? This strategic, rhetorical use of a metaphorical proverb functions as both a penitent confession and an invitation to perceive the crisis in a way most likely to move the prophet himself, and ultimately Yahweh (via Isaiah's intercessory prayer), to pity and action on Jerusalem's behalf. "See," Hezekiah is saying, "this city's inhabitants are precious sons—helpless, surrounded, and in deadly peril. Its leaders are powerless women, utterly incapable of delivering either their children or themselves."[30] Hezekiah, the once-rebellious monarch whose international politics stood at odds with Isaiah's prophetic word, now depicts both self and subjects trapped in the most fragile and dangerous of situations. Surely Isaiah and Yahweh will take pity. Surely, in Queen Puduhepa's words, "to a woman in travail the god yields her wish."

ISAIAH 36-37: CONCLUSION

The story told in Isaiah 36–37(38) plays a strategic role in the book of Isaiah as a whole, as scholars such as P. Ackroyd, C. Conrad, and C. Seitz have recognized in recent years. Significant for its function as a bridge between chapters 1–39 and 40–66, it most certainly also drew readers' attention in its own right by virtue of its miraculous denouement. Why and how was Jerusalem saved? According to Sennacherib's own annals, Hezekiah bought Jerusalem's survival at a high price. 2 Kgs 18:13-16 states that Hezekiah saved his city by contritely paying Assyria's king an enormous quantity of silver and gold from the temple and palace treasures. But for readers of the Isaiah scroll, the crisis ends without payment of any tribute. Rather, one-hundred-and-eighty-five thousand Assyrian soldiers are struck down in a single night by the "angel of the Lord"; and the once-proud Sennacherib is forced to return home—a stunning rebuke of the Rabshakeh's claim that trust in Yahweh is folly.

Given the importance of Hezekiah's proverb, both for the monarch's turning from reliance on Egypt to trust in Yahweh alone, and for the crisis that occasions its utterance, we may well ask whether 37:3b influenced other portions of Isaiah's vision as well. Surveying the scroll as a whole, we discover that in two other contexts where trust in God's strength and readiness to deliver are at issue, imagery focussing upon the ability or inability to bring to birth appears.

BRINGING TO BIRTH
IN THE BOOK OF ISAIAH

Striking though it be in his message to the prophet Isaiah, Hezekiah's natal proverb sits comfortably within its broader Isaian context, given the book's plethora of figurative references to children (infants, toddlers, or fully-grown sons and daughters; Chapter 2) and to women (Chapters 3, 4, and 5). Two Isaian texts echo in particularly striking ways the childbirth imagery of Hezekiah's proverb situation: Isa 26:18 and Isa 66:7-9. Considered together (in canonical order), these three texts constitute a recurring, developing motif that transcends the modern-day boundaries of Proto-, Deutero-, and Trito-Isaiah, contributing to the reader's construal of Isaiah as a coherent literary work.

217

Isaiah 26:18

Isaiah 26:18 is part of a lament appearing within Isaiah 24–27, the so-called "Isaian Apocalypse." The chapter begins with an eschatological salvation song celebrating God's final victory on behalf of Israel and its "mighty city," Jerusalem. The liturgical hymn form helps "to bridge the gap between the fears and tensions of the present, in which the final triumph appears remote and improbable, and the certainty of ultimate victory and joy" by drawing the reader "more directly into the confidence of this ultimate victory by drawing forth his own confession of its certainty" (Clements 1980b:211). Rhetorically, therefore, the hymn genre underscores the theme of trust in Yahweh prominent in this text (see especially vs. 4 and, in the preceding chapter, Isa 25:9). We note the contrast in verses 5-6 between Zion, the once-humbled city whose future security Yahweh guarantees,[31] and the ostensibly "secure city" leveled by Israel's God. "In that day," the prophet proclaims:

> this song shall be sung / In the land of Judah:
> Ours is a mighty city; / He makes victory our inner and outer wall.
> Open the gates, and let / A righteous nation enter . . .
> Trust in the Lord for ever and ever,
> For in Yah the Lord you have an everlasting Rock
> For He has brought low those who dwelt high up,
> Has humbled the secure city,
> Humbled it to the ground, / Leveled it with the dust—
> To be trampled underfoot, / By the feet of the needy,
> By the soles of the poor. (Isa 26:1-6; *Tanakh*)

Following this confidence in salvation is a communal lament by persons whose continual suffering threatens to obviate their hope. The lament begins with a confession of trust borne of God's way in the world. Verse 7a, "the path is level for the righteous man," voices (proverbially?) the belief that God smooths life's way for the upright—a common, though not unquestioned, biblical affirmation. But if the righteous receive rewards, so also the wicked should be punished. Should their offenses go unchecked, not only will they continue to do evil, but also God's justice and majesty will appear to be undermined (vs. 10). In verse 11, the lamenters appeal directly to God to destroy their enemies. Verses 12-15 contain expressions of assurance that Yahweh, who is righteous, indeed will intercede on behalf of the oppressed while slaying the wicked.

Verse 16, the beginning of a poetic description of the lamenters' distress, has challenged many a translator. *Tanakh* renders the verse:

> O Lord! In their distress, they sought You;
> Your chastisement reduced them
> To anguished whispered prayer. (*Tanakh*)

Among the difficulties with this translation, however, is the rendering of the noun *lahas* ("incantation, charm") as "prayer,"[32] a meaning it bears nowhere else.[33] Outside Isaiah, *lahas* appears, explicitly associated with snake charming, in Jer 8:17 and Eccl 10:11 (respectively):

> Lo, I will send serpents [*nehasîm*] against you,
> Adders [*sip'onîm*] that cannot be charmed ['*en lahem lahas*],
> And they shall bite you—declares the Lord. (*Tanakh*)

> If the snake [*hannahas*] bites because no spell was uttered [*belo' lahas*], no advantage is gained by the trained charmer.

Skilled charmers (*nebon lahas*) stand among those leaders whose demise Isa 3:3 foretells. In verse 20 of the same chapter, *hallehasîm* ("amulets") appear among various objects Yahweh will strip from the bodies of Jerusalem's upperclass women. The juxtaposition of snakes, symbols of fertility in Israel's ancient Near Eastern world (McCullough 1962:289-91), women (in Isa 3:20), and childbirth imagery (in Isa 26:16-18) is intriguing. Does the latter indeed describe an anguished plea for supernatural assistance, but in a form of address (an incantation) specifically associated with women's pain in childbirth and parturition's attendant rituals? Given our lack of information concerning fertility objects and childbirth practices in ancient Israel, we cannot answer this question with certainty. Nonetheless, the presence of *lahas* in verse 16 suggests that its link with childbirth imagery may be stronger than many contemporary translations suggest.

Verses 17-18 continue with the lamenting community's anguish, employing the discontinuous terms of a woman in travail:

> Like a pregnant woman [*harah*]
>   approaching childbirth [*taqrîb laledet*],
> Who writhes [*tahîl*] and cries out in her pangs [*bahabaleha*],
> So were we before you, O Lord!

We conceived [*harînu*]; we writhed [*halnu*];
We gave birth to nothingness [*yaladnu ruah*].
We accomplished no salvation on earth;
No inhabitants of the world are born. (*Tanakh*)[34]

We noted in Chapter 3 that within Israel's ancient Near Eastern world, travailing woman similes were employed stereotypically to describe the psychological anguish and physiological reactions of persons facing impending doom. Not surprisingly, therefore, verse 17 illumines the speakers' anguish and dismay. But this text differs from previously examined examples of travailing woman similes.[35] Although such tropes normally do not encourage readers to contemplate the birth of anyone (or anything), in this instance the poem moves from a vivid description of maternal pain to delivery's outcome—or in this case, to the lack thereof. By describing itself as a woman in labor, the lamenting community—like the Hittite Queen Puduhepa—undoubtedly intends to appear pitiful, incapacitated, desperately needing divine help. But by its admission in verse 18a, "we gave birth to nothingness" (*ruah*, commonly translated "breath," "wind," or "spirit"), the community also acknowledges its utter inability to bring about sorely-needed salvation. These righteous sufferers have "conceived" and their "labor" is anguished indeed. But they cannot birth "a new thing on earth" (Jer 31:22b). Such an accomplishment lies beyond human resources; only God can perform that task.

In its canonical form, verse 18 is followed by a reference to resurrection. Commentators disagree concerning whether this reference indicates the resurrection of individuals (O. Kaiser 1974:215-20) or the faithful community whose lament it follows. The chapter concludes, at any rate, with instructions and encouragement from an unidentified voice (vs 20; *Tanakh*):

Go, my people, enter your chambers,
And lock your doors behind you.
Hide but a little moment, / Until the indignation passes.

Your suffering is not over, the voice explains, but in just a "little moment," God will initiate a final judgment upon the earth. In the midst of anguish and an overwhelming sense of futility, then, the lamenting community is urged to sing of its trust in Yahweh, to affirm God's dealings with the world, to anticipate the destruction of the wicked and to suffer patiently, expecting divine recompense.

Isaiah 66:1-16

Isaiah 66:1-16, part of the scroll's concluding chapter, is striking both for its divine warrior imagery (and the ultimate undoing of God's enemies) and for its climatic, joyous conclusion to personified Zion's story. The initial oracle begins with the messenger's formula, "Thus says the Lord" (vs. 1)—the poet's claim that not his but Yahweh's words follow—and continues with God's scornful dismissal of an earthly temple.

Because our reader knows that the post-exilic Jewish community erected a new temple in Jerusalem between 520-515 BCE (certainly an auspicious time in the post-exilic community's history), the oracle in Isa 66:1-16 can be linked with that period.[36] Clearly, the author of these verses regards the temple builders of his day as obstacles to, not instruments of, divine will.

The poem then shifts abruptly between affirmation of some ("the poor and brokenhearted, who is concerned about my word") and condemnation of others ("who slaughter oxen and slay humans . . . who offer incense and worship false gods"). These enemies, we learn in verse 5, are Jews ("your kinsmen who hate you"), not foreigners. Perhaps Isa 66:1-16 includes non-Jewish, as well as Jewish, foes among the victims of Yahweh's imminent attack—verses 15-16, for example, contain phrases that elsewhere in Isaiah appear in oracles about God's judgment upon foreign nations. Clearly, however, the traditional division between Israel and the nations has, during the strife of the post-exilic period, become a new division between the wicked and the righteous; and Jews can count members of their own community among Yahweh's enemies.[37]

Now just as the theophany begun in verse 6 and resumed in verses 15-16 describes Yahweh's imminent, ultimate victory over the Lord's foes, so verses 7-14 depict the other side of the coin, i.e., the deliverance awaiting those faithful persons enduring their oppressors' derision. Employing childbirth imagery to describe the future salvation of Jerusalem and her inhabitants, the poet celebrates an event precisely the opposite of Hezekiah's proverb situation in Isa 37:3b:

> Before she writhed [tahîl], she gave birth [yaladah];
> Before her pangs came upon her,
>   she bore [himlîtah][38] a son [zakar].

> Who has heard the like? / Who has seen such things?
> Can a land pass through travail [*yuhal*][39] / In a single day?
> Or is a nation delivered [*yiwwaled*] / All at once?
> Yet Zion travailed [*halah*]
> And at once bore [*yaledah*] her sons [*baneha*]!
> Shall I position for birth [*'asbîr*] but not bring forth?
> —says the Lord.
> Shall I who cause birth [*hammôlîd*] shut [the womb]?
> —says your God. (66:7-9; my transl.)

Here, Jerusalem—not its inhabitants but the city itself—is depicted as a pregnant woman miraculously spared a prolonged, painful, and exhausting labor. Indeed, her children (literally "sons") are born before labor pains begin. Announcement of this astonishing, never-before-witnessed event is followed by two rhetorical questions placed in God's mouth: "Shall I position for birth (*'asbîr*) but not bring forth? Shall I who cause birth shut the womb?" These questions seek to reassure those whose own prolonged suffering at the hands of their foes has forced them to question whether Yahweh is able and trustworthy to act on their behalf. But verse 9a also evokes memory of Hezekiah's proverb, for the verb *'asbîr* ("[Shall] I position for birth?") recalls the reference to *masber* (the birth canal) in Isa 37:3b. Through this "textual echo," readers recall a crucial moment in the past when the Lord miraculously rescued Jerusalem; and they are emboldened to believe that at any moment Yahweh again will act on their city's behalf, bringing salvation to its righteous inhabitants and destruction to their enemies.

Mother Zion escapes the birth pangs that, according to Gen 3:16, have been everywoman's lot since Eve, the first progenitrix. Indeed, hints suggest that Isa 66:1-14 intends to stir thoughts of the first woman's punishment for human rebellion against God. When verses 12-14 depict a new paradisiacal realm featuring streams of prosperity and wealth flowing to Jerusalem, we recall the river that flowed from Eden, dividing to water the entire earth.[40] Moreover, the image of a mother comforting her son—called *'îs* ("man") in verse 13—recalls Eve's remark at the birth of Cain: "I have gained a male child (*'îs*) with the help of the Lord" (Gen 4:1). The noun *'îs* appears hundreds of times in the Hebrew Bible, of course. Its use to refer to an infant or small boy is unusual, however; so its appearance in conjunction with a mother and child in Isa 66:13 further links this text with Eve's story in the minds of readers steeped in their religious traditions.

Note the difference in strategy motivating the use of natal imagery in Hezekiah's proverb performance on the one hand and Isa 66:1-16 on the other. In the former, the metaphorical proverb invites the reader to perceive Jerusalem's plight in a way most likely to move Isaiah, and ultimately Yahweh, to pity and action on the city's behalf. In the latter, the metaphor convinces the reader that God is able and ready—momentarily—to intervene on behalf of the faithful, not only as an avenging warrior utterly destroying enemies but also as a divine midwife overseeing the painless, speedy births of Zion's sons.[41] So confident is the poet of Yahweh's imminent intervention that he speaks as if the deliverance already were accomplished.

Did the author of the childbirth imagery in Isa 66:1-16 compose with Isa 37:3b in mind? Did he intentionally reverse Hezekiah's proverb so that a metaphorical description of a city's desperate situation was transformed into a metaphorical account of its imminent salvation? The answer to this question can never be known with certainty. But our reader brings both Isaiah 26 and 36—37 to his reading of Isa 66:7-9; he knows the story of Jerusalem's miraculous rescue and the destruction of Sennacherib's troops by the Lord's messenger.[42] And lexical correspondence suggests that he will discern within the latter tradition a poetic vehicle by which to convey the tenor of Zion's glorious future. Already we have pointed to the presence of 'asbîr in Isa 66:9 and of masber in Isa 37:3b. Both forms of the root sbr are rare; the verb appears in the Hiphil only at Isa 66:9, and the noun appears only in Hezekiah's proverb and in Hos 13:13. Note, as well, that whereas Isa 66:7b announces the birth of a single male child (zakar), verse 8b proclaims the multiple births of Zion's sons, baneha, employing the same (admittedly common) plural noun appearing in Isa 37:3b.

These observations suggest that the reader of this poetic description of Zion's painless delivery will construe the relationship between entities in Hezekiah's proverb and context situations differently from the four correlation options identified and discussed earlier in this Chapter. Steeped in Isaiah's woman Zion imagery, he may correlate Jerusalem "herself" with the woman lacking strength to bring forth her sons (Isa 37:3b). Isaiah 66:7-9, then, depicts Yahweh's reversal of Jerusalem's earlier proverbial plight. She may lack strength to deliver, but Israel's God does not.

CONCLUSION

In this Chapter, we have scrutinized a childbirth proverb spoken by an important king to a major prophet at a crucial moment on the eve of God's miraculous rescue of Jerusalem and investigated two additional texts in Isaiah containing (in)ability-to-bring-to-birth imagery. Isaiah 26:17-18 begins with a hymnic expression of Zion's strength, enjoining the righteous to trust in Yahweh. But singing gives way to a communal lament in which the supplicants invoke childbirth imagery to describe their pain, despair, and helplessness. In the climactic Isaiah 66:7-9, Jerusalem's redemption is described with imagery opposite the proverb situation in Isa 37:3b. Indeed, because the metaphors in 37:3b and 66:7-9 are two sides of the same coin, their relationship is as close, if not closer, than that between Isaiah 66 and other Isaian texts depicting Zion as both woman and mother.

How, then, does the inability/ability to give birth motif function for competent redactors and readers? It appears first in a description of desperate, helpless human beings who care deeply about Jerusalem and who struggle to trust in Yahweh in the face of anguish and their own failure to bring about salvation (26:18). Their lament is not answered immediately, and their suffering continues. They are, however, assured of deliverance, urged to trust God, and encouraged to be patient. The motif reappears in a pivotal text about a specific, crucial, and memorable crisis wherein the inability-to-bring-to-birth metaphor, expressed proverbially, elicits from Isaiah an intercessory prayer leading to Jerusalem's miraculous deliverance—clearly demonstrating Yahweh's power and trustworthiness and stunningly refuting the Rabshakeh's blasphemous words. Finally, it appears in an announced demonstration of Yahweh's ability to deliver Zion, bringing forth her sons so quickly and painlessly that the world is astonished. Once a widow bereaved of her children, Zion will raise her offspring in a new paradisiacal age—a fitting fate for the beloved bride of Isaiah 62.

CONCLUSION

The book of Isaiah testifies to faith in tension with history, to forgiveness in the face of culpability, to wrestlings with questions admitting no easy answers, even if they are God's answers, and to hope in the midst of oppression, frustration, disappointment, and death. Without apology, it steadfastly asserts that all creation and all of history are firmly under Yahweh's control, and that obdurate humans must bear punishment for their transgressions. But it also insists that God can abrogate even the divine plan itself, so that forgiveness and grace abound.

Books have been written on numerous Isaiah-related topics receiving nary a sentence in this study. Isaiah's vision is too complex, multifaceted, and rich ever to be summarized in a single work, regardless of its length. I have intended to identify and trace two significant Isaian themes—the book's rhetoric of rebellion, and the ultimate status of Jerusalem and her rivals—concentrating especially upon the contributions of child and female tropes to those themes. Performing that task, however, I have discerned one of the vision's essential affirmations: Israel faces a choice—ongoing rebellion against its God, or penitence and obedience to Yahweh's teaching. Those in Zion who repent of Israel's rebelliousness and live according to the divine will joyfully anticipate the ultimate fulfillment of Yahweh's plan. Those persisting in rebellion against God face fiery destruction. The reader must decide between these two options, but the text does not set forth his choices in unbiased terms. Rather it seeks, through various rhetorical strategies, to align readers with those who confess, lament, and praise, awaiting the fulfillment of the unfolding prophetic vision within which they and history are moving.

Reader-oriented methodologies have yet to make significant inroads into studies of Israel's prophetic literature. Too often, such methods are set up as a "straw man" and then dismissed with so unreflective a comment as "it would take four hours to listen to Isaiah in its entirety. Who could remain attentive for that long?" But the literature itself suggests, through myriad features identified in this study, that certain readers undertook sequential readings of even extensive prophetic works. Consider, in addition to Isaiah, the book of Ezekiel, where prophecies correlate with historical events, presented in chronologically sequential order and marked by a string of sequential dates. J. A. Darr's reader-oriented approach has served us well, though we have introduced an innovation: our reader, part of Israel's cognoscenti, *presumes* to read in ways and at a level unavailable to the majority of his contemporaries.

In its intention to persuade, Israel's prophetic literature takes second seat to no other. Repeatedly, I have asked how our familial model and selected metaphors enabled attempts (by authors and redactors) to persuade readers to particular perceptions of reality. Our understanding of how metaphors and related tropes "mean" and function requires that we take figurative uses of language seriously—in our case, female and child tropes. In the course of investigating such imagery, we have found that scholars too often seek to "get at" the meaning *around* or *in spite of* the medium. But our approach demonstrates the benefits of recognizing that the medium and the message are inextricable: we cannot grasp one without the other. In Chapter 3, for example, we discovered that a stereotypical simile, put to other purposes, functioned not as an expression of human weakness, but rather as an image of divine power. In Chapter 6, an ancient myth about woman's lot in childbirth was reversed as well, such that an *end* to the punishing pain instituted with the loss of paradise became a *prelude* to paradise returned. We cannot know whether these uses already were part of our reader's extratextual repertoire. They are unique, however, within our Hebrew Bibles.

In Chapter 2, we not only specified certain ancient Israelite associations with offspring, but also traced a larger and important theme, Isaiah's rhetoric of rebellion, wherein child imagery plays a significant role. In Chapter 3, we identified pervasive, if sometimes inaccurate, associated commonplaces with women. These, in turn, informed our investigation (Chapters 4 and 5) of the Isian "ladies' lots" theme. Jerusalem's experiences and prospects are certainly at issue throughout Isaiah, and not just in chapters 40–66. But Zion's relations with Yahweh and Israel are not the only concerns this theme addresses. Her international relations with rivals are of central importance as well. Some scholars would lift up Isaiah as an example of biblical universalism. In our study, however, we have been impressed by Isaiah's emphasis upon Jerusalem's exaltation over the nations. Peoples who serve her and her God have a place in that future. But those that will not have none, as Isa 60:12 clearly states:

> For the nation and kingdom that will not serve you shall perish; those nations shall be utterly laid waste. (60:12)

This verse, be it poetry, or prose (as many commentators suggest), forthrightly articulates a pervasive perspective in Isaiah's ladies' lots theme. Indeed, I have noted that elsewhere, other Isaian texts conventionally labeled "later supplements" or "prosaic additions" succinctly encapsulate aspects of both our themes. They should, therefore, draw intense interest not only from reader-oriented critics, but also from redaction critics interested in how Isaiah's final redactors interpreted the material before them.

Finally, we examined a neglected, but crucially-placed proverb performance in the Hezekiah-Isaiah narratives to determine its meaning, function, and significance not only for its specific setting, but also for evaluating Hezekiah's role in Isaiah 1–39. Beyond that task, we noted two additional texts—one sequentially earlier (Isaiah 26), the other later (Isaiah 66), related to Hezekiah's inability-to-bring-to-birth imagery. These texts, too, contribute to the reader's construal of Isaiah as a cohesive literary work.

Taking seriously the rhetorical nature of language, and especially figurative uses of language, immeasurably enriches our reading of all Israel's prophetic literature, including Isaiah. An historically-informed, reader-oriented approach reveals otherwise obscured aspects of Isaiah's unfolding meaning and message. In adopting this approach, of course, I have not intended to supplant historical-critical methods. Rather, I have pursued yet another way of responding to the command, "Read this [scroll]" (Isa 29:11-12).

NOTES

NOTES TO CHAPTER 1:
READING ISAIAN METAPHORS

[1] Unless otherwise indicated, "Isaiah," "Isaian," and "Isaianic" refer to the book of Isaiah rather than to the eighth-century prophet.

[2] M. A. Tolbert notes the persistence in New Testament studies of the "quest of the historical Jesus": "If the authors of biblical books speak with many voices and diverse points of view, surely Jesus himself spoke with only *one*. . . . The singular, authoritative Word of God is restored to modern Protestantism by seeking the singular, authoritative voice of the historical Jesus" (1989:11-12). We suggest that an analogous phenomenon explains, in part, scholars' preoccupation with the prophets' original words. If the rise of critical biblical scholarship took away with one hand traditional beliefs about the (ultimately divine) origins of *all* the Bible's prophetic literature, it gave back with the other the possibility of identifying the actual oracles of the divinely-inspired prophets.

[3] Even E. Conrad, whose critique of historical criticism is particularly sharp at points, concedes that his own reading reflects "the wealth of scholarship that the historical critical reading of Isaiah represents" (1991:1). His diachronic analysis of "fear not" oracles (1985), for example, is crucial to his discussion of Isaiah's royal narratives (1991:34-51).

[4] Such assertions run counter to the theories of many early proponents of multiple Isaian authorship. R. Pfeiffer, e.g., could confidently claim that Isaiah 40—66 found its place in the book of Isaiah only because "sufficient space remained on the scroll" after Isaiah 1—39 had been copied (1941:447-48). His extreme view has not commended itself generally, even among scholars insisting upon the original (and, in the case of Proto-Isaiah, long-lived) independence of one or more of the scroll's major sections.

[5] More extensive summaries of scholarship appear in B. Childs (1979:316-325), M. Sweeney (1988:1-25), and R. Rendtorff (1984; 1991b).

[6] Rendtorff concedes that distinguishing between these two approaches in this way risks oversimplification, since some scholars retain interest in both diachronic and synchronic analyses (1991:22-23).

[7] These critics further divide into two sub-groups: those who believe that originally independent sections of Isaiah came together

only *late* in the scroll's history of composition and "for reasons that are unclear or accidental" (Seitz 1991:15); and those believing that much earlier in its history, two or more of Isaiah's major sections were shaped in relation to each other, and so must be interpreted within the literary context of the book as a whole. C. Seitz further distinguishes between those of the latter group who separate the origin and development of the First Isaian corpus from that of Isaiah 40—55 and 56—66, "even as the search for redactional unity proceeds," and those who admit the redactional "merger" of two or more sections. But Seitz acknowledges that these three approaches in Isaiah studies "are frequently unrelated, mutually inconsistent, or even at odds with each other" (1991:14; and see further 14-30).

[8] On efforts to trace Isaiah's diachronic development see Sweeney (1988:1-25) and C. Seitz (1988:13-22, 105-26; 1991:1-35).

[9] As we shall see, e.g., the intimate relationship between the first four chapters of Isaiah's vision on the one hand, and Isaiah 56—66 on the other, suggests that these earliest chapters were at least constructed, and perhaps composed, with the latest chapters fully in mind.

[10] Conrad carefully notes that the term "objective" does *not* carry a claim of utter objectivity (1991:29).

[11] Hence, we focus not only upon certain traditionally-cited structures and transitional texts in Isaiah but also upon patterns that may only become visible during a sequential reading focused especially upon our recurring tropes.

[12] Like Darr, I concur with M. H. Abrams (1977:426) that "literary works are intentional (that is, they do function rhetorically, and such functions can be ascertained with a certain degree of empirical surety)." I respond to S. Fish's question, "Is there a text in this class?" with a resounding "yes"; and features of that text both abet and constrain readers' interpretations of it. Nonetheless, a text only becomes fully a "coherent literary work" as its potential for coherence is actualized by the reader in dialogue with text and "extratext."

[13] In referring to rhetoric, I mean the many ways poetic texts manipulate and attempt to persuade their readers, rather than formal codifications of rhetorical speech as outlined in ancient Greek and Roman rhetorical handbooks. Of course, there are points of similarity between the two.

[14] Obviously, this third lens is of primary importance for P. Miscall's synchronic readings of Isaiah, described above.

[15] I place our reader at 400 BCE for at least two reasons: first, this is a likely, though not universally-accepted, date by which to posit Isaiah's existence in its final form. Second, it enables us to avoid wrestling with Hellenism's considerable influence upon Israel's long-lived conventional ideas regarding children and women (see T. Frymer-Kensky 1992:203-212).

[16] My use of the masculine pronoun is intentional. We know, of

course, that women were trained as scribes in ancient Mesopotamia, especially (though not exclusively) the *naditu* women in Old Babylonian Sippar; and I do not reject out of hand the possibility that Israelite women also functioned as scribes during at least some periods in Israel's history. With the monarchy's demise, however, two institutions most likely to train and support female scribes—the harem and the queen mother—ended in Israel. It seems wise, therefore, to image our reader as male. Moreover, I discover little in Isaiah's child and female imagery to support arguments for female authorship of passages containing such tropes. The presence of female imagery—even in diverse and copious amounts—does not necessarily prove (or, for that matter, disprove) female authorship. Much less should we expect to detect a "feminist" trajectory within our texts. One can plausibly speculate that women's associations with both children and females could differ from men's in significant ways. But such speculation does not lead inevitably to the conclusion that women's uses of female and child imagery were always, or even often, innovative. Rather, Isaiah's familial tropes presupposed and reenforced traditional relationships, structures, and values within ancient Israel's society.

[17] Scrolls are themselves more sequential than books. One cannot simply flip a scroll open to the appropriate "page." To the contrary, one must unroll it sequentially, even if the goal is a particular pericope near the end.

[18] Indeed, it would be flatly impossible in the scope of my study to specify—much less to follow—all textual features readers will identify, interpret, trace, and perhaps reassess as their dialectic with the text progresses. In this context I trace reader reaction to only two kinds of recurring tropes—child imagery and female imagery—though their reading of relevant texts is thoroughly contextual. Nevertheless, methodological and theoretical models set forth in this chapter can illumine other recurring Isaian metaphors.

[19] These and other textual features also betray the expectation that *at least certain readers* would read Isaiah sequentially.

[20] J. Barton finds the same phenomena at work in early New Testament times: "for people in our period, . . . genre is not a central concern in reading Scripture" (1988:148).

[21] In *Oracles of God* (1988:149-50), Barton dismisses the notion of sequential readers of Isaiah and other biblical books. His arguments are scarcely convincing, however. First, they rest upon the presupposition that all ancient readers would have read Isaiah *in exactly the same way*. Yet Isaiah's perpetuators and promulgators surely presumed different levels of reading competency among their contemporaries. Laypersons might never expect to read or hear Isaiah from beginning to end, but that does not mean that no one else could or would. Second, Barton's assertion that Isaiah would not have been perceived in New Testament times as a "closed, unitary whole," ignores the

book's obviously chiastic structure, which strongly suggests a work edited as a whole (see Alonso Schökel 1988:192). Third, Barton's claim that Isaiah was read as "a collection of fragments . . . in which every pericope, indeed every sentence or even every word, had a meaning independent of its context," describes only a single hermeneutical method, one associated especially with the *rabbis*. Yet the rabbis did not limit themselves to a *single* way of reading and interpreting scripture. To the contrary, the reading strategy Barton ascribes (anachronistically?) to the earliest New Testament period constituted but one of many approaches the rabbis used to discover in the texts to hand a host of different levels of meaning (M. Fishbane 1982:91-110). These points, plus the text's many coordinating features, strongly indicate that readings other than a fragmented, pericopal reading of Isaiah were possible.

[22] Soskice extensively discusses the importance of models for generating metaphors (1985:50): "Our suggestion is that model and metaphor are closely linked; when we use a model, we regard one thing or state of affairs in terms of another, and when we use a metaphor, we speak of one thing or state of affairs in language suggestive of another. This close association of model and metaphor is important not only for explaining how metaphors work but for explaining why metaphors can be so useful" (1985:150-51). A familial model, e.g., generates numerous metaphors: God the Father; Jerusalem the maiden and wife of God; Israel as the children of God and of Zion, their mother, etc.

[23] The situation differs in New Testament studies, owing to keen interest in the parables of Jesus.

[24] Helpful discussion appears in Soskice (24-53), P. Macky (1990:31-56), and especially M. Johnson (1981:3-47).

[25] Soskice quotes, e.g., from V. Woolf's metaphorical description of Mrs. Ramsay in *To the Lighthouse*: "Never did anybody look so sad. Bitter and black, half-way down, in the darkness, in the shaft which ran from the sunlight to the depths, perhaps a tear formed; a tear fell; the waters swayed this way and that, received it, and were at rest. Never did anybody look so sad" (Woolf 1938:32-33). Woolf's metaphor certainly brings together associations from more than a single entity. But what is being described, Soskice notes, "is not both a private grief *and* a shaft of some kind but simply some private, sickening grief" (47).

[26] Because both synecdoche and metonymy operate within a single domain, however, there is no guarantee that either will be "felt" (Sapir 1977:14).

[27] Obviously, we cannot know all the webs of culturally-conditioned commonplaces surrounding terms in an ancient metaphorical utterance; our resource, the extant literature, is surely but part of a once-larger corpus. Ostensibly novel texts—like Jer 31:22b, "For the

Lord has created a new thing on the earth: a woman encompasses a man"—flaunt our efforts at interpretation. Imagine how much more difficult our task would be, however, had innovation been prized most highly by Israel's poets.

[28] Despite differences between symbols and metaphors, much of what one can say about ancient Israel's recurring metaphors appears precisely in Wheelwright's discussions of symbols.

[29] Soskice points to the importance of recovering associated commonplaces surrounding terms in a metaphorical utterance when she invites her readers to consider "the cognitive significance of 'kingship' to a people whose history was that of Israel and compare this with the flaccid notions the modern reader is likely to associate with the term" (1985:108).

[30] Quoting C. D. Lewis (1947:72).

NOTES TO CHAPTER 2:
CHILD IMAGERY AND THE RHETORIC OF REBELLION

[1] Before Immanuel knows how to reject bad (or "sour") and choose good (or "sweet"), the lands of Rezin and Pekah will be depopulated (Isa 7:15-16). Before Maher-shalal-hash-baz can say "Daddy" and "Mommy," both Damascus and Samaria will be plundered by Assyria (Isa 8:4). See M. L. Gruber (1989:68-69).

[2] S. B. Pomeroy states that "no known society positively prefers girl babies to boys" (1983:208; citing Dickemann 1979:321-67). All known biblical and extra-biblical examples of the birth announcement concern the birth of a male infant (S. Parker 1989:67-68). Daughters had a place within the ideal ancient Near Eastern family, of course. Both biblical and extra-biblical texts depict seven sons and three daughters as the perfect complement (e.g., Job, *CTA* 3.3.3-4; Coogan 1990:137). J. Pringle (1983:132) notes Hittite midwives' even-handed responses to the births of both male and female infants: "If a boy were born, the Midwife in B gave him the 'goods of a male child,' saying, 'Let a female child be born in a year forth.' If a girl were born, there was the same procedure in reverse, 'the goods of a female child,' saying 'Let a male child be born in a year forth.'"

[3] See also Deut 4:9-10; 11:19; 31:12-13; Josh 4:6-7; Ps 78:4; and W. Brueggemann (1982:14-39).

[4] NRSV and *Tanakh* follow MT. However, LXX reads *nosîm*, "creditors," understanding the line to mean, "O my people, your exactors strip you, and creditors rule over you."

[5] Translation of verse 10 is difficult: some have suggested that the repeated monosyllables are meant to imitate childish prattle, so attempts to arrive at a meaningful translation are ill-conceived.

[6] 2 Macc 7:27 suggests that children were weaned at approximately three years of age. See also the "Instruction of Any" (Robins 1989:114): "When you were born after your months, [your mother]

was yet yoked to you, her breast in your mouth for three years."

[7] Limited studies of ancient Palestinian burial sites have revealed that thirty-five percent of those interred had perished before the age of five years; almost half had not lived to be eighteen (Meyers 1988:112).

[8] Hence, one recoils in horror at the prospect of such a fate befalling one's own people (e.g., 2 Kgs 8:12), but may express grizzly glee in anticipation of just such injury against the dependents of one's enemies (see Ps 137:9 and Nah 3:10).

[9] S. B. Parker argues persuasively that though Isa 9:5 announces a royal birth, the birth announcement (with the basic, but adaptable, pattern yld bn l + pronominal suffix) was not limited to court settings. Rather, it was used more broadly to announce the birth of a (male) child to its father, and then to other family members and friends who would rejoice at news of the nativity (1989:64-65).

[10] Many commentators identify Isa 8:23—9:6 (ET Isa 9:1-7) as an accession oracle, rather than as the announcement of a recent or anticipated royal birth. They point to Ps 2:7 ("the Lord said to me, 'You are my son, I have fathered you [yelidtîka] this day'") and Ps 89:27-28 ("He shall say to me, 'You are my father, my God, the rock of my deliverance.' I will appoint him first-born, highest of the kings of the earth"; see also 2 Sam 7:14). It is true that both enthronement psalms refer to the Davidic king as God's (adopted) son. But significant differences distinguish them from Isa 9:5. The speaker is different; and the emphasis of the begetting imagery and familial metaphors is, in the psalms, on the intimate linking of deity and king, whereas in Isa 9:5 it is on the great joy elicited by the announced birth of a royal child. Both H. Wildberger (1972:379-80) and S. Parker (1988:136-138) conclude that Isa 9:5 is the birth announcement of a royal heir.

[11] C. Cohen (1973:75-81) shows that a "widow" metaphor was used of once-independent cities that had become the vassals of other states. On cities personified as females, see Chapters 4 and 5 below.

[12] In addition to the two texts cited below, note Isa 60:4. Jerusalem herself is depicted as a nursling in Isa 60:16.

[13] On links between Isaiah 66 and the opening chapters of Genesis, see Chapter 6 below.

[14] A Ugaritic text (van Selms 1954:100) describes a son's obligations to his father—e.g., guiding him home when the latter is drunk, plastering his leaking roof, and washing his soiled clothes. The Egyptian "Instruction of Any" (Robins 1989:114) teaches Egyptian youths how and why they must respect their aging mothers: "Double the food your mother gave you, support her as she supported you; she had a heavy load in you, but she did not abandon you. . . . As you grew and your excrement disgusted, she was not disgusted, saying 'What shall I do!' When she sent you to school, and you were taught to write, she kept watching over you daily, with bread and beer in her house." A Sumerian proverb (Gordon 1959:485-86) bemoans the fate of an ideal

mother who experiences poverty, despite seven grown sons, the perfect number: such a mother ought to be economically secure.

[15] Examining eight familial and sex crimes that carry the death penalty in Deuteronomy, L. Stulman (1992:47-63) concludes that "D is in the process of limiting the fringe powers vested in the paterfamilias and consolidating those powers in regional tribunals under commmunity/ state authority" (63).

[16] Kugel (1981:291) cites Isa 1:4 to make his point that "the second clause always adds something to the first clause paired with it, such as 'Ah, sinning nation,' (and more than this) 'people heavy with transgression,' (and more than this they are a) 'family of evil-doers,' (and more than this they are) 'wicked children' (and more than this that they) 'abandoned the Lord,' and so forth." Note, too, that as the sense of sinfulness is expanded, the subjects—nation, people, family, wicked children—become, in one sense or another, smaller.

[17] "Here [vs. 9], the thought is not that a spiritual remnant has been spared from destruction because its members have repented and turned back to God. Just the opposite is true. The remnant is just as sinful and deserving of punishment as those who have already been overthrown" (Willis 1985:165).

[18] Here, the "children" speak in the first person plural, acknowledging that their survival is strictly due to Yahweh's forebearance. On the significance of such first person plural forms for Isaiah as a whole, see Conrad (1991:83-116). He argues that Isaiah's implied audience, hearing the scroll performed orally, identifies with the surviving "we" of 1:9-10, 2:5; 16:6; 17:14; 32:15; 33:2, 21-22; 42:24; and 47:4.

[19] Yahweh's "plan" for Israel and the nations is an important, recurring concern in Isaiah (see further Chapter 4 below; also, e.g., Jensen 1986:443-55; Conrad (1991:52-82).

[20] Isa 40:1-11 is significant not for its shift in tone, to which our reader is well-accustomed, but rather for its ambiguity. Will our reader construe this material as a return to the divine council whence the prophet received his initial commission (6:1-13)? That commission was to persist until cities, houses, and lands lay desolate (6:11). Isaiah 40:1-11, by contrast, focuses upon the certainty of God's word of hope for Jerusalem, but also on a "second chance" for all Israel, including its persistently sinful leadership. The reader does not rule out Isaiah as the speaker in 40:6 (against Conrad 1991:118). To the contrary, Isaiah's ability to address times and experiences beyond his own lifetime is well-established by this point in the scroll.

[21] Early rabbinical interpreters clearly were loath to implement Deut 21:18-21 in any but the most extreme and specific cases. Their hermeneutic of leniency led them to limit the law's applicability by claiming, e.g., that it pertained to males, but not to females, to boys, but not to adults, and only to sons who were at least thirteen years and a day of age, since male children were not required to observe the

commandments until they had attained that milestone.

22 An example of rhetorical irony (Alonso Schökel 1988:157-58): "This really means: you do not have to remind me, I know it already, and do not think you will be able to justify yourself and be absolved."

23 NRSV: "and your interpreters transgressed against me."

24 If, by "these things," is meant what has preceded this verse, then Israel is encouraged to remember the web of themes spun out thus far, including affirmations that Yahweh is its creator from the womb (44:2), its source of life, blessing, and fertility (44:3), and the incomparable God whose control of history is so complete (44:6-8) that worshipping any other deity is pure folly (44:9-20).

25 Note the reappearance of metallurgy imagery, first introduced in Isaiah 1:22-25. We shall return to this text in Chapter 5.

26 Reading 'arîs with the LXX and 1QIsª; MT has saddîq.

27 R. N. Whybray speaks of "the 'children' of the erring 'mother'" (1975:148). In this poem, however, Zion is not an erring mother. Rather, she is the victim of her children's disobedience, and suffers for their sins.

28 E. Conrad (1991:147) notes "a movement toward pluraliza- tion that represents a movement also toward disintegration and diversi- ty. . . . The Lord's reference to the community as 'servant' and 'chosen one' eventually becomes pluralized to 'servants' (54:17; 65:8, 9, 14, 15; 66:14) and 'chosen ones' (65:9, 15, 22)."

29 Almost from the outset, the reader of Isaiah has experienced sudden and dramatic shifts from words of judgment to promises of salvation for both Israel and the nations (see, e.g., Isaiah 19, in which Egypt is both threatened with harsh servitude and blessed as the people of Yahweh). In these latter chapters, readers recognize that such sudden shifts in tone are, in a sense, mimetic of the sudden shifts in circumstances (e.g., 4:2; 10:25; 29:5-6; 60:22b) with which Yahweh encourages the faithful and threatens the wicked.

30 Some commentators emend MT mena'ep to mena'epet so that this form, too, is feminine.

31 Literally, "she acts the harlot."

32 This obviously offensive gesture is, within modern American culture, both regarded as childish and associated with children. Whether such was the case in ancient Israel cannot be known. Psalm 35:21 refers to (adult) males opening their mouths wide, but says nothing about a protruding tongue.

33 Sorceresses were regarded by the biblical authors as illicit practitioners of magic (Deut 18:10-11; Jer 27:9; Ezek 13:17-23; Isa 47:9-13). Adultery and harlotry, both aberrations of socially-sanctioned conjugal activity within marriage, also were well-established metaphors for illegitimate religious and political activities, as we shall see.

34 In the following verses, these leaders are personified as a woman whose "harlotries," stereotypically, are international activities

and idolatry. Such activity will be useless, however, for her idols will be blown away. Only those who take refuge in Yahweh will "inherit my holy mountain" (57:13). We shall return to this text with its harlotry imagery in our Chapter 5.

[35] Forms of *ps'* and *ht'*, first paired in Isa 1:28, appear in synonymous parallelism in 43:24, 25, 27; 44:22; 53:12; 58:1; and 59:12.

[36] Elsewhere in Isaiah, *khs* apears only in the charge that the people of Israel are "faithless children" (*banîm kehasîm*; 30:9).

[37] The same word appears in Isa 1:5, part of Isaiah's indictment of Yahweh's rebellious children.

[38] *Tanakh* has "and uttering them with the throat."

[39] For recent discussions of this lament, see E. C. Webster (1990: 89-102), R. J. Clifford (1989:93-102), and C. C. Broyles (1989).

[40] So P. Hanson (1975:92-93). In Mic 7:20, the names of certain of Israel's patriarchs apparently refer to the contemporary community: "You will keep faith with Jacob, loyalty to Abraham, as you promised on oath to our fathers in days gone by." See also Isa 51:1-3, where Abraham and Sarah are presented as the ancestral couple whence descended all Israel.

[41] M. S. Odell (1991:217-33) examines prayers of the Babylonian Ersahunga genre, "a prime example of the expression of the individual's trust in his god despite that god's apparent absence" and finds the supplicant using familial imagery in appeals to his god: "May thy heart like the heart of a child-bearing mother return to its place, like a child-bearing mother, like a begetting father, return to its place" (225).

[42] In addition to the following, see also Isa 41:25.

[43] After completion of this chapter I discovered that R. J. Clifford has also glimpsed the significance of Isaiah 60–62, the description of Zion's glorification (see below, our Chapter 5), and the laments that both precede and follow it: "[Isaiah 60–62] are the middle of a vast chiasm: lament (59:1-19) + entry of Yahweh into the city (59:20/60–62/entry (63:1-6 + lament (63:7–64:12). The chiasm seems to say that glorification of the city, i.e., the entrance of Yahweh into it, can only come about through judgment and repentance"(1993:16). I would rather say that, in response to the true confessions and laments of rebelliousness by Yahweh's children, the way is paved for Yahweh, the divine warrior, fully to enact God's world-wide plan, bringing salvation to all those in Zion who repent (including foreigners and eunuchs), while utterly destroying persistent rebels.

[44] In 62:1, the same word (*hsh*) appears in the prophet's avowal *not* to keep silent.

[45] So P. Hanson (1975:179-80) and, cautiously, C. Westermann (1969:413-14).

[46] See Chapter 6 below. By describing the "deliverance" of Jerusalem's children prior to the destruction of rebels, Isaiah 66 honors the order of events presaged in Isa 1:27-28.

NOTES TO CHAPTER 3:
THE WAYS WOMEN ARE

[1] T. Frymer-Kensky (1992a) insists that, "there is nothing distinctively 'female' about the way that women are portrayed in the Bible, nothing particularly feminine about either their goals or their strategies. The goals of women are the same goals held by the biblical male characters and the authors of the stories." Her assertion notwithstanding, an additional comment requires modification. She states that "the Bible presents no characterisitics of human behavior as 'female' or 'male,' no division of attributes between the poles of 'feminine' and 'masculine'" (14). As we shall see, however, the Bible does betray a variety of stereotypical associations surrounding women, their experiences and behaviors. Were there no differences between certain widely-held associations with women and men, a phrase like "On that day the Egyptians will be like women" (Isa 19:16a) would be meaningless.

[2] Mesopotamian women, J.-J. Glassner writes, "are mainly identified . . . as belonging to someone else, subordinate to their father, husband and children respectively. This is clearly seen in the way they are referred to by the scribes, who usually omit to mention the women's proper name preferring to call her **dam** PN, 'wife of so-and-so.'" (1989:82). The Bible contains stories of extraordinary women, and of everyday women caught in extraordinary situations. But the gist of Glassner's remark is as true for most biblical women as it is of Mesopotamian women.

[3] "[S]ince the overarching and integrating institutions of the society (in particular, legal and religious institutions) . . . belong to the public sphere and are designed and governed by men, the values they articulate and seek to impose are essentially male values, although formulated as 'general' rules and norms" (Bird 19891:290). While Frymer-Kensky's remarks concerning the nonpresence in public life of the goddess Uttu, who "mirrors and models the life of a Sumerian wife," cannot simply be applied to ancient Israelite women, they strike a congruent chord (1992a:24). Modeling by a female deity is not simply descriptive, she observes, but also prescriptive: "On the one hand, divine modeling for women's family roles gives women esteem within these roles so that these roles become a source of self-satisfaction and nourishment. On the other hand, this same divine modeling makes cultural attitudes and stereotypes part of the realm of the sacred, lending powerful support to these attitudes and inhibiting change." Through their depictions of women's experiences, actions, and roles, and through their uses of female imagery, the creators of ancient Israel's laws, narratives, poems, and proverbs commended certain roles and activities for women, while condemning others.

[4] The Egyptian "Instruction of Any" urges young men to allow their wives some freedom running the household (Robins 1989:114):

> Do not control your wife in her house, when you know she is efficient; don't say to her: "Where is it? Get it!" When she has put it in the right place. Let your eye observe in silence, that you may recognize her skill; it is a joy when your hand is with her, there are many who don't know this.

That such instruction was needed suggests that Egyptian men also exercised (prudently, the Instruction of Any urged) final authority within the domestic sphere.

[5] C. Meyers correctly warns against anachronistically reading later attitudes toward women into earlier periods of Israel's history (in 1989:265-278). Yet her identification of women's considerable contributions to pre-monarchical society does not inevitably support the contention that women and men shared equal power and status. Women can do extraordinary amounts of work and still be regarded as inferior to males.

[6] See P. Bird (1989a:291) and T. Frymer-Kensky (1992a:120). So also Meyers: "anthropologists have pointed out that formal rights may favor males but that daily informal interaction may exhibit a 'balance of gender power' or even some signs or areas of female dominance" (1989:268-69).

[7] According to Ezek 16:9-14, Yahweh extravagantly fulfills the obligation to provide his wife, personified Jerusalem, with food, oil, and clothing. In Hosea 2, adulteress Israel mistakenly credits her "lovers" with bestowing Yahweh's gifts of bread, water, wool, flax, oil, and drink (vss. 5-9).

[8] See also Jer 8:10 and Job 31:10. D. R. Hillers (1964:63) quotes a curse from the Esarhaddon Treaty (428-29): "May Venus, the brightest of the stars, make your spouses lie in the lap of your enemy before your eyes."

[9] S. Rollin refers to the plight of foreign women who, as a result of military campaigns, found themselves in Mesopotamia, forced to live as slaves, beggars, or prostitutes (1983:37).

[10] Of course wealth could afford women a greater degree of freedom and authority than poor women—and even poor men—enjoyed.

[11] Reading with LXX; MT has "low."

[12] NRSV understands *pot* in light of 1 Kgs 7:50, where it refers to the sockets in the lintel and threshold upon which the inner doors of the temple turn.

[13] In Ezek 16:50, personified Sodom and her daughters are accused of haughtiness (*wattigbehênah*).

[14] See also Prov 21:9 and 25:24.

[15] A Sumerian proverb suggests that young females were regarded as less aggressive than young males: "A chattering maiden—her mother has silenced her; / A chattering young man—his mother could not silence him as well!" (Gordon 1959:139).

[16] See, e.g., P. Trible (1978:166-199); R. Weems (1988); K. P.

Darr (1991); S. A. White (1989:161-77); T. Craven (1983); C. Camp (1981:14-29; 1985); and T. Frymer-Kensky's strong, balanced discussion of the successful rhetorical strategies employed by female biblical characters (1992a:128-40).

[17] Note the feminine singular suffixes in these two verses. The referent for these pronouns is the city.

[18] Outside Isaiah, plant life is linked with illicit religion in a variety of texts, e.g., Deut 12:2; 1 Kgs 14:23; 2 Kgs 16:4; 17:10; 2 Chr 28:4; Jer 2:20; 3:6, 13; 17:2 Ezek 6:13. See Holladay (1961:170-76).

[19] We shall discuss maternal love in a separate section below.

[20] See CTA 24.47-50 and M. D. Coogan (1990:137).

[21] See further on this topic below, Chapters 4 and 5, discussing the fate of certain cities, including Jerusalem, within Isaiah.

[22] K. Grosz's comments about women in Nuzi are interesting in this context: "It is true that limitations were imposed on women more often than on men, simply because women in patrilineal societies are the ones who cross the family borders. When they marry they do not become members of their husband's lineage—only their children do. Thus, women could be termed a 'foreign element' in their husbands' families—an element recruited in order to perpetuate the lineage, but simultaneously potentially dangerous to it in the event of the husband's death" (1989:178).

[23] Wives did have legal rights, however, as J. R. Wegner notes: "the Bible clearly distinguishes marriage (acquisition of a woman's sexual-reproductive function) from slavery (acquisition of the entire woman). The Israelite wife had many legal rights (spelled out in Ex. 21:10-11; Num. 30:1-16; and elsewhere) that clearly distinguish her status from that of a slave" (1992:41; see also 1988).

[24] "Three relationships demand absolute fidelity by one partner for the other," T. Frymer-Kensky writes (1992a:146): "the loyalty of vassal to suzerain, the allegiance of wife for husband, and Israel's devotion to God. Love language is used for all three."

[25] So also T. Frymer-Kensky: "Marriage in Israel was certainly not 'egalitarian' in the modern sense of the world [sic]. At the same time, it was not the hierarchy of master and servant, but a bond between loving intimates" (1992a:147).

[26] Unlike some of the literature of Israel's neighbors, Israel's literature reflects no social concern for overpopulation. See Frymer-Kensky (1977:147-55) and A. Kilmer (1972:160-77).

[27] When references to childlessness appear in the Hebrew Bible, it is simply presupposed that the woman's body is "at fault." The only possible exception is 2 Kgs 4:14, where we are told that a wealthy woman from Shunem "has no son, and her husband is old."

[28] By rewarding women who bore children and devaluing those who did not, E. Fuchs observes, Israel's culture helped to insure that what men most wanted from women—sons to continue the male

line—would be what women most desired for themselves (1985: 117-36). According to I. Seibert, some women in Israel's ancient Near Eastern world attempted to avoid conception through the use of magical stones, etc. Moreover, women sometimes chose abortion, although the legal penalties could be extremely severe: "according to law," Seibert writes, women guilty of abortion "were impaled and denied internment [sic]" (1974:28).

[29] A Sumerian proverb (Gordon 1959:181) employs both maternal joy at the birth of a child, and maternal sorrow at the death of a child, as lenses through which to perceive the ups and downs of life at court: "The palace—one day it is a mother who has given birth; the next day, it is a mother in mourning!"

[30] Largely because of childbirth's dangers, female life expectancy was only about thirty years, as opposed to forty years for males (Meyers 1988:112-13).

[31] The gravity of such a situation eludes J. Robinson, who writes, "for a woman to carry a child to the moment of birth and then be unable to deliver it implied the most public humiliation possible for her, and since the Hebrews believed that suffering was a punishment for sin, it marked her off as a particularly wicked person" (1976:178). What was at stake was not shame, but survival.

[32] In the Vassal-Treaties of Esarhaddon, Belet-ili appears in a curse against those who would damage or destroy the treaty tablet: "May Belet-ili, the Lady of all creatures, put an end to birth giving in your land, so that the nurses among you shall miss the cry of babies in the streets" (Wiseman 1969:538).

[33] See, e.g., C. Fontaine (1987:95-126); D. H. Englehard (1970); H. A. Hoffner (1966:198-203); J. Pringle (1983:128-41); S. Rollin (1983:34-45); I. Seibert (1974:28-29); Lambert (1969).

[34] According to Lev 12:1-5, if a woman bore a son her impurity lasted thirty-three days and twice as long if the child were female.

[35] Although occasionally referring to women's religious practices (e.g., 1 Sam 28; 1 Kgs 15:9-15; 2 Kgs 23:7; Jer 7:17-18; 44:15-19; Ezek 8:14; 13:17-23), biblical writers' assessments of those practices are generally negative. (Of course, they criticize many of the men's religious practices, as well.) T. Frymer-Kensky assumes, too readily I believe, that the many references to Yahweh's control of conception, pregnancy, and delivery reflect ancient Israelite women's belief that "no other god could be invoked" in matters of reproduction (1992a: 97). Possibly, however, the assertions that Yahweh controls women's wombs are polemical attempts to ascribe solely to Yahweh powers popularly attributed to goddesses and to midwives skilled in childbirth rituals and incantations. Her summary of the Bible's account of Yahweh's role in reproduction is accurate; whether it adequately expresses actual women's presuppositions and practices is a separate question.

[36] Certainly the plethora of small female figures exhibiting pro-

nounced breasts and/or labia, uncovered in Palestine and elsewhere in the ancient Near East, testify to concern for female fertility and lactation in Israel's world.

[37] Compare L. Archer's comments (1983:283-84) about the sparcity of legal references to Jewish women's involvement in death rituals.

[38] Akkadian versions of the myth also have been found throughout the Neo-Assyrian period.

[39] Pringle 1983:130-31; Lambert 1969:33-34; Seibert 1974:28-29.

[40] But see Meyers 1988:99-109; she argues that the passage actually refers to the unremitting toil imposed upon women, despite the sexual and reproductive demands of their husbands upon them.

[41] Tablet 11, lines 113-119 in E. A. Speiser (1969:94).

[42] See also Isa 13:7-8a; Jer 22:23; 30:6; 49:24; 50:43; Mic 4:9, 10 (all kayyôledah). Related similes (kehôlah and kemabkîrah in Jer 4:31; kemô 'eset ledah in Jer 13:21) bear the same connotations. In Isa 19:16, there is no reference to labor, but in that context to be "like women" is to "tremble with fear."

[43] Just as the travailing woman simile says nothing about the figurative or literal emergence of new life (contra P. Trible 1978:64 and S. Ackerman 1992:167), so also it connotes nothing about the past sexual history of those whose behavior it illumines. Hence the problem with Follis' observation that when bat-siyyôn is likened to a woman in travail (Mic 4:10 and Jer 4:31), she is "certainly not virginal" (1987:182).

[44] On Isa 42:10-17 as a single unit, see K. Darr (1987a:560-71). My argument has been accepted, and further strengthened, by Dion (1991:113-24). See also my forthcoming (but long in press) essay, "Two Unifying Female Images in the Book of Isaiah" (1994).

[45] For this translation of 'p'h, see K. Darr (1987a:567-68).

[46] These observations are based, of course, upon the literature to hand. Travailing woman similes may have functioned in other ways in ancient Israel as well.

[47] Perhaps it never occurred to the ancient Yahwists to ponder their deity's origins. It is possible, however, that such speculations once existed, but came to be regarded as theologically inappropriate and so were suppressed.

[48] In Gen 6:1-4, one finds an account of sexual intercourse between divine beings (benê ha'elohîm) and human women. In its present context the myth functions in several ways: to explain why the human lifespan is limited; to shed light on the origins of the legendary Nephilim; and to justify further God's decision to destroy life on earth, save for the inhabitants of Noah's ark. See S. Niditch (1985).

[49] In addition to the texts discussed below, see also Prov 27:1, which speaks of a day giving birth to events, and Ps 87:4, which figuratively describes the births of Philistia, Tyre, and Cush in Zion.

[50] Tanakh translates "came into being."

[51] However, the biblical authors (except the Yahwist) tend to use

Hiphil forms of the verb to refer to the male act of begetting children; the Qal form most often describes the female act of bearing offspring.

[52] It is possible, of course, that Ps 90:2 is meristic: first male begetting is envisioned, then female bearing. But because they exhibit complementary parallelism ("were birthed"/"brought forth"), it is perhaps more likely that both verbs refer to the (female) act of giving birth. See also the discussion of Isa 59:4 below. Isa 45:10 moves from begetting (the Hiphil form of *yld*) to bearing. References to "father" and "women," however, make the shift explicit.

The Polel imperfect form of *hîl* in verse 2aß can be either second masculine singular or third feminine singular (the forms being identical in biblical Hebrew). Moreover, the Septuagint presupposes *tehôlal* (Polal) rather than *tehôlel*, rendering this verb, like *yulladû* in vs. 2a, a passive construction. Because it is likely that religious sensibilities led the Septuagint's translators to avoid the image of God giving birth, it is not necessary to emend an intelligible MT at this point. Questions of number and gender are more crucial, however, for if the verb is indeed a third feminine singular form, then we are left with the task of identifying who "she" is. A. Weiser (1962) believes that she is mother earth. His solution leads, however, to the awkward image of mother earth giving birth to the earth—that is, to the land in its entirety. It seems better, therefore, to follow *Tanakh* in identifying the verb as a second person masculine singular form (so also BDB, s.v. *hûl* [*hîl*], and the NRSV), recognizing that the poet has used childbirth imagery in order better to illumine the mystery of Yahweh's creative activity.

[53] The Qumran Targum makes explicit Sea's origins: "Did you shut the Sea within doors? When it gushed from the womb *of the deep*" (emphasis mine). See M. H. Pope (1973:293).

[54] Though the former, negative response may indeed be implied, the latter notion is present, as well. Again, masculine verb forms are used, even when the female act of bearing is envisioned. The verb in verse 29b is a Qal perfect third masculine singular form of the verb *yld* with a third masculine singular object suffix (literally, "and the frost of heaven, who birthed him [it]?").

[55] These two verbs also are paired in Isa 23:4 (the city of Sidon bewails its childlessness), and in Isa 54:1 and 66:7, 8 (references to Jerusalem's miraculous offspring). An additional text, Isa 26:17-18, will be discussed in Chapter 6.

[56] See also Num 11:12 (*Tanakh*), where an angry Moses complains to God, "Did I conceive [*harîtî*] all this people, did I bear them [*yelidtîhû*], that You should say to me, 'Carry them in your bosom as a nurse carries an infant,' to the land that You have promised on oath to their fathers?" Clearly, Moses believes that the answer to his questions is, "No I did not; *you* did."

[57] Concomitantly, the mother's physical comfort depended upon her ability to nurse her child at regular intervals.

[58] The verb is a Piel imperfect third masculine singular form of the root *hbl*, which twice appears in a reference to human female conception in Cant 8:5.

[59] This verse follows the normal course of events—conception, pregnancy, birth. See Hos 9:11, where a similar sequence reverses the normal order, thereby rendering the threat even more unsettling.

[60] E. Fuchs (1985:128-29) adopts A. Rich's distinction between the institution of motherhood, and its personal and psychological aspects: "the social and legal *institution* of motherhood is distinctly different from the personal and psychological aspect of motherhood; the latter refers to 'the *potential relationship* of any woman to her powers of reproduction and to children,' whereas the former refers to the mechanism aimed at 'ensuring that that potential and all women—shall remain under male control' [A. Rich 1976:xv]. The institution of motherhood is a powerful patriarchal mechanism." Idealizing "maternal attributes" helps both to perpetuate institutionalized motherhood and to ensure women's compliance by shaping and rewarding maternal behaviors.

[61] K. M. O'Connor (1992:181) suggests that such cannibalism accusations may be more symbolic than actual. Though her observation has validity, the depiction of women carrying out such activity also heightens the passage's rhetorical effect precisely because it flies in the face of strong associations with maternal nurture, compassion, and devotion.

[62] The argument is by analogy: just as a mother could never forget, or fail to have compassion for, her nursing infant, so Yahweh cannot forget, or lack compassion for, Jerusalem. This is *not* a metaphorical depiction of Zion as the "son of her womb," C. Seitz's claim notwithstanding (1991:203-4).

[63] See "mourning" in *IDB*. T. Frymer-Kensky notes the frequency of references to laments by Sumerian goddesses on behalf of family members, and in public laments over their destroyed cities (1992a:36-38).

[64] Little is known of the nature and extent of women's involvement in this festival. On the basis of Judg 21:16-24, S. Ackerman reasonably conjectures that women's contributions included dancing. The song of the vineyard in Isa 5:1-7 hints that women contributed music as well, since its reference to a male "beloved" suggests a female singer (1992:162).

[65] My translation of *niqqatah*, "to be cleaned out [of a plundered city]"; NRSV has "ravaged." "Despoiled" creates a nice play in English on the previous depiction of Zion's spoiled and haughty daughters.

[66] K. Horney (1967:135) notes that "a woman becomes doubly sinister in the presence of the bloody manifestations of womanhood"; see also J. Galambush (1992:103-5).

[67] *Defilement*. Both BDB and KB identify *nîdah* (a term occurring only here in the Hebrew Bible) as a variant of *niddah*, a men-

strous women or a defiled thing (also Albrekson 1963:64). NRSV has "mockery," derived from *nwd*, "to mock." "Mockery" commends itself because of the reference to derisive laughter (*shq*) in verse 7b. As we shall see, however, menstrual metaphors and word plays in subsequent verses commend "menstruant," a meaning that will certainly suggest itself to the reader, even as the idea of mockery also is present. Indeed, *nîdah* may appear precisely because it suggests both the mockery of verse 7 and the menstrual imagery of verses 8-9 and 17.

Indecency. NRSV has "nakedness," contextually appropriate, though no stripping of Lady Jerusalem has yet explicitly been described. If *nîdah* is "menstrous woman," "indecency" translates *'erwatah* well; of course, "vulnerability" is also appropriate to this context.

Retreats. MT *wattasab 'ahôr*; NRSV has "turns her face away," but *'ahôr* suggests, as an adverb, "behind," and as a noun, the "hinder side." The same root will appear in the phrase, "she did not consider her *'aharît*, her end(time)" or future. Basic to the root's meaning is "behind," a meaning suggestive in a context including references to a menstruant and to the uncleanliness in her garments.

Uncleanness. Tum'ah can refer to various kinds of cultic impurity, including sexual activity (e.g., Num 5:19). In Lev 15:25-26, 30, however, it refers to a woman's normal or abnormal discharge of blood. Given the reference to "in her skirts" (*besûlêha*), and the reference to (or word play upon) the *niddah*, the reader is likely to construe in *tum'atah* a metaphorical reference to menstrual blood.

Skirts. Sûl, the skirt of a robe, refers to God's train in Isa 6:1 and to the high priest's robe in Exodus 28 and elsewhere. It often appears in passages depicting cities as personified women.

68 In Jer 2:33-34, associations with the polluting blood of the menstruant inform an accusation of violent and unjust bloodshed: "How well you direct your course to seek lovers! / So that even to wicked women you have taught your ways. / Also on your skirts is found the lifeblood of the innocent poor, / though you did not catch them breaking in" (NRSV). W. Holladay (1986:56) reads "on your palms" (*bekappayik*; cf. LXX) instead of "on your skirts" (*biknapayik*; MT), because "when used metaphorically [*kanap*] has sexual connotations (Deut 23:1; Ezek 16:8), and this would particularly be the case with the mention of blood; such connotations are inappropriate here." Certainly the language is figurative, in the sense that the offending parties are addressed in the feminine singular. But within this figure, the reference to "your skirts," that is, the loose-flowing ends of garments, is quite literal; and the reference to blood(shed) evokes not sexual intercourse, but menstruation. In this metaphorical address to females wearing stained garments, then, two different sorts of associations with blood are active. Of primary significance is the blood of the innocent poor; also present, however, is the polluting blood of the menstruant (*dam* [pl.] designates menstrual blood in Lev 20:18). See

Kedar-Kopfstein (1978:234-50); and Galambush (1992:94-95).

[69] According to Deut 22:28-29, if a women who is not bethrothed is involved in sexual intercourse, be it by force or by "consent" (which, in fact, is not hers to give), the man must pay her father the virgin's bride-price (fifty shekels of silver) and marry her. "Because he violated her," the text states, "he shall not be permitted to divorce her as long as he lives" (vs. 29b). Exod 22:16 deals with intercourse described as consensual (he seduces, rather than rapes, her). As in Deuteronomy, the male is required to pay her father the bride-price and marry her, unless her father refuses to permit the marriage. In that case, he still must pay him fifty shekels of silver.

A betrothed woman who has sexual intercourse with a man within a town is regarded as an adulteress since, even in the case of rape, she presumably could have cried out and been heard. According to Deut 22:24, both she and the man are to be stoned to death. When a betrothed woman and a man have intercourse "in the open country," however, the presumption is that she was raped, since her cries would have gone unheard. In that case, only the man is to be killed; she is presumed innocent. (See Frymer-Kensky 1992a:56-59).

[70] N. H. Walls (1992: 21) observes that "females who do not complete [the] transition [to wife and mother]—who remain independent of male domination—are a threat to the social and ideological structure of patriarchal and androcentric society. . . . They are no longer girls who will develop into women, but simply unmarried females marginal to accepted feminine categories and outside of the normal structures for securing social rank."

[71] One of their functions, therefore, is to alert females to the danger of becoming a prostitute, or of acting in ways (e.g., traveling about at night without proper escort) that might encourage others to identify them as "loose women."

[72] The "out-of-bounds" woman ('issâ zarâ) comes in a variety of forms: prostitute, adulteress, foreigner, foolish woman. In Proverbs 1–9, she poses a tempting threat to the son—a threat the sage/father seeks to obviate through a variety of rhetorical strategies. See C. A. Newsom (1989:142-60) and G. A. Yee (1989:53-68). Scholars have long debated whether the 'issâ zarâ of Proverbs is in fact a non-Israelite. In the Egyptian Wisdom of Any, the geographical strangeness of the seductress is explicitly stated: "Beware of a woman who is a stranger, one not known in her town; don't stare at her when she goes by, do not know her carnally. A deep water whose course in unknown, such is a woman away from her husband" (quoted in Robins 1989: 114). I see no reason to rule out the ethnically foreign woman as one manifestation of 'issâ zarâ, the "out-of-bounds" woman who is also called a nokrîyyâ, a foreign or alien woman. But an Israelite woman who behaved in ways deemed socially inappropriate, like her ethnically foreign counterparts, could be regarded as an 'issâ zarâ.

[73] Adultery is called a "great sin" in Gen 20:9 and a "sin against God" in Gen 20:6, 39:9; Ps 51:6. This characterization of adultery is also found in texts from Ugarit and Egypt (Goodfriend 1992a:82).

[74] H. McKeating also notes that when Israel's wisdom literature speaks of adultery, the husband's wrath, along with loss of reputation, is chief among its threats (1979:60).

[75] See Deut 22:20-21, 23-24; T. Frymer-Kensky notes the significance of stoning as the penality for adultery: "Stoning is a very special penalty, reserved for those offenses which completely upset the hierarchical arrangements of the cosmos" (1992a:192; so also L. Stulman 1992:59).

[76] A woman accused of adultery by her husband was forced to undergo a drinking-oath trial, described in Num 5:11-31. See T. Frymer-Kensky (1984:11-26) and M. Fishbane (1974:25-45).

[77] Here, we are reminded of P. Haas' claim that legal materials are "symbolic attempts to work out in concrete behavioral terms the implications of deeply held values and principles" (1989:84).

[78] According to M. Greenberg, capital punishment was the penalty of adultery in all cases. Others suggest, however, that ancient Israelite men, like their Mesopotamian counterparts (Frymer-Kensky 1992a:193), could choose whether or not to initiate proceedings against offenders, and retained the right of pardon (see H. McKeating [1979:59] on Prov 6:34-35).

[79] See Hos 2:2-3; Jer 13:26-27; Ezek 16:36-39; 23:26-29. In each of these texts, the victim is not an actual woman, but rather a personified people (Hos 2:2-3) or city.

[80] According to Ezek 23:25, Oholibah's former lovers will cut off her nose and ears.

[81] See G. A. Yee (1992:105-6).

[82] See also her article, "Prostitution (OT)" under the name E. A. Goodfriend (1992:509).

NOTES TO CHAPTER 4:
THE LADIES' LOTS: ISAIAH 1–39

[1] See, most recently, F. W. Dobbs-Allsopp (1993); also A. Fitzgerald (1972, 1975), E. Follis (1987), and T. Frymer-Kensky, who cites as the earliest known instance of such imagery the stele of Merneptah, which declares that Palestine has become a "widow" to Egypt (1992a:172). We shall turn to the city as widow below.

[2] In a private communication, Peter Machinist has noted that Mesopotamian cities were occasionally personified, but usually gender either was not marked, or was masculine.

[3] Other Hebrew terms for city include *mahoz* (m.) and *qeret* (f.).

[4] For a contrary view, see T. McDaniel (1968:198-209). On the Sumerian "weeping goddess," see S. N. Kramer (1983).

[5] The phrase *bat-PN* refers to cities (and nations) other than

Jerusalem/Zion fifteen times: in Isaiah (Gallim, Tarshish, Sidon, Babylon); Jeremiah (Egypt, Babylon); Zechariah (Babylon); Psalms (Tyre, Babylon); and Lamentations (Edom). *Bat-siyyôn* appears twenty-six times: in 2 Kings; Isaiah; Micah; Zephaniah; Jeremiah; Lamentations; Zechariah; and Psalms. (For extrabiblical examples of the *bat-PN* epithet, see Dobbs-Allsopp 1993:84.) "Daughter, my people," appears fourteen times: in Isaiah; Jeremiah (5x in ch. 8); and Lamentations (5x). The correct translation of *bat-'amî* is contested.

[6] The plural *benôt-PN* (Isa 3:16, 17; 4:4; 16:2; Ezek 16:27, 57; Cant 3:11) refers either to a city's female inhabitants, or to towns and settlements surrounding a major urban center. See Follis (1987:174-75).

[7] The phrase "virgin daughter" is connected with Jerusalem/Zion (2 Kgs 19:21=Isa 37:22; Lam 2:13); "my people" (Jer 14:17); Judah (Lam 1:15); Egypt (Jer 46:11); Sidon (Isa 23:12); and Babylon (Isa 47:1). "The virgin Israel" occurs in Amos 5:2; Jer 18:13; 31:4b, 21. Scholars disagree about the meaning of such phrases. For example, Fitzgerald, understands "virgin Israel" in Amos 5:2 to be "the exiles of the Northern Kingdom" (1975:178-79), while Galambush argues that Amos calls upon the "house" or ruling family (or inhabitants) to lament the demise of the "virgin," the capital, Samaria (1992:36).

[8] Neither *bat-PN* nor *betulat-(bat)-PN* is applied to ancient Near Eastern cities generally (Bourguet 1987:482-84).

[9] As Galambush (1992:21) observes, however, Lewy was unclear concerning what came first—the notion that the goddess (city) and god were married (leading to the construction of a temple in the city), or the presence of the sanctuary in the city (leading to the notion that the goddess [city] and god were married). From a different perspective, M. Wakeman argues for the original primacy of the goddess: in early Sumer, the goddess Innana was patron of the city, Uruk, and "the man who managed the temple estate was the husband (or lord, *en*) chosen by [her]" (1985:12; see also 1982).

[10] So also E. J. Adler (Goodfriend) who writes, "it is possible for a city to be called 'mother' to its inhabitants for reasons other than parturition, so that a sexual union and a partner for this 'mother' aren't a necessity" (1989:146).

[11] On the metaphorial use of *znh*, "to fornicate, be a harlot," see above, Chapter 3.

[12] Adler (1989) can argue for the pentateuchal origins of the prophets' adultery/prostitution metaphors because she believes the Decalogue, the Priestly source, and Exodus 32–24 "represent some of the oldest strata in the Bible" (390-90). She accepts that the Pentateuch accurately records the covenant-making experience at Sinai, including the exact words by which that experience was articulated. In contrast to Adler, Galambush distinguishes between poetic personifications of cities as (adulteress) women and the distinct, though related,

metaphor of the (male) people "whoring (*znh*) after other gods" which appears in certain extraprophetic texts (1992:27, 36-38).

[13] In both the Code of Hammurabi (§177) and the Middle Assyrian Laws (§28), a woman whose son was a minor is called an *almattu*.

[14] The major surviving city laments are "Lament over the Destruction of Ur," "Lament over the Destruction of Sumer and Ur," "Nippur Lament," "Eridu Lament," and "Uruk Lament." They are believed to date from no later than 1925 BCE. These laments, in turn, greatly influenced liturgical laments used, apparently, in cultic ceremonies marking the destruction and restoration of sanctuaries, as well as in particular festivals and in rituals to avert evil (Dobbs-Allsopp 1993).

[15] He follows leads by W. Gwaltney (1983) and D. Hillers (1992).

[16] On Isaiah 1–4 as a redactional unit, see M. Sweeney (1988).

[17] W. G. E. Watson notes "the complete congruence of gender (all feminine), which reinforces the similes" (1984:258).

[18] Kramer 1969:457. See also his "Lamentation over the Destruction of Sumer and Ur" (627): "Of the widespread stall of Nanna—torn down were their hedges,/ The garden huts were despoiled."

[19] "The Lament over Ur," 125-29 (Dobbs-Allsopp 1993:69). The translator notes: "both the 'garden hut'. . . and 'pulled-up harvest shed'. . . refer to temporary structures erected during harvesting. Thus, LU compares the destruction of Ningal's temple to these dilapidated structures after they have been abandoned following the harvest."

[20] With the exception of the first person plural suffixes in verse 9, verses 9-20 have second masculine plural suffixes. They are not, therefore, addressed to personified Jerusalem.

[21] Recall that the pillar of cloud/fire not only guided the Israelites, but also protected them from Pharaoh's approaching army (Exod 14:19-20). See M. Sweeney (1988:179-80) and P. Miscall (1993:52).

[22] Isa 10:27b-32 is fraught with difficulties. The text of verse 27b is surely corrupt; and scholars have suggested a number of possible historical campaigns lying behind the particular enemy approach described therein. Our reader may or may not possess sufficient knowledge to associate this text with a specific historical setting, or to rule out other settings based on its details. The climax of these verses, however, is the king of Assyria's threatening gesture against Zion. The significance of that gesture will be assessed on the basis of various evidence: not only the historical knowledge that Assyria did *not* destroy Jerusalem, but also information derived from sequentially prior texts concerning Assyria's role in Yahweh's divine plan, the eventual termination of that role, and divine assurances in, for example, 10:24-27a.

[23] A related view (e.g. G. Gray 1956:231) takes the participle's female gender more seriously (Gray translates our phrase in Isa 12:6, "inhabitress of Sion"), but regards it nonetheless as a collective designation ("what is meant is the entire population of the city").

24 Though Holladay (1989:429) translates "let enthroned Zion say" (see below), he notes that "the participle *yosebet* is poised between 'enthroned' and 'inhabitant [feminine] of,' given the presence of *yosebê*, 'inhabitants of' in the following colon."

25 The words, "The oracle (*massa'*) concerning Babylon that Isaiah son of Amoz saw," introduces an extensive oracle against Babylon in Isa 13:2–14:27. Ten subsequent superscriptions will introduce oracles against the Philistines (14:28), Moab (15:1), Damascus (17:1), Egypt (19:1), the "wilderness of the sea" (21:1), Dumah (21:11), the desert plain (21:13), the valley of vision (= Jerusalem [22:1-14]; oracles against two court officials, Shebnah and Eliakim, in verses 20-25), and Tyre (23:1). In addition, destruction threatens Assyria in 14:24-27, Jacob in 17:4-6, and Ethiopia in 18:1-7.

26 Here, I part company with J. G. Williams (1977:59), who takes texts like Isa 10:5-19 at face value. Williams writes, "If I am correct in concluding that the alas-form expresses a true lament over the dying and the dead, then [Isa 10:5-19] represents YHWH's sadness over the pretentions of the foreign instrument of his word. It is as though YHWH had high hopes for Assyria also." Such utterances may indeed be sincere when the destruction of one's own city or nation is at issue (but see Amos 5:2, where a premature lamentation functions as a threat). When the "lamented" party is Israel's foe, however, its expressions of sorrow must be understood as sarcastic and mocking.

27 The address to Philistia's gate is an example of synecdoche (the gate stands for the city as a whole). See J. D. Sapir (1977:12-19) and I. Provan (1991:76). As noted, addresses to a city's walls or gates are a characteristic of both Mesopotamian and Israelite city laments (Dobbs-Allsopp 1993:180).

28 *qen mesulah* lacks the prefixed *ke*, which is understood from the previous *ke'ôp-nôded*.

29 The critic knows—though the first-time reader does not—that a subsequent reference to birds in flight will evoke quite different associations. In Isa 31:4-5, the simile *kesipparîm 'apôt*, "like birds hovering," is used to describe Yahweh's protective activity on Zion's behalf. Unlike *ndd*, which can bear associations of *fearful* fleeing, the Hebrew verb *'wp* connotes soaring or hovering (in order to defend nestlings? see Deut 32:11; and J. C. Exum 1981:336); among its subjects are not only birds (e.g., Gen 1:20; Deut 4:17) and Yahweh (see also 2 Sam 22:11 = Ps 91:5), but also the wings of the seraphim (Isa 6:2). The phrase *kesipparîm 'apôt* functions, then, as a compelling figure of God's protection. Aviary imagery conveying weakness in one context becomes an image of strength in another.

30 NRSV has "the destruction of my beloved people."

31 Commentators debate the original place of Tyre and Sidon in this oracle. Whatever the text's prehistory, however, its juxtaposition of these seaports is intelligible. (see, e.g., Erlandsson 1970:98; Dobbs-

Allsopp 1993:116-17).

[32] See, e.g., Erlandsson 1970:97-102; Kaiser 1974:159-72; and Wildberger 1978:853-84.

[33] The Syriac omits le'mor, permitting the translation: "The sea has spoken, O stronghold of the sea: 'I have not labored, . . . '" So rendered, J. Galambush notes, "Sidon is addressed as the stronghold of the sea, who is bereaved by the death of the sea's children, who in turn can logically be only the people of Sidon" (1992:39).

[34] Note the sequence giddaltî . . . rômamtî, as in 1:2b.

[35] P. C. Schmitz (1992:17) notes that "the role of Sidon as the mother city of Tyre was recalled on Seleucid coins of Sidon bearing the legend 'm sr, 'mother of Tyre.'"

[36] W. G. E. Watson's translation, by contrast, recalls the ruined city's glory days: "Can this be your joyful city, / To whom, since ancient times, / Her tribute they brought to her at her feet, / Obliged to reverence at a respectful distance?" "Tyre," he claims, "is depicted as a haughty queen with a respectable ancestry welcoming her subject kings who, after grovelling as prescribed (forehead to ground at a distance from the throne) approach and kneel to lay tribute at her feet" (1976:373). Watson cites some interesting ancient Near Eastern parallels to his translation, but his rendering of qadmatah as "her tribute" seems forced. See H. Wildberger (1978:856, 874).

[37] Israel's associations with trade and traders were mixed. On the negative side, D. C. Snell (1992:628-29) notes, "The passage in Ezek 28:5-7 about the Phoenician city of Tyre seems to see trade as a source of sin. And one Heb word for profit, besa', usually has the sense of 'unjust gain,' as in Exod 18:21 where Moses' father-in-law advises him to appoint as judges 'able men from all the people, such as fear God, men who are trustworthy and hate gain (RSV: a bribe).'"

[38] S. von Rin (1963:23-24) comments on the "ingenious pun" of nskhh, which can mean either "worn out, passionate," or "forgotten." He likewise notes that forms of zkr can mean either "be remembered," or "be lain with." For the latter he compares Arabic dkr, "penis," and zkr in Mishnaic Hebrew. W. G. E. Watson (1984:185) notes that zkr evokes both "to remember" and "male" (though he inexplicably claims that zkr, "male" is "unattested in Hebrew").

[39] R. Youngblood contends that "ariel" means "city of God," but acknowledges a play on words, such that the "city of God" is threatened with becoming an "altar-hearth" (1979:461).

[40] Note that Isa 26:5b employs feminine grammatical forms throughout, though the NRSV translation does not reflect their presence. Because Jerusalem speaks from the ground/dust in 29:4, poetic personification is more pronounced there than in 26:5b.

[41] Or perhaps simply tolerated by a benevolent deity, as is Anat by El. N. H. Walls notes that "Anat is called the daughter of El explicitly when she is most rebellious against the divine patriarch" (1992:109).

NOTES TO CHAPTER 5:
THE LADIES' LOTS: ISAIAH 40–66

[1] Jer 31:2.

[2] So Seitz (1990:245), reading with the MT, "*we'amar*."

[3] So D. Petersen (1977:20), reading *w'wmrh* with 1QIsa[a].

[4] With the Septuagint, and possibly 1QIsa[a], reading MT *we'amar* as a first person singular form.

[5] It does not suffice to say with Seitz that "the reason for the lack of explicit clarification of the heavenly court scene and the obscure voices in 40:1-11 is that the backdrop of Isaiah 6 has been presupposed, from an editorial perspective, for the reader of this key passage" (1990:241). Bringing knowledge of Isaiah 6 to a reading of 40:1-11 does not resolve all of the reader's questions.

[6] Such texts may, however, cause him to reconsider his earlier construal, confirming its validity or altering it in light of new evidence.

[7] Indeed, it seems the most plausible meaning, since "herald to Zion" begs the question of the herald's identity.

[8] "Worm" Israel is addressed using feminine singular grammatical forms in the salvation oracle of 41:14-16, presumably because *tôla'at*, "worm," is a feminine noun. And reassuring words concerning Jerusalem's future occasionally appear (41:27; 44:26, 28).

[9] In 43:2, Yahweh promises Israel, "When you pass through the waters, I will be with you; and through the rivers, they shall not overwhelm you." Not surprisingly, many commentators detect an allusion to the exodus from Egypt. But the phrase "pass through the rivers" may signify a harrowing ordeal, expressed metaphorically as passing through the mythical waters of chaos. Such a meaning makes sense in the present context and is certainly a more compelling interpretation than J. McKenzie's claim that "cross the rivers" refers to "the transportation of captives" (1968:91). In Isa 44:27, Yahweh claims to dry up the rivers of the deep: "who says to the deep, 'Be dry—I will dry up your rivers.'" Recall that in Isa 8:7-8, Assyrian invasion was likened to an inundating river.

[10] *herpah* "reproach, shame" refers to sexual disgrace in 2 Sam 13:13, Ezek 16:57, and Prov 6:33, to barrenness in Gen 30:23 and Isa 4:1, and to widowhood in Isa 54:4.

[11] In portraying the city's destruction, J. Galambush notes, the poem speaks of the loss of her men (vs. 3) and her children. It says nothing, however, about the deaths of adult Babylonian women. Personified Babylon assumes their role (1992:41, 43). Galambush further claims that "the city's 'widowhood,' . . . is simultaneously the death of its male inhabitants/protectors, and its consequent vassal status" (43). It is not clear to me, however, that the text presumes Lady Babylon to be married to her male inhabitants.

[12] J. Galambush's discusses looking and seeing in 1992:104-6.

[13] So *Tanakh*; NRSV has "O captive Jerusalem."

[14] Within the commentary itself, Muilenburg identifies the fifth strophe as verses 11-14 (638), though he concedes that the difficult verse 15 "stands in immediate sequence to verse 14" (641).

[15] The translation is by S. Ackerman (1990:40).

[16] NRSV has "for, in deserting me." See the commentaries.

[17] The Hebrew word is *yad*, "hand," but Ackerman translates "phallus" on the basis of usage in Ugaritic mythological texts and the Dead Sea Scrolls (39). Many commentators concur.

[18] The verb *zarah*, used frequently of the rising sun, occurs in each of these three verses; forms of *'ôr*, "light," occur in verses 1 and 3.

[19] *'arapel* describes the deep darkness wherein Yahweh dwells in 2 Kgs 8:12.

[20] Translation by J. McKenzie (1967:39), slightly modified.

[21] So also P. Hanson, who concedes that "the nations are the object of Israel's exploitation elsewhere in chapter 60 (by implication throughout the chapter, explicitly in v. 11b and v. 14)." Hanson also emends the text to "restore" its poetic meter (1975:51, 56-57).

[22] See R. N. Whybray (1975:236) and, e.g., Gen 19:31; Deut 21:15, 16, 17; 2 Sam 13:15; Deut 22:13, 16.

[23] O. R. Gurney (1974) demonstrates that Mesopotamian temples tended to have names connoting peace and stability, while gates were named using military metaphors. Here, however, Zion's once-vital defenses need serve no other purposes than to demonstrate Yahweh's salvific power and to praise God.

[24] C. Westermann, to the contrary, identifies the speaker of verses 6 and 7 as the prophet: "In v. 1 he said of himself that he could not keep silent until . . . Thus, v. 6f must refer to the people to whom he addresses his proclamation, in so far as they accept this, hold now to the word of salvation, and always hold it up before God" (1969:377).

[25] Both words for crowns in verse 3, Anderson notes, have a broad range of meanings: *'ateret* (vs. 3a) can designate a royal crown (Jer 13:18; Ezek 21:26; Ps 21:4; Esth 8:5); a woman's decorative tiara (Ezek 16:12; 23:42), or a symbol of honor or glory (Prov 4:9; 14:24; 16:31; 17:6; Job 19:9; 31:36; Lam 5:16). Figuratively, it refers to Samaria in Isa 28:1-3 and to Yahweh in Isa 28:5. *Sanîp* (*qere*; vs. 3b) also connotes royalty (Zech 3:5; "turban"), a woman's ornament (Isa 3:23), and a sign of honor (Job 29:14). Other crown vocabulary, by contrast, appears to have a more specialized or limited range of meanings: "the term *nezer* is always conected with authority, either of the king (2 Sam 1,10; 2 Kgs 11,12; Ps 89,40; 132,18) or of the high priest (Exod 29,6; 39,30; Lev 8.9). The term *misnepet* is used exclusively for the turban or mitre of the high priest (e.g. Exod 28.37). The term *pe'er* may refer to priests (Exod 39,28; Ezek 44,13) or to the ornamental headgear of women (Isa 3,20), men (Ezek 24,17), or a bridegroom" (1986:78).

[26] Biddle also recognized the presence of wedding imagery, both

in the sons whom Zion will wear as wedding jewelry (Isa 49:14-18) and in Yahweh's rejoicing over her "as the bridegroom" when she weds her "sons" (1991:183). Both R. N. Whybray (248) and J. Muilenburg (720) emend "your sons" to "your builder."

NOTES TO CHAPTER 6:
NO STRENGTH TO DELIVER

[1] Isaiah 36–39 also appears, with variations, in 2 Kgs 18:13–20:19. Scholars disagree about the original locus of these chapters. The majority view holds that Isaiah 36–39 was copied from Kings. This judgment has been challenged, however, by K. A. D. Smelik (1986:70-76; 1992) and, more recently, by C. R. Seitz (1991).

[2] Paroemiologists acknowledge that proverbs are difficult to define. C. A. Parker offers a good, brief definition: a proverb is, she writes, "a message coded by tradition and transmitted to evaluate and/or affect human behavior" (1973:80). C. R. Fontaine's definition attends more fully to literary and anthropological issues, as well as to the importance of a contextual understanding of the "traditional saying," her phrase for proverbs appearing outside Israel's canonical wisdom corpus (Proverbs, Job, Ecclesiastes):

> the traditional saying [is] a statement, current among the folk, which is concise, syntactically complete, consisting of at least one topic and comment which may or may not be metaphorical, but which exhibits a logical relationship between its terms. Further, the saying may be marked by stylistic features (mnemonics, rhythm, alliteration, assonance, etc.) or be constructed along recognizable frames ("Better A than B . . .," etc.) which distinguish it from other genres (or folk idioms). The referents which form the image are most likely to be drawn from the experience of common, "everyday" life, but the meaning (message) of the saying may vary from context to context, and any "truth claim" for that message must be considered "relative" rather than "absolute." The transmission of the saying, however achieved, is *always* purposeful, but specific details of contextual use may be necessary to determine the purpose in any given situation. (1982:64)

[3] Of course, not all short utterances are proverbs, and not all proverbs are terse. By the same token, not all poetic utterances are proverbs, while many proverbs conform to standard syntactical and metrical patterns of everyday prose.

[4] Returning to Fontaine's definition of the traditional saying, I note that Hezekiah's proverb consists of two topics and two comments:

Topic A: babes; Comment A: are positioned for birth
Topic B: strength; Comment B: is lacking to deliver

[5] "Narrativity," writes J. G. Williams, "is the telling of a process of acts, events, or experiences. It would obviously not be present except in very compact form in proverbs, which make up a genre lying to the contrary extreme of narrative forms. But the use of tightly controlled narrative phrases empowers many of the proverbs" (1987:273-74).

[6] Though the proverb is metaphorical in its application to the situation, it contains no internal metaphors.

[7] See also Seitel 1972, 1977.

[8] This diagram appears in a version of Seitel 1969 reprinted in *Folklore Genres* (129).

[9] Note also the plurals in the well-known proverb shared by Jeremiah (31:29) and Ezekiel (18:2), "parents have eaten sour grapes, and children's teeth are blunted."

[10] Actually the message is delivered by envoys. Their use of the messenger formula, "Thus says Hezekiah," however, purportedly ensures that Hezekiah's words are repeated precisely and accurately. Note that Isaiah employs the messenger formula to convey Yahweh's response in verse 6.

[11] So Fontaine (1982:252). In terms of Seitel's model, the relationship would be as follows: in the proverb situation, A=babes positioned for birth, while B=no strength to deliver. Analogously, in the context situation C=the need to repel Assyria, while D=the lack of strength to do so.

[12] True, the city's inhabitants are not actually present in the interaction situation. According to Seitel's definition, their identification with an entity in the proverb situation would exemplify third person correlation. But because Hezekiah is king, he can speak not only for himself but also for his subjects.

[13] Although Isaiah also is among the city's inhabitants, Hezekiah logistically (he *sends* messengers *to* Isaiah, rather than summoning the prophet) and rhetorically distances Isaiah from himself through the proverb performance and the words that follow: "Perhaps the Lord *your* God will take note of the words of the Rabshakeh, . . . and will mete out judgment for the words that the Lord *your God* has heard—if you will offer up prayer for the *surviving remnant* (37:4; emphasis mine). J. J. M. Roberts has noted a similarly strategic function of pronouns in Isaiah's exchange with Ahaz in Isaiah 7 (1985:197).

[14] Of course, a proverb cannot be paraphrased without loss of content and impact. My attempts are strictly for purposes of clarification.

[15] When Isaiah criticizes Judah's participation in the rebellion, he does not single out Hezekiah; rather, he rebukes Jerusalem's leaders as a group. See, e.g., Isa 30:1 ("Oh, disloyal sons!") and 31:1 ("Ha! Those who go down to Egypt for help. . . .").

[16] Naturally, we cannot suppose that everyone in any culture, ancient or modern, would respond to the proverb in *exactly* the same

way. A woman who had been through the experience described, or a person who had witnessed (or heard) a close relative in such a situation, likely would react differently from someone lacking experience in such matters.

[17] In the Sumerian Hymn to Enlil, we learn of events that, though part of everyday happenings in nature, cannot occur without Enlil, the overseer of the world: "Nintur could not kill, could not slay. The cow would not lose its calf in its pen, the ewe not bring forth a premature lamb in its sheepfold" (T. Frymer-Kensky 1992a:49-50). The Babylonian Epic of Atra-Hasis does not describe pregnant women unable to complete delivery. It does, however, depict barrenness as a punishment inflicted upon those human beings who survived the flood and whose noise threatens the sleep of the god Enlil. See W. G. Lambert and A. R. Millard (1969).

[18] Lambert marks with an asterisk those portions of the text where he cannot discern the flow of meaning.

[19] More common is the metaphor of the unborn babe as a boat trying to escape a dangerous quay. Lambert finds the boat image "curious," but says nothing about the fact that unborn infants float in their mothers' amniotic fluid (Glassner 1989:80-81).

[20] In the Akkadian "Poem of Erra," the god Isum berates the god Erra for destruction he wrought against land and cities alike. According to Cagni's translation (1977:54), Isum attributes to the person in charge of the city a wish that both he and his mother had died in childbirth: "Ah, had I remained inclosed in [your] womb on the day you gave birth to me! / Ah, had there been an end to our [li]ves' and had we died toge[ther]'!"

[21] Line 50 is clearly the rubric for the preceding text.

[22] According to Hos 13:13, infant Ephraim lacks the wisdom to position itself in the birth canal when labor signals approaching parturition. Unlike Hezekiah, Hosea blames the baby for the inability to bring to birth.

[23] As in the Telepinus myth.

[24] As in the Middle Assyrian medical text.

[25] C. Seitz (1991) has recently addressed afresh the question of how Hezekiah's words and actions are to be understood in their present context, as part of his larger argument about the original locus of the Hezekiah-Isaiah narratives (for Seitz, their Isaiah setting is primary) and the role of those narratives in the ongoing growth of the Isaiah scroll. He refers only briefly to Hezekiah's message to Isaiah in Isa 37:3-4 and does not touch on the proverb's content. Seitz's larger argument requires that no significant tension exist between the assessment of Hezekiah he finds in chapters 36-37(38) on the one hand and the contents of Isaiah 1–35 on the other. But does Seitz correctly conclude (1) that the depiction of Hezekiah in Isaiah 36-37 is thoroughly positive and (2) that this positive presentation of Hezekiah is

not at odds with preceding portions of the scroll? Clearly I am in some measure of disagreement (as well as agreement) with his argument, though space constraints do not allow me to present here a satisfactory account of our differences and my reasons for differing.

Unlike Seitz, however, I suggest that neither a refusal to read Isaiah 36–37 through the lens of a reconstructed rebellion by Hezekiah, nor the absence of *explicit* references to him from 1:2 until 36:1, rules out the possibility that certain oracles in chapters 1–35 can influence the reader's understanding of his proverb's *interaction situation*. The relevance of sequentially prior oracles for determining how Hezekiah is assessed in chapters 36–37 does not turn on the presence of an explicit, critical word about the king in Isaiah 1–35, but rather on whether the reader comes to believe that Hezekiah has participated, whether directly or indirectly, in acts consistently condemned by the prophet in sequentially prior texts.

C. Conrad (1991), who also argues for a favorable view of Hezekiah, likewise passes quickly over Hezekiah's initial communiqué to Isaiah, including his proverb performance (42).

[26] The noun is *sarah*; NRSV translates "distress." In Jer 49:24 (see also Jer 4:31), this word appears in a simile about birth pangs. BDB suggests (II. [*srr*]) that a Hiphil form of the root *srr* referred specifically to the pain accompanying labor (Jer 4:31; 49:24; see also Jer 48:41; 49:22). The noun *sarah* is particularly appropriate in this context, therefore, since it presages Hezekiah's proverb situation and, we shall argue, his own plight depicted figuratively.

[27] *Tôkehah*; this verb suggests what God is doing to Hezekiah and his nation, i.e., chastizing them for relying on Egyptian aid. NRSV renders it "rebuke."

[28] Both NRSV and *Tanakh* translate "disgrace," but this feminine noun, from the root *na'as* (to spurn, contemn), probably means "contempt." It is a *hapax legomenon*, and may suggest the king of Assyria's attitude toward both Judah and its God (as revealed by the Rabshakeh's words).

[29] Wayne Booth notes that "the deliberate use of a recognizable metaphor (a special case of the deliberate use of any abnormality, any figuring) inevitably invites judgments of the speaker's character" (1979:174). His observation is interesting in light of Hezekiah's ambivalent character at the beginning and end of Isaiah 36–39. M. Sweeney observed in a private communication that Hezekiah is like his proverb: almost the ideal king, his actions nevertheless bring the Assyrians to Jerusalem's door and raise the spectre of Babylonian exile (to which he offers a rather cavalier response in Isa 39:8). Hezekiah can bring to the point of birth, but he cannot quite pull off the delivery.

[30] In light of the pejorative connotations associated with likening men to women in biblical and extra-biblical sources, Hezekiah possibly intends not only to depict himself and his advisors as powerless but

also to suggest self-debasement, an appropriate attitude in light of his earlier decision to form an alliance with Egypt. See D. Hillers (1964: 66-68) and W. L. Holladay (1966:237).

[31] Although not referred to by name, Jerusalem undoubtedly is the "mighty city" referred to in verse 1.

[32] So also the NRSV; its translation of *saqun*, "they poured out [a prayer]," identifes the form as a Qal pf. 3 c. p. of *suq*, "to pour out, melt" (see also Job 28:2), but such an identification is by no means certain.

[33] BDB notes the noun's possible associations with snake-charming (see Jer 8:17 and Eccl 10:11).

[34] The phrase is difficult. Clements (1980b:216) translates, "and the inhabitants of the world have not fallen," claiming that the reference is to "the wicked who abuse the faithful, and make life hard for them." O. Kaiser (1974:209; see also the NRSV) points to the noun *nepel*, meaning "untimely birth, abortion" (Ps 58:9) to support his translation, "and no inhabitants of the world are born."

[35] Excepting the occurrence in Isa 42:14 which, as we have seen, is unique in the Hebrew Bible.

[36] This statement presupposes that the reader will construe the contiguous lines of these verses in relation to one another. Traditionally, critics have denied their unity. As noted in our Chapter 1, however, P. Hanson has argued convincingly for the post-exilic emergence of oracles detailing both the punishment awaiting the wicked, and the salvation Yahweh will grant on behalf of the faithful (1975:161-86). The reader, therefore, would be accustomed to making sense of such shifts in the course of moving through the text.

[37] In addition to P. Hanson, see A. Rofé (1985). Though critical of Hanson's ideological bias toward the so-called "visionary group," Rofé agrees that these texts bespeak intracommunal strife within the post-exilic community.

[38] This Hiphil perfect 3 fem. sing. form of the verb *mlt* ("to slip away") depicts the infant effortlessly slipping from the womb.

[39] The form *yuhal*, occuring only here in the MT, is masculine; however "land" (*eres*) is feminine. BHS suggests, without textual support, that the text be emended to read '*am eres*. However R. N. Whybray argues (1975:284) that this is an example of the impersonal passive construction (see GKC §121a).

[40] Note the Hebrew Bible's motif of a sacred stream that flows from Zion (e.g., Isa 33:20-24; Zech 14:8; Ezek 47:1-12; and Joel 4:18 [ET 3:18]), related closely to the Eden myth with its river that nurtures the garden and divides to water the world. See J. D. Levenson (1976: 7-36); R. Clifford (1972); and K. P. Darr (1987b:272-79).

[41] J. F. A. Sawyer discusses Isa 66:7-14 with insight (1989: 96-98).

[42] Possibly, the same hands are responsible for both the inclusion of Isaiah 36–37 and the creation of Isa 66:1-16.

BIBLIOGRAPHY

Abrams, M. H. 1953. *The Mirror and the Lamp: Romantic Theory and the Critical Tradition.* New York: Oxford Univ.
——. 1977. "The Deconstructive Angel." *Critical Inquiry* 3:425-38.
——. 1988. *A Glossary of Literary Terms.* 5th edn. New York: Holt, Rinehart and Winston.
Abusch, T., *et al.*, eds. 1990. *Lingering Over Words.* Atlanta: Scholars.
Ackerman, S. 1990. "Sacred Sex, Sacrifice and Death: Understanding a Prophetic Poem." *Bible Review* 6:38-44.
——. 1992. "Isaiah." In *The Women's Bible Commentary.* C. Newsom and S. Ringe, eds. Louisville: Westminster/John Knox. Pp. 161-68.
Ackroyd, P. R. 1978. *Isaiah I-XII: Presentation of a Prophet.* SVT 29. Pp. 16-48.
——. 1982. "Isaiah 36-39: Structure and Function." In *Von Kanaan bis Kerala..* W. C. Delsman *et al.*, eds. AOAT 211. Neukirchen-Vluyn: Neukirchener Verlag.
Adler, E. J. 1989. "The Background for the Metaphor of Covenant as Marriage in the Hebrew Bible." Ph.D. diss., Univ. of California at Berkeley. (See also under E. A. Goodfriend.)
Albrektson, B. 1963. *Studies in the Text and Theology of the Book of Lamentations.* Lund: CWK Gleerup.
Alonso Schökel, L. 1988. *A Manual of Hebrew Poetics.* Rome: Pontifical Biblical Institute.
——. 1987. "Isaiah." In *The Literary Guide to the Bible.* R. Alter and F. Kermode, eds. Cambridge, MA: Belknap. Pp. 165-83.
Anderson, B. W. 1978. "'The Lord Has Created Something New'—A Stylistic Study of Jer 31:15-22." *CBQ* 40:463-78.
——. 1988. "The Apocalyptic Rendering of the Isaiah Tradition." In *The Social World of Formative Christianity and Judaism.* Fest. H. C. Kee. J. Neusner *et al.*, eds. Philadelphia: Fortress. Pp. 17-38.
Anderson, T. D. 1986. "Renaming and Wedding Imagery in Isaiah 62." *Biblica* 67, 1:75-80.
Archer, L. J., 1983. "The Role of Jewish Women in the Religion, Ritual and Cult of Graeco-Roman Palestine." In *Images of Women in Antiquity.* A. Cameron and A. Kuhrt, eds. London & Canberra: Croom Helm. Pp. 273-87.
Asher-Greve, J. M. 1985. *Frauen in altsumerischer Zeit.* Bibliotheca Mesopotamica, 18. G. Buccellati, ed. Malibu: Undena Publications.
Baker, D. W. 1992. "Tarshish." In *ABD* 6. D. N. Freedman, ed. New York: Doubleday. Pp. 331-33.

Barton, J. 1988. *Oracles of God.* New York/Oxford: Oxford Univ.

Berlin, A. 1985. *The Dynamics of Biblical Parallelism.* Bloomington: Indiana Univ.

Biddle, M. E. 1991. "The Figure of Lady Jerusalem: Identification, Deification and Personification of Cities in the ANE." In *The Biblical Canon in Comparative Perspective.* W. W. Hallo *et al.*, eds. Lewiston, NY: Mellen. Pp. 173-94.

Bird, P. 1974. "Images of Women in the Old Testament." In *Religion and Sexism.* R. R. Ruether, ed. New York: Simon and Schuster. Pp. 41-88.

———. 1987. "The Place of Women in the Israelite Cultus." In *Ancient Israelite Religion: Essays in Honor of Frank Moore Cross.* P. D. Miller *et al.*, eds. Philadelphia: Fortress. Pp. 397-419.

———. 1989a. "Women's Religion in Ancient Israel." In *Women's Earliest Records From Ancient Egypt and Western Asia.* B. S. Lesko, ed. Pp. 283-98.

———. 1989b. "'To Play the Harlot': An Inquiry into an Old Testament Metaphor." In *Gender and Difference in Ancient Israel.* P. L. Day, ed. Minneapolis: Fortress. Pp. 75-94.

———. 1992. "Gender and Poverty: Biblical Perspectives." Unpub. paper (Biblical Studies Working Group, Ninth Oxford Institute for Wesleyan Studies, Oxford, UK, July 30, 1992).

Black, M. 1962. *Models and Metaphors: Studies in Language and Philosophy.* Ithaca: Cornell Univ.

———, ed. 1968a. *The Importance of Language.* Ithaca: Cornell Univ.

———. 1968b. *The Labyrinth of Language.* New York: New American Lib.

———. 1979a. "More About Metaphor." In *Metaphor and Thought.* A. Ortony, ed. Cambridge: Cambridge Univ. Pp. 19-43.

———. 1979b. "How Metaphors Work: A Reply to Donald Davidson." In *On Metaphor.* S. Sacks, ed. Chicago: Univ. of Chicago. Pp. 181-92.

Booth, W. 1961. 1983. *The Rhetoric of Fiction.* 2nd edn. Chicago and London: Univ. of Chicago.

———. 1979. "Metaphor as Rhetoric: The Problem of Evaluation." In *On Metaphor.* S. Sacks, ed. Chicago: Univ. of Chicago.

———. 1979. "Afterthoughts on Metaphor." In *On Metaphor.* S. Sacks, ed. Chicago and London: Univ. of Chicago. Pp. 173-74.

Bourguet, D. 1987. *Des Métaphores de Jérémie.* EB 9. Paris: Gabalda.

Bowman, C. H. 1978. "The Goddess 'Anatu in the Ancient Near East." Ph.D. diss., Univ. of California at Berkeley.

Brettler, M. 1989. *God is King: Understanding an Israelite Metaphor.* JSOTSup 76. Sheffield: JSOT.

Brown, F. *et al.* 1974 edn. *A Hebrew and English Lexicon of the Old Testament.* Oxford: Clarendon.

Broyles, C. C. 1989. *The Conflict of Faith and Experience in the Psalms: A Form-Critical and Theological Study.* JSOTSup 52. Sheffield: JSOT.

Brown, F. *et al.* 1974 edn. *A Hebrew and English Lexicon of the Old Testament*. Oxford: Clarendon. (= BDB)

Brueggemann, W. 1982. *The Creative Word: Canon as a Model for Biblical Education*. Philadelphia: Fortress.

Burke, K. 1957. *The Philosophy of Literary Form*. Revised abr. edn. Vintage paperbacks, New York: Vintage Books. Originally published, Baton Rouge: Louisiana State Univ., 1941.

———. 1964. "Literature as Equipment for Living." In *Perspectives by Incongruity*. S. E. Hyman, ed. Bloomington: Indiana Univ. Pp. 100-09.

Cagni, L. 1977. *The Poem of Erra*. Malibu: Undena.

Cameron, A. and A. Kuhrt, eds. 1983. *Images of Women in Antiquity*. London & Canberra: Croom Helm.

Camp, Claudia. 1981. "The Wise Women of 2 Samuel: A Role Model for Women in Early Israel?" *CBQ* 43:14-29.

———. 1985. *Wisdom and the Feminine in the Book of Proverbs*. Sheffield: Almond.

Carr, D. 1993. "Reaching for Unity in Isaiah." *JSOT* 57:61-80.

Childs, B. S. 1979. *Introduction to the Old Testament as Scripture*. Philadelphia: Fortress.

Clements, R. E. 1980a. *Isaiah and the Deliverance of Jerusalem: A Study of the Interpretation of Prophecy in the Old Testament*. Sheffield: JSOTSup 13.

———. 1980b. *Isaiah 1—39*. NCB. Grand Rapids and London: Wm. B. Eerdmans and Marshall, Morgan & Scott.

———. 1982. "The Unity of the Book of Isaiah." *Int* 36:117-29.

———. 1985. "Beyond Tradition History: Deutero-Isaianic Development of First Isaiah's Themes," *JSOT* 31:95-113.

Clifford, R. J. 1972. *The Cosmic Mountain in Canaan and the Old Testament*. Harvard Semitic Monograph Series 4. Cambridge: Harvard Univ.

———. 1989. "Narrative and Lament in Isaiah 63:7—64:11." In *To Touch the Text: Biblical and Related Studies in Honor of Joseph A. Fitzmyer, S.J.* M. P. Horgan and P. J. Kobelski, eds. New York: Crossroad.

———. 1993 "The Unity of the Book of Isaiah and Its Cosmogonic Language." *CBQ* 55:1-17.

Cohen, Chayim. 1973. "The Widowed City." *JANESCU* 5:75-81.

Conrad, Edgar. 1985. *Fear Not Warrior*. Brown Judaic Studies 75. Chico: Scholars.

———. 1988. "The Royal Narratives and the Structure of the Book of Isaiah." *JSOT* 41:67-81.

———. 1991. *Reading Isaiah*. Minneapolis: Fortress.

Coogan, M. D. 1990. "Job's Children." In *Lingering Over Words*. T. Abusch, *et al.*, eds. Pp. 135-47.

Craven, T. 1983. *Artistry and Faith in the Book of Judith*. SBLDS 70. Chico: Scholars.

Crenshaw, J. L. 1981. *Old Testament Wisdom: An Introduction*. Atlanta: John Knox.
——. 1985. "Education in Ancient Israel." *JBL* 104:601-15.
Crocker, J. C. 1977. "The Social Use of Rhetorical Forms." In *The Social Use of Metaphor*. Philadelphia: Univ. of Pennsylvania.
Cross, Frank M., Jr. and David Noel Freedman. 1955. "The Song of Miriam." *JNES* 14:237-50.
Darr, J. A. 1987. "'Glorified in the Presence of Kings': A Literary-Critical Study of Herod the Tetrarch in Luke-Acts." Ph.D. diss. Vanderbilt Univ.
——. 1992. *On Character Building: The Reader and the Rhetoric of Characterization in Luke-Acts*. Literary Currents in Biblical Interpretation. D. N. Fewell and D. M. Gunn, eds. Louisville: Westminster/John Knox.
Darr, K. P. 1987a. "Like Warrior, Like Woman: Destruction and Deliverance in Isaiah 42:10-17." *CBQ* 49:560-71.
——. 1987b. "The Wall Around Paradise: Ezekielian Ideas about the Future." *VT* XXXVII, 3:272-79.
——. 1991. *"Far More Precious than Jewels": Perspectives on Biblical Women*. Louisville: Westminster/John Knox.
Day Lewis, C. 1947. *The Poetic Image*. London: J. Cape.
Day, P. L., ed. 1989. *Gender and Difference in Ancient Israel*. Minneapolis: Fortress.
Dickemann, M. 1979. "Female infanticide, reproductive strategies and social stratification: a preliminary model." In *Evolutionary Biology and Human Social Behaviour*. N. A. Chagnon and W. Irons, eds. North Scituate, MA: Duxbury. Pp. 321-67.
Dion, P. E. 1991. "The Structure of Isaiah 42:10-17 as Approached through Versification and Distribution of Poetic Devices." *JSOT* 49:113-24.
Dobbs-Allsopp, F. W. 1993. *Weep, O Daughter of Zion: A Study of the City-Lament Genre in the Hebrew Bible*. Bib et. Or. 44. Rome: The Pontifical Institute.
Driver, S. R. and J. C. Miles. 1935. *The Assyrian Laws*. Oxford: Clarendon.
Eagleton, T. 1983. *Literary Theory: An Introduction*. Minneapolis: Univ. of Minnesota.
Englehard, D. H. 1970. "Hittite Magical Practices: An Analysis." Ph.D. diss., Brandeis Univ.
Erlandsson, S. 1970. *The Burden of Babylon: A Study of Isaiah 13:2—14:23*. Lund: CWK Gleerup.
Exum, J. C. 1981. "Of Broken Pots, Fluttering Birds and Visions in the Night: Extended Simile and Poetic Technique in Isaiah." *CBQ* 43: 331-52.
Fischer, H. G. 1989. "Women in the Old Kingdom and the Heracleopolitan Period." In *Women's Earliest Records*, B. S. Lesko, ed. Pp. 5-24.

Fish, S. E. 1970 (1972). "Literature in the Reader: Affective Stylistics."
In *New Literary History* 2 (123-162); rev. and repr. in *Self-Con-
suming Artifacts: The Experience of Seventeenth-Century Literature*, pp. 353-427. Berkeley: Univ. of California.

———. 1990. *Is There a Text in This Class? The Authority of Interpretive
Communities*. Cambridge, MA: Harvard Univ.

Fishbane, M. 1974. "Accusations of Adultery: A Study of Law and
Scribal Practice in Numbers 5:11-31." *HUCA* 45:25-45.

———. 1982. "Jewish Biblical Exegesis: Presuppositions and Principles." In *Scripture in the Jewish and Christian Traditions*. F. E.
Greenspahn, ed. Nashville: Abingdon.

Fitzgerald, A. 1972. "The Mythological Background for the Presentation of Jerusalem as a Queen and False Worship as Adultery in
the OT." *CBQ* 34:403-416.

———. 1975. "*BTWLT* and *BT* as Titles for Capital Cities." *CBQ* 37:
167-83.

Follis, E. R. 1987. "The Holy City as Daughter." In *Directions in Biblical
Hebrew Poetry*, E. R. Follis, ed. Sheffield: JSOTSup 40. Pp. 173-84.

———. 1992. "Zion, Daughter of." In *ABD* 6. D. N. Freedman, ed. New
York: Doubleday. P. 1103.

Fontaine, C. R. 1982. *Traditional Sayings in the Old Testament: A
Contextual Study*. Bible and Literature Series 5. Sheffield: Almond.

———. 1987. "Queenly Proverb Performance: The Prayer of Puduhepa
(KUB *XXI*, 27)." In *The Listening Heart: Essays in Wisdom and the
Psalms in Honor of Roland E. Murphy, O. Carm.* K. G. Hoglund *et
al.*, ed. JSOTSup 58. Sheffield: JSOT. Pp. 95-126.

Franke, Chris A. 1991. "The Function of the Satiric Lament Over
Babylon in Second Isaiah (XLVII)." *VT* 4:408-18.

Frye, N. 1982. *The Great Code*. New York: Harcourt Brace
Jovanovich.

Frymer-Kensky, Tikva. 1977. "The Atrahasis Epic and Its Significance
for Our Understanding of Genesis 1—9." *BA* 40:147-55.

———. 1984. "The Strange Case of the Suspected Sotah (Numbers
5:11-31)." *VT* 34:11-26.

———. 1992a. *In the Wake of the Goddesses: Women, Culture, and the
Biblical Transformation of Pagan Myth*. New York: The Free Press.

———. 1992b. "Deuteronomy." In *The Women's Bible Commentary*. C.
Newsom and S. Ringe, eds. Pp. 52-62.

Fuchs, E. 1985. "The Literary Characterization of Mothers and Sexual
Politics in the Hebrew Bible." In *Feminist Perspectives on Biblical
Scholarship*. Biblical Scholarship in North America 10. A. Y.
Collins, ed. Chico: Scholars. Pp. 117-36.

Galambush, J. 1992. *Jerusalem in the Book of Ezekiel: The City as
Yahweh's Wife*. SBLDS 130. Atlanta: Scholars.

Gesenius, F. H. W. 1821. *Philologisch-kritischer und historischer
Commentar über den Jesaia*. Leipzig: F. C. W. Vogel.

Glassner, J.-J. 1989. "Women, Hospitality and the Honor of the Family." In *Women's Earliest Records*. B. S. Lesko, ed. Pp. 71-90.

Goodfriend, E. A. 1992a. "Adultery." In *ABD* 1. D. N. Freedman, ed. New York: Doubleday. Pp. 82-6. (See also under E. J. Adler.)

——. 1992b. "Prostitution." In *ABD* 5. D. N. Freedman, ed. New York: Doubleday. Pp. 505-10.

Gordon, E. I., ed. 1959. *Sumerian Proverbs: Glimpses of Everyday Life in Ancient Mesopotamia*. Philadelphia: Univ. of Pennsylvania.

Gray, G. B. 1912. *The Book of Isaiah: A Critical and Exegetical Commentary on the Book of Isaiah 1—39*, 1. ICC 18. New York: Charles Scribner's Sons.

Greenberg, Moshe. 1960. "Some Postulates of Biblical Criminal Law." In *Yehezkel Kaufmann Jubilee Volume*. M. Haran, ed. Jerusalem: Magnes. Pp. 5-28.

Grosz, K. 1989. "Some Aspects of the Position of Women in Nuzi." In *Women's Earliest Records*. B. S. Lesko, ed. Pp. 167-80.

Gruber, M. I. 1983. "The Motherhood of God in Second Isaiah." *RB* 90:351-59.

——. 1989. "Breast-Feeding Practices in Biblical Israel and in Old Babylonian Mesopotamia." *JANES* 19:61-83.

Gwaltney, W. C., Jr. 1983. "The Biblical Book of Lamentations in the Context of Near Eastern Lament Literature." In *Scripture in Context II: More Essays on the Comparative Method*. W. W. Hallo *et al.*, eds. Winona Lake: Eisenbrauns. Pp. 191-211.

Haas, P. 1989. "'Die He Shall Surely Die': The Structure of Homicide in Biblical Law." *Semeia* 45:67-87.

Hamborg, G. R. 1981. "Reasons for Judgement in the Oracles Against the Nations of the Prophet Isaiah." *VT* XXXI:145-59.

Hanson, P. 1975. *The Dawn of Apocalyptic*. Philadelphia: Fortress.

Harrelson, W. 1980. *The Ten Commandments and Human Rights*. Philadelphia: Fortress.

Harries, K. 1979. "The Many Uses of Metaphor." In *On Metaphor*. S. Sacks, ed. Chicago: Univ. of Chicago.

Harris, R. 1989. "Independent Women in Ancient Mesopotamia?" In *Women's Earliest Records*. B. S. Lesko, ed. Pp. 145-56.

——. 1990. "Images of Women in the Gilgamesh Epic." In *Lingering Over Words*, T. Abusch *et al.*, eds. Pp. 219-30.

Hillers, D. R. 1964. *Treaty-Curses and the Old Testament Prophets*. Bib. et Or. 16. Rome: Pontifical Biblical Institute.

——. 1972. *Lamentations*. AB 7a. Garden City: Doubleday.

——. 1992. *Lamentations: A New Translation with Introduction and Commentary*. AB 7a. 2nd rev. edn. New York: Doubleday.

Hoffner, H. A. 1966. "Birth and Name-Giving in Hittite Texts." *JNES* 27:198-203.

Holladay, W. L. 1961. "On Every High Hill and Under Every Green Tree." *VT* 11:170-76.

——. 1966. "Jer. xxxi 22B Reconsidered: 'The Woman Encompasses the Man.'" *VT* 16:236-39.

——. 1986. *Jeremiah 1: A Commentary on the Book of Jeremiah, Chapters 1—25.* P. Hanson, ed. Hermeneia. Philadelphia: Fortress.

Horney, K. 1967. *Feminine Psychology.* Edited and with an Introduction by H. Kelmar. New York: Norton.

Hrushovski, B. 1984. "Poetic Metaphor and Frames of Reference." *Poetics Today* 5:5-43.

Iser, W. 1972. "The Reading Process: A Phenomenological Approach." *New Literary History* 3:279-99.

——. 1978. *The Act of Reading: A Theory of Aesthetic Response.* Baltimore and London: The Johns Hopkins Univ.

Jacob, E. 1962. "Mourning." *IDB* 3. New York and Nashville: Abingdon. Pp. 452-54.

Jensen, J. 1986. "Yahweh's Plan in Isaiah and in the Rest of the Old Testament." *CBQ* 48:443-55.

Johnson, M., ed. 1981. *Philosophic Perspectives on Metaphor.* Minneapolis: Univ. of Minnesota.

Kaiser, B. B. 1987. "Poet as 'Female Impersonator': The Image of Daughter Zion as Speaker in Biblical Poems of Suffering." *JR* 67:164-82.

Kaiser, O. 1972. *Isaiah 1-12.* R. A. Wilson, trans. OTL. London: SCM.

——. 1974. *Isaiah 13—39.* R. A. Wilson, trans. OTL. London: SCM.

Kedar-Kopfstein, B. 1978. "*dam.*" *TDOT* III. Grand Rapids, MI: W. B. Eerdmans. Pp. 234-50.

Kilmer, A. 1972. "The Mesopotamian Concept of Overpopulation and Its Solution as Represented in the Mythology." *Or.* 41:160-77.

Kjärgaard, M. S. 1986. *Metaphor and Parable.* Acta Theologica Danica XI. Leiden: E. J. Brill.

Knierim, R. 1985. "Criticism of Literary Features, Form, Tradition, and Redaction." In *The Hebrew Bible and Its Modern Interpreters.* D. Knight and G. Tucker, eds. Fortress and Scholars: Philadelphia and Chico. Pp. 123-65.

Koehler, L. and W. Baumgartner, eds. 1958. *Lexicon in Veteris Testamenti Libros.* 2 Volumes. Leiden: E. J. Brill.

Kramer, S. N. 1969a. "Lamentation over the Destruction of Ur." In *ANET.* 3rd edn. J. B. Pritchard, ed. Pp. 456-63.

——. 1969b. "Lamentation over the Destruction of Sumer and Ur." In *ANET.* 3rd edn. J. B. Pritchard, ed. Pp. 611-19.

——. 1983. "The Weeping Goddess: Sumerian Prototypes of the *Mater Dolorosa.*" *BAR* 46:69-80.

Kugel, J. 1981. *The Idea of Biblical Poetry: Parallelism and its History.* New Haven and London: Yale Univ.

Kuhrt, A. 1989. "Non-Royal Women in the Late Babylonian Period: A Survey." In *Women's Earliest Records.* B. S. Lesko, ed. Pp. 215-39.

Lambert, W. G. 1960. *Babylonian Wisdom Literature*. Oxford: Clarendon.
——. 1976. "A Middle Assyrian Medical Text." *Iraq* 31:28-39.
—— and A. R. Millard. 1969. *Atra-Hasis: The Babylonian Story of the Flood*. Oxford: Clarendon.
Lanahan, W. 1974. "The Speaking Voice in the Book of Lamentations." *JBL* 93:41-49.
Lesko, B. S., ed. 1989. *Women's Earliest Records from Ancient Egypt and Western Asia*. Atlanta: Scholars.
Levenson, J. D. 1976. *Theology of the Program of Restoration of Ezekiel 40—48*. Missoula: Scholars.
Lewy, J. 1944. "The Old West Semitic Sun God Hammu." *HUCA* 18:436-43.
Locher, C. 1986. *Die Ehre einer Frau in Israel*. Freiburg: Universitäts Verlag and Göttingen: Vandenhoeck & Ruprecht.
Luckenbill, D. D., ed. 1927. *Ancient Records of Assyria and Babylonia*. Vol II. J. H. Breasted, ed. Chicago: Univ. of Chicago.
Macky, P. W. 1990. *The Centrality of Metaphors to Biblical Thought: A Method for Interpreting the Bible*. Studies in the Bible and Early Christianity 19. Lewiston/Queenston/Lampeter: Mellen.
Malul, M. 1988. *Studies in Mesopotamian Legal Symbolism*. Neukirchen-Vluyn: Butzen & Bercker Kevelaer.
McCullough, W. S. 1962. "Serpent." *IDB* 4. New York and Nashville: Abingdon. Pp. 289-91.
McKeating, H. 1979. "Sanctions against Adultery in Ancient Israelite Society, with Some Reflections on Methodology in the Study of Old Testament Ethics." *JSOT* 11:57-72.
McKenzie, J. L. 1967. *Second Isaiah*. AB. Garden City, NY: Doubleday.
Meyers, C. 1988. *Discovering Eve: Ancient Israelite Woman in Context*. New York and Oxford: Oxford Univ.
——. 1989. "Women and the Domestic Economy of Early Israel." In *Women's Earliest Records*. S. B. Lesko, ed. Pp. 265-78.
Miller, P. D. 1984. "Meter, Parallelism and Tropes: The Search for Poetic Style." *JSOT* 28:99-106.
Miscall, P. D. 1991. "Isaiah: The Labyrinth of Images." *Semeia* 54:103-21.
——. 1993. "Isaiah: New Heavens, New Earth, New Book." In *Reading Between Texts*. D. N. Fewell, ed. LCBI. Louisville: Westminster/John Knox.
de Moor, J. C. 1987. *An Anthology of Religious Texts from Ugarit*. New York: E. J. Brill.
Muilenberg, J. 1956. "Isaiah 40—66." In *IB* 5. Nashville: Abingdon.
Newsom, C. A. 1984. "A Maker of Metaphors: Ezekiel's Oracles Against Tyre." *Interp* 38:151-64.

——. 1989. "Women and the Discourse of Patriarchal Wisdom: A Study of Proverbs 1—9." In *Gender and Difference in Ancient Israel*. P. L. Day, ed. Pp. 142-60.

—— and S. H. Ringe. 1992. *The Women's Bible Commentary*. Louisville: Westminster/John Knox.

Nielsen, K. 1989. *There is Hope for a Tree: The Tree as Metaphor in Isaiah*. JSOTSup 65. Sheffield: JSOT.

Niditch, S. 1985. *Chaos to Cosmos: Studies in Biblical Patterns of Creation*. Chico: Scholars.

O'Connor, K. M. 1992. "Lamentations." In *The Women's Bible Commentary*. C. Newsom and S. Ringe, eds. Pp. 178-82.

Odell, M. S. 1991. "An Exploratory Study of Shame and Dependence in the Bible and Selected Near Eastern Parallels." In *The Biblical Canon in Comparative Perspective*. Scripture in Context IV. Ancient Near Eastern Texts in Studies 11. K. L. Younger, Jr. *et al.*, eds. Lewiston/Queenston/Lampeter: Edwin Mellen. Pp. 217-33.

Ortner, S. and H. Whitehead, eds. 1981. *Sexual Meanings: The Cultural Constructions of Gender and Sexuality*. Cambridge: Cambridge Univ.

Parker, C. A. 1973. "Aspects of a Theory of Proverbs: Contexts and Messages in Swahili." Ph.D. diss., Univ. of Washington.

Parker, S. B. 1988. "The Birth Announcement." In *Ascribe to the Lord: Biblical and Other Studies in Memory of Peter C. Craigie*. L. Eslinger and G. Taylor, eds. JSOTSup 67. Sheffield: JSOT. Pp. 133-49.

——. 1989. *The Pre-Biblical Narrative Tradition*. Resources for Biblical Study 24. Atlanta: Scholars.

——. "The Beginning of the Reign of God: Myth and Liturgy in Psalm 82." Unpublished manuscript.

Petersen, D. L. 1977. *Late Israelite Prophecy: Studies in Deutero-Prophetic Literature and in Chronicles*. SBLMS 23. Missoula: Scholars.

Pfeiffer, R. H. 1941. *Introduction to the Old Testament*. New York and London: Harper & Brothers Publishers.

Pomeroy, S. B. 1983. "Infanticide in Hellenistic Greece." In *Images of Women in Antiquity*, A. Cameron and A. Kuhrt, eds. Pp. 207-19.

Pope, M. H. 1973. *Job*. 3rd edn. AB. Garden City: Doubleday.

Pringle, J. 1983. "Hittite Birth Rituals." In *Images of Women in Antiquity*. A. Cameron and A. Kuhrt, eds. London and Cranberra: Croom Helm. Pp. 128-41.

Pritchard, J. B. 1969. *ANET*. 3rd edn. Princeton: Princeton Univ.

Provan, I. 1991. *Lamentations*. NCBC. Grand Rapids: Eerdmans.

Reiner, E. 1966. "La Magie babylonienne." In *Le Monde du Sorcier*. Georges Condominas *et als.*, ed. Paris: Editions du Seuil.

——. 1985. *Your thwarts in pieces, Your mooring rope cut: Poetry from Babylonia and Assyria*. Michigan Studies in the Humanities 5. Ann Arbor: Univ. of Michigan.

Rendtorff, R. 1984. "Zur Komposition des Buches Jesaja." *VT* 34:295-320.

———. 1985. *The Old Testament: An Introduction.* J. Bowden, trans. Philadelphia: Fortress.

———. 1989. "Jesaja 6 im Rahmen der Komposition des Jesajabuches." In *The Book of Isaiah—Le Livre d'Isaïe.* J. Vermeylen, ed. BETL 81. Leuven: Peeters. Pp. 73-82.

———. 1991a. "Jesaja 56,1 als Schlüssel für die Komposition des Buches Jesaja." In *Kanon und Theologie.* Neukirchen Vluyn: Neukirchen.

———. 1991b. "The Book of Isaiah: A Complex Unity. Synchronic and Diachronic Reading." *Society of Biblical Literature 1991 Seminar Papers 30.* E. H. Lovering, Jr., ed. Atlanta: Scholars. Pp. 8-20.

Rich, Adrienne. 1976. *Of Women Born.* New York: Norton.

Richards, I. A. 1936. *The Philosophy of Rhetoric.* Oxford: Oxford Univ.

Rin, S. von, 1963. "Ugaritic-Old Testament Affinities." *BZ* 7:23-24.

Roberts, J. J. M. 1985. "Isaiah and His Children." In *Biblical and Related Studies Presented to Samuel Iwry.* A. Kort and S. Moschauser, eds. Winona Lake: Eisenbrauns. Pp. 193-203.

Robins, G. 1989. "Some Images of Women in New Kingdom Art and Literature." In *Women's Earliest Records.* B. S. Lesko, ed. Pp. 105-16.

Robinson, J. 1976. *The Second Book of Kings.* Cambridge: Cambridge Univ.

Rofé, A. 1985. "Isaiah 66:1-4: Judean Sects of the Persian Period." In *Biblical and Related Studies.* A. Kort and S. Morschauser, eds. Winona Like: Eisenbrauns. Pp. 205-18.

Rollin, S. 1983. "Women and Witchcraft in Ancient Assyria." In *Images of Women in Antiquity.* A. Cameron and A. Kuhrt, eds. Pp. 34-45.

Sacks, S. (ed.) 1979. *On Metaphor.* Chicago and Oxford: Univ. of Chicago.

Sapir, J. D. 1977. "The Anatomy of Metaphor." In *The Social Use of Metaphor: Essays on the Anthropology of Rhetoric.* J. D. Sapir and J. C. Crocker, eds. Pp. 3-32.

———. 1977. *The Social Use of Metaphor.* J. D. Sapir and J. C. Crocker, eds. Philadelphia: Univ. of Pennsylvania.

Sawyer, J. F. A. 1989. "Daughter of Zion and Servant of the Lord in Isaiah: A Comparison." *JSOT* 44:89-107.

Schmitz, P. C. 1992. "Sidon." In *The Anchor Bible Dictionary*, Vol 6. D. N. Freedman, ed. New York: Doubleday. Pp. 17-18.

Scott, R. B. Y. 1956. "Isaiah 1—39: Introduction and Exegesis." In *IB* 5. New York and Nashville: Abingdon. Pp. 151-381.

Seibert, Ilse. 1974. *Woman in Ancient Near East.* Marianne Herzfeld, trans. G. A. Shepperson, rev. Leipzig: Edition Leipzig.

Seitel, Peter. 1969. "Proverbs: A Social Use of Metaphor." *Genre* 2:143-61; reprinted in *Folklore Genres.* D. Ben-Amos, ed. Austin: Univ. of Texas. Pp. 125-43.

——. 1976. "Proverbs and the Structure of Metaphor among the Haya of Tanzania." Ph.D. diss., Univ. of Pennsylvania.

——. 1977. "Saying Haya Sayings: Two Categories of Proverb Use." In *The Social Use of Metaphor: Essays on the Anthropology of Rhetoric.* J. D. Sapir and J. C. Crocker, eds. Philadelphia: Univ. of Pennsylvania. Pp. 75-99.

Seitz, C. 1988. "Isaiah 1—66: Making Sense of the Whole." In *Reading and Preaching the Book of Isaiah.* C. Seitz, ed. Philadelphia: Fortress. Pp. 105-26.

——. 1990. "The Divine Council: Temporal Transition and New Prophecy in the Book of Isaiah." *JBL* 109:229-47.

——. 1991. *Zion's Final Destiny: The Development of the Book of Isaiah: A Reassessment of Isaiah 36—39.* Minneapolis: Fortress.

Setel, T. D. 1985. "Prophets and Pornography: Female Sexual Imagery in Hosea." In *Feminist Interpretation of the Bible.* L. M. Russell, ed. Philadelphia: Westminster. Pp. 86-95.

Smelik, K. A. D. 1986. "Distortion of Old Testament Prophecy: The Purpose of Isaiah xxxvi and xxxvii." In *Crises and Perspectives.* J. de Moor *et al.*, eds. Leiden: E. J. Brill. Pp. 70-93.

Snell, D. C. 1992. "Trade and Commerce." In *ABD* 6. D. N. Freedman, ed. New York: Doubleday. Pp. 625-29.

Soskice, J. M. 1985. *Metaphor and Religious Language.* Oxford: Clarendon.

Speiser, E. A. 1964. *Genesis: Introduction, Translation, and Notes.* AB. Garden City: Doubleday & Company.

——., trans. 1969. "The Epic of Gilgamesh." In *ANET.* 3rd edn. J. B. Pritchard, ed. Pp. 72-99.

Sternberg, M. 1978. *Expositional Modes and Temporal Ordering in Fiction.* Baltimore: Johns Hopkins.

Stinespring, W. F. 1965. "No Daughter of Zion: A Study of the Appositional Genitive in Hebrew Grammar." *Encounter* 26:133-41.

Stulman, L. 1992. "Sex and Familial Crimes in the D Code: A Witness to Mores in Transition." *JSOT* 53:47-63.

Sweeney, M. A. 1987. "New Gleanings from an Old Vineyard: Isaiah 27 Reconsidered." In *Early Jewish and Christian Exegesis: Studies in Memory of William Hugh Brownlee.* C. A. Evans and W. F. Stinespring, eds. Atlanta: Scholars. Pp. 51-66.

——. 1988. *Isaiah 1—4 and the Post-Exilic Understanding of the Isaianic Tradition.* BZAW 171. Berlin and New York: de Gruyter.

Taylor, J. Glen. 1988. "A First and Last Thing to Do in Mourning: KTU 1.161 and Some Parallels." In *Ascribe to the Lord: Biblical and Other Studies in Memory of Peter C. Craigie.* L. Eslinger and G. Taylor, eds. JSOTSup 67. Sheffield: JSOT.

Tolbert, M. A. 1989. "Reading the Bible with Authority: Feminist Interrogation of the Canon." Unpublished manuscript.

Tompkins, J. 1980. "An Introduction to Reader-Response Criticism." In *Reader-Response Criticism*. J. Tompkins, ed. Baltimore & London: Johns Hopkins Univ.

Trible, P. 1978. *God and the Rhetoric of Sexuality*. Philadelphia: Fortress.

Van Dijk, J. *et al.*, eds. 1985. *Early Mesopotamian Incantations and Rituals*. Yale Oriental Series. Babylonian Texts 11. New Haven and London: Yale Univ.

Van Selms, A. 1954. *Marriage & Family Life in Ugaritic Literature*. Pretoria Oriental Series 1. London: Luzac & Company, Ltd.

———. 1973. "Isaiah 28:9-13: An Attempt to Give a New Translation." *ZAW* 85:332-39.

———. 1989. "L'unité du livre d'Isaïe." *The Book of Isaiah—Le Livre d'Isaïe*. J. Vermeylen, ed. BETL 81. Leuven: Peeters. Pp. 11-53.

Wakeman, M. K. 1985. "Ancient Sumer and the Women's Movement." *JFSR* 1:7-27.

———. 1984. "Sacred Marriage." *JSOT* 22:21-31.

Walls, Neal H. 1992. *The Goddess Anat in Ugaritic Myth*. SBLDS 135. Atlanta: Scholars.

Watson, W. G. E. 1984. *Classical Hebrew Poetry: A Guide to its Techniques*. JSOTSup 26. Sheffield: JSOT.

———. 1976. "Tribute to Tyre (Is. XXIII 7)." *VT* 26:371-74.

Webb, Barry G. 1990. "Zion in Transformation: A Literary Approach to Isaiah." In *The Bible in Three Dimensions*. D. J. A. Clines *et al.*, eds. JSOTSup 87. Sheffield: JSOT. Pp. 65-84.

Webster, E. C. 1990. "The Rhetoric of Isaiah 63—65." *JSOT* 47: 89-102.

Weems, Renita. 1988. *Just a Sister Away: A Womanist Vision of Women's Relationships in the Bible*. San Diego: LuraMedia.

Wegner, J. R. 1988. *Chattel or Person: The Status of Women in the Mishnah*. New York: Oxford Univ.

———. 1992 "Leviticus." In *The Women's Bible Commentary*. C. Newsom and S. Ringe, eds. Pp. 36-44.

Weidner, E. 1969. "Treaty Between Ashurnirari V of Assyria and Mati'ilu of Arpad." In *ANET*. 3rd edn. J. B. Pritchard, ed. Pp. 532-33.

Weinfeld, M. 1983. "Zion and Jerusalem as Religious and Political Capital: Ideology and Utopia." In *The Poet and the Historian*. HSS 26. R. Friedman, ed. Chico, CA: Scholars.

Weiser, A. 1962. *The Psalms*. H. Hartwell, trans. OTL. Philadelphia: Westminster.

Wenham, G. J. 1976. "*betûlah* 'A Girl of Marriageable Age.'" *VT* 22:326-48.

Westermann, C. 1969. *Isaiah 40—66*. D. G. M. Stalker, trans. OTL. Philadelphia: Westminster.

Wheelwright, P. 1962. *Metaphor and Reality*. Bloomington: Indiana Univ.

White, S. A. 1989. "Esther: A Feminine Model for Jewish Diaspora." In *Gender and Difference in Ancient Israel*. P. L. Day, ed. Pp. 161-77.

Whiting, R. M. 1989. *State Archives of Assyria 3*. Helsinki: Helsinki Univ.

Whybray, R. N. 1975. *Isaiah 40—66*. NCB. London: Oliphants.

Wiken, U. 1984. "Shame and Honour: A Contestable Pair." *Man* 19:635-47.

Wildberger, H. 1962. "Jesajas Verstndnis der Geschichte." *VTSup* 9:83-117.

——. 1972. *Jesaja*. BKAT 10/1. Neukirchener-Vluyn: Neukirchener.

——. 1978. *Jesaja 13—27*. BKAT 10/2. Neukirchener-Vluyn: Neukirchener.

——. 1982. *Jesaja 28—39*. BKAT 10/3. Neukirchener-Vluyn: Neukirchener.

Williams, J. G. 1977. "Irony and Lament: Clues to Prophetic Consciousness." *Semeia* 8:51-69.

——. 1987. "Proverbs and Ecclesiastes." In *The Literary Guide to the Bible*. R. Alter and F. Kermode, eds. Cambridge: Belknap. Pp. 263-82.

Willis, J. 1985. "An Important Passage for Determining the Historical Setting of a Prophetic Oracle—Isaiah 1.7-8." *ST* 39:151-69.

Wilshire, L. 1975. "The Servant-City: A New Interpretation of the 'Servant of the Lord' in the Servant Songs of Deutero-Isaiah." *JBL* 94:356-67.

Wilson, J. A. 1969. "Joy at the Accession of Mer-ne-Ptah." In *ANET*. 3rd edn. J. B. Pritchard, ed. P. 378.

Wiseman, D. J., trans. 1969. "The Vassal-Treaties of Esarhaddon." In *ANET*. 3rd edn. J. B. Pritchard, ed. Pp. 534-41.

Woolf, V. 1938. *To the Lighthouse*. London: J. M. Dent & Sons.

Yee, G. A. 1989. "'I Have Perfumed My Bed with Myrrh': The Foreign Woman (*'issâ zarâ*) in Proverbs 1—9." *JSOT* 43:53-68.

——. 1992. "Hosea." In *The Women's Bible Commentary*. C. Newsom and S. Ringe, eds. Pp. 195-202.

Youngblood, R. 1979. "Ariel, 'City of God.'" In *Essays on the Occasion of the Seventieth Anniversary of The Dropsie University*. A. I. Katsh and L. Nemoy, eds. Philadelphia: The Dropsie Univ.

INDEXES

AUTHORS

271

238, 240
Sapir, J. D. 39-40, 231, 249
Sawyer, J. F. A. 177-78,
181, 257
Schmitz, P. C. 250
Scott, R. B. Y. 138
Seibert, I. 100, 240, 241
Seitel, P. 207-210, 254
Seitz, C. 17, 19, 27, 166,
217, 229, 243, 251, 253,
255-56
Smelik, K. A. D. 253
Snell, D. C. 250
Soskice, J. M. 37-40, 45,
231, 232
Speiser, E. A. 117, 241
Sternberg, M. 57
Stinespring, W. F. 128
Stulman, L. 234, 246
Sweeney, M. A. 15, 93-94,
115, 228, 229, 248, 256
Taylor, J. G. 171
Tolbert, M. A. 228
Trible, P. 238, 241
Van Dijk, J. 99
Wakeman, M. K. 247
Walls, N. H. 128, 245, 250

Watson, W. G. E. 53, 248, 250
Webb, B. G. 18, 19
Webster, E. C. 236
Weems, R. 238
Wegner, J. R. 113, 239
Weidner, E. 117
Weinfeld, M.
Weiser, A. 242
Wenham, G. J. 128
Westermann, C. 76, 186, 193,
198, 200-201, 236, 252
Wheelwright, P. 41, 232
White, S. A. 239
Whiting, R. M. 99
Whybray, R. N. 66, 178, 191-
97, 199-201, 235, 252,
253, 257
Wildberger, H. 233, 250
Williams, J. G. 249, 254
Willis, J. 137, 234
Wilson, J. A. 132
Wiseman, D. J. 117, 240
Woolf, V. 231
Yee, G. A. 87-88, 120, 245,
246
Youngblood, R. 250

BIBLICAL REFERENCES

GENESIS
1 105
1:20 249
2:7-22 106
3:15 91
3:16 100, 222
4:1 222
6:1-4 241
11:30 179
16:2 98
17:5 198
17:15 198
19:18 96
19:31 252
20:6 246
20:9 246
20:18 98

22:12 96
25:21 179
28:14 179
29:6 252
29:31 179
30:1 98
30:2 98
30:23 251
32:28 198
35:6-7 198
35:10 198
35:16-19 98
35:17 214
38:24 120
39:9 246
39:30 252

EXODUS
11:15 172
14:19-20 248
18:21 250
20:12 54
21:10-11 239
21:15 55
22:16 245
28 244
28:37 252
32-34 247
39:28 252
44:13 252

LEVITICUS
8:9 252
12:1-5 240
15:25-26 244